DAILY GRACE

BRYAN CHAPELL

SALEM
BOOKS

an imprint of Regnery Publishing
Washington, D.C.

DAILY GRACE

365 DAILY DEVOTIONS REFLECTING GOD'S UNLIMITED GRACE

BRYAN CHAPELL

ISBN: 978-1-68451-296-6
eISBN: 978-1-68451-314-7

Library of Congress Control Number: 2021947535

Published in the United States by Salem Books
An Imprint of Regnery Publishing
A Division of Salem Media Group
Washington, D.C.
www.SalemBooks.com

Manufactured in the United States of America

10 9 8 7 6 5 4 3 2 1

Books are available in quantity for promotional or premium use. For information on discounts and terms, please visit our website: www.SalemBooks.com.

BRYAN CHAPELL

is the author of *Each for the Other,*
Unlimited Grace,
Praying Backward,
and *Holiness by Grace*

DAILY GRACE
INTRODUCTION

In my early years in ministry, I often sought to compel obedience by haranguing people into guilty or fearful submission to God's standards. Then, the Lord crushed my pride and healed my heart with the compelling power of the grace of the Gospel. Since that time, everything that I have preached, taught, or written has sought to shine the beautiful grace of the Lord Jesus Christ upon all of life to ignite the joy that is the true strength of Christian obedience and witness.

Daily Grace continues the project of shining the sweetness and power of grace into every aspect of life by providing a year's worth of daily devotions. Each reveals how the grace of God in Jesus Christ provides strength for today and hope for tomorrow. The devotional thought is preceded by a related Bible verse and followed by a brief prayer. Each thought has been carefully chosen from one of my previous books or messages that has been particularly meaningful to readers, listeners, friends, and family.

TRANSFORMED FROM THE INSIDE OUT

A key reason to meditate on Scripture with a focus on how we live in response to God's grace is to keep straight the order of Scripture's imperatives and indicatives. The imperatives (what we should *do*) are always a *consequence* of the indicatives (who we *are* by God's grace). What we do is never the *cause* of God's love for us. We obey in *response* to God's love. We were beloved long before we obeyed or knew to do so. His grace toward us precedes, enables, and motivates our efforts toward holiness. Grace not only precedes God's imperatives, it is also the ultimate power that enables us to obey His standards as we are transformed from the inside out.

Relishing the grace God has provided for us through Jesus Christ's sacrifice for our sin stimulates humility, gratitude, sacrifice, obedience, and praise. We delight to revere God for the love He has shown us. Our obedience is not so much to gain earthly benefits as to express gratitude for God's eternal blessings. We pursue holiness to bless the Heavenly Father who has been gracious to us, rather than to bribe a divine tyrant to be favorable toward us. We obey not merely to experience the blessings of obedience but to honor the God who provides them. Heaven's priorities become our own because expressing love for the One who first loved us provides our greatest joy and deepest satisfaction.

Since God's love for us is the soil in which our love for God grows, we do not identify His grace simply for spiritual sentiment. Grace is supremely practical and powerful. Regular focus on the good news that Jesus died for our sin despite our undeserving status ignites love for God in the hearts of believers that makes them willing and able to honor Him. We turn to Him for help when we realize we are helpless apart from Him. We pray for the aid we need, when we know He promises never to turn away from those who seek Him.

By identifying such grace throughout Scripture, we fan into flame zeal for our Savior. Our goal is stimulation of a profound love for God that bears holy fruit. When God's people see how resolute and rife His love for them is, then they rejoice to live for Him. Grace compels this holiness as our hearts respond to His mercy with a compelling love for whatever pleases Him.

Grace *motivates* lives of praise, and also *empowers* them. This may surprise many believers because it is common to think of grace as an excuse not to obey God rather than as the fuel of godliness. In order to discern how grace empowers godliness, we need to consider the sources of power for living in ways that please our Savior.

THE POWER OF KNOWLEDGE

One obvious source of spiritual power is knowledge. We need to know what to believe and to do in order to apply God's Word to our lives. If we do not *know* what to believe, then we cannot honor the truths about God; and, if we do not *know* what to do, then we cannot truly please God.

Yet, as important as it is to know what to believe and what to do, such knowledge is still insufficient for living the Christian life. If we have no will or ability to act on the knowledge we have, then we cannot please God. That's why excavating the message of grace from all of Scripture is so important. The love for God that the Gospel of grace stimulates in us provides power for Christian living that knowledge alone cannot.

We all have acquaintances who know a lot about the Bible, but whose lives or attitudes seem remote from the heart that gave it. Something must accompany knowledge of God for godliness to thrive in our lives—and that something is love for God.

THE POWER OF LOVE

To help us grasp the full power of love for God, we must consider a critical question: What is the primary reason that temptations gain power over believers? Sin's power has already been defeated; we are no longer its slaves (Romans 6:14–17). By virtue of the Holy Spirit's renewal of our minds and indwelling of our hearts, sin has no more dominion over us (Romans 12:1–2; Galatians 2:20; 1 John 4:4).

We may choose to sin, but we are not powerless against it. We *can* think and act in accord with God's desires. Believers have been spiritually born again as "new creations" that are able—even though it may require much struggle and grievous setbacks—to resist Satan's temptations by the means of God's grace.

So, if sin no longer sits in the driver's seat of our hearts, why do we yield to temptations? The sad answer is, because we love them. Consider this: If a sin did not attract us, it would have no power over us.

We turn from God to temptations because we are drawn to sin's temporary pleasures and false promises (Hebrews 11:25; James 1:14–15). We love the object of our lust, or greed, or ambition, more than we love the Savior. That's why we pursue the sin rather than the Savior. And, when broken hearts protest, "No, I still love Jesus," we need wise and caring counsel that responds, "Yes. That is true. You do still love Jesus, but when you yielded to temptation you loved the sin more." Sin is not necessarily a denial of love for Christ; it is simply a denial of Jesus as our first love in that situation, trial, or temptation.

The understanding that sin takes control of our lives through our love of it leads to another critical question: What will drive love for sin from our hearts? First, it helps to know that the pleasures of sin are temporary and that its consequences are ruinous. That's why Scripture gives us warnings about sin's harmful effects on us and our loved ones. Sadly, when we are in love with sin, we tend not to heed these warnings and deceive ourselves that the sin's benefits will outweigh its damages.

So, what else will keep love for sin from controlling our hearts? The answer is: a surpassing love. When love for Christ surpasses all other loves, it expels sin's control over our hearts. We want to please Him above all other pleasures. We may still experience the attraction of sin, but the desire to satisfy our Savior is stronger. Love for Him overpowers love for sin. That's why Jesus said, "If you love me, you will keep my commandments" (John 14:15).

With this understanding of the power of love for Jesus, we are prepared to ask a final, critical question: If a surpassing love for Christ makes living for Him our highest priority and greatest joy, then what will fill our hearts with such love? The answer comes in the words of John Newton's famous hymn: "Amazing grace ... that saved a wretch like me."

THE POWER OF GRACE

Grace fills our hearts with the surpassing love for God that compels genuine Christian living (2 Corinthians 5:14-15). When we grasp the wonder of the love of God for us, then love for Him grips our minds, fills our hearts, and empowers our lives by diminishing all other loves. Igniting such a compelling love for God is the beautiful and powerful effect of identifying the grace of God that flows through all the Bible.

That's why the devotions that follow in *Daily Grace* constantly shine the light of God's grace on every passage of Scripture. Such light fills the Christian heart with reasons and resources to love the Savior and live for Him. The light of grace enables lives of praise.

Since hearts filled with love for God are emptied of love for the world, each devotion highlights an aspect of grace that can increase love for Him. The Bible assures us of the blessed consequence: without love for the world, its temptations lose their power. We simply are less tempted to do what we have less desire to do. A preeminent love for God makes doing His will the believer's greatest joy, and this joy is our strength (Nehemiah 8:10).

Daily Grace will help you meditate on how you can apply the Bible to your life in a grace-centered way. As you discern how God's grace radiates in Christ's love for you, then you will delight to love Him. That means you will delight to love what and whom He loves. Such delight in His delight not only provides the power for personal holiness but stimulates love for the unlovely, provision for the needy, and care for all that Christ loves. His heart will become your heart and, as a consequence, His ways will become your ways. Embracing Jesus's love for you will cause you to love to live for Him.

DAILY GRACE

365 DAILY DEVOTIONS

1

Blessed be the God and Father of our Lord Jesus Christ,
the Father of mercies and God of all comfort, who comforts
us in all our affliction, so that we may be able to comfort
those who are in any affliction, with the comfort with which
we ourselves are comforted by God. (2 Corinthians 1:3–4)

Every year the calendar starts over at January 1. But just because the calendar changes doesn't mean our circumstances do. Maybe you're facing the affliction of a health scare or a financial hardship. Maybe you're in a rocky relationship or have problems at work.

Whatever affliction you're facing right now, do not think that it or its lessons are worthless. The comfort God provides in earthly difficulty becomes more real to those God intends us to reach because we have *really* known it.

My wife tells of being unable to hear the thoughts of a famous speaker, until that woman sat in a chair and unknowingly revealed a shoe with a hole in the sole. Suddenly all the women listening knew that the woman speaking of God's comfort through deprivation *really* knew what she was speaking about.

None of us should want affliction—or waste it. When we know more of God's eternal comforts through our earthly afflictions, we are best able to share the truths of eternity with those needing God.

> **PRAYER:** Father, You know the difficulties I'm experiencing and will provide as You know best for my eternity. May confidence in this grace give me comfort in affliction that You have prepared me to share with others in need!

2

We know that a person is not justified by works of the law but through faith in Jesus Christ, so we also have believed in Christ Jesus, in order to be justified by faith in Christ and not by works of the law, because by works of the law no one will be justified. (Galatians 2:16)

One of my favorite people I met early in my church ministry. Maudette had lived alone as a widow for many years. But even in her advanced years, she tended her garden with great devotion. Her care resulted in beautiful flowers for our church each week that Maudette arranged around the platform.

When she died, a minister from Maudette's distant family suggested that she had *earned* God's favor by tending her garden for the benefit of our church. The minister was trying to be cordial, but all who knew Maudette knew the better truth she lived.

Maudette's garden was an expression of *her love* for Christ—not an effort to make Him love her.

Her hope was not in her flowers. Her hope was in her Savior! Like Maudette, may you have a great faith in your Savior's love, not in any work of your own that will fade with the flowers of this earth!

PRAYER: *Lord, may I never imagine that I can earn Your grace or favor. May my daily service to You be motivated by my gratitude for the unfading mercy You provided for me in the finished work of Jesus Christ, my Savior.*

3

*I appeal to you therefore, brothers, by the mercies of God, to
present your bodies as a living sacrifice, holy, and acceptable
to God, which is your spiritual worship. (Romans 12:1)*

For many years, I thought God's acceptance hinged on my righteousness. I read passages like Romans 12:1 as a threat. This is what my heart heard: "Present your bodies as a living sacrifice *and then you will be* holy and acceptable to God."

It was as though God were wagging His finger at me and saying, "Now you be a good living sacrifice, and *then* you will be holy and acceptable to Me." The word, "holy," should have been a clue to my mistake. Nothing that we will do will make us acceptable to God. Our best works are only "filthy rags" to Him (Isaiah 64:6).

What I missed was that the words, "holy and acceptable," are not statements of what we will become, but declarations of what we are. How can that be possible for sinners like us? Don't miss the opening words: "by the mercies of God."

God's mercies in Christ make us holy and acceptable. That's why we offer ourselves as holy sacrifices in lives of worship that praise our merciful God. It's not our works that make us holy, but His. Our sacrifice doesn't make Him love us; Jesus's did. That's why we live for Him as a sacrifice of praise.

PRAYER: *Father, thank You for being merciful to me! Help my heart to grasp the greatness of that mercy so that I will offer my life to You as a sacrifice of praise that You have made holy and acceptable despite my many weaknesses and flaws.*

4

I will give you a new heart, and a new spirit I will put
within you. And I will remove the heart of stone from
your flesh and give you a heart of flesh. (Ezekiel 36:26)

For most of my friend's adult life, he tried to reach his harsh-talking and hard-hearted aunt with the message of Christ's love. Still, the older woman's heart seemed untouched.

After she passed away, her family gathered to divide her belongings. The family surprisingly found a few religious books and decided they should go to my "religious" friend. Yet, because the books reeked of tobacco and a stuffy house, he stored them in his attic without looking inside.

Years later, he stumbled across the books, and found in one a handwritten letter from his aunt. In her own hand, she confessed her sins and claimed Jesus as her Savior. My friend was shocked.

Though he would have offhandedly affirmed, "God can reach anyone," he really didn't expect that to happen with his aunt. Yet, her letter confirmed that no matter how hard the heart, God's grace is greater. He can take a stony heart and make it soft for Jesus.

Real change is possible, and to be prayed for, because grace is real and powerful. Consider someone in your life whose heart you think is too hard for God. Pray for God to soften their hearts. He can. After all, He softened yours!

> **PRAYER:** Lord, help me not to give up on sharing the Gospel with those whose hearts seem hard, knowing that Your Spirit can make a heart of stone soften and beat for Jesus.

5

Do not present your members to sin as instruments for unrighteousness, but present yourselves to God as those who have been brought from death to life, and your members to God as instruments for righteousness. For sin will have no dominion over you, since you are not under law but under grace. (Romans 6:13–14)

Many of us struggle to reconcile our desire to please God with the fact that we still sin. We ask the question, "God, will I ever be able to please You?"

The Apostle Paul makes it clear in Romans 6 that we are no longer under the control of sin. The grace of God has brought new life that *should* no longer engage in sinful pursuits or passions. But with the *should* is also a *can*—a promise of new ability.

Sin no longer has dominion over us; we are no longer slaves to sin. Yes, we all stumble and fall sometimes. But we do not have to remain defeated. We do not have to grovel in the dirt of our discouragement or surrender to repetitive failure.

God has granted us new life that is not powerless to resist sin. We have been freed from the guilt *and* power of sin. So, instead of groveling, we focus on believing; instead of surrendering, we start anew.

We believe the Bible's promise of power for a new life, rejecting Satan's lie that there is no hope or help for us. Then, by believing we *can*, we start to live again in the power that is ours by Christ's grace.

> **PRAYER:** Lord, thank You for delivering me from slavery to sin. Help me to really believe in that deliverance so that I can start this day presenting myself to You as one who has been brought from death to life in Christ.

6

You shall love the Lord your God with all your heart and with all your soul and with all your strength and with all your mind, and your neighbor as yourself. (Luke 10:27)

Love for God produces more love. That is why Jesus says love for God is the greatest commandment. When loving Him is our highest priority and greatest desire, then we also love what and whom He loves. As a result, our love for God becomes the basis for living for Him and caring for others.

The grace of God that stimulates such love for God will not allow us to settle into a cozy sweater of self-absorbed satisfaction that ignores a hurting world. A heart captivated by grace beats with God's love and concern for His world.

That's why Jesus commands us to love God with all our heart, soul, strength, and mind, *and* our neighbor as ourselves. If we love God deeply, we will love our neighbors too, reflecting His love for us in the way that we love others. Because we love Jesus, we love all those He loves.

> **PRAYER:** Father, I know that we live in a hurting world. Please help me to sense deeply Your grace toward me, so that as my heart responds in love for You, I will love all that You love.

If I then, your Lord and Teacher, have washed your feet, you also ought to wash one another's feet. For I have given you an example, that you also should do just as I have done to you. (John 13:14–15)

Many years ago, my wife, Kathy, and I were given a small wooden plaque that has become one of our most treasured possessions. Not because it's made of anything fancy but because of the message it bears: "Home is where each lives for the other and all live for God."

The plaque has survived multiple moves, an occasional bump, and even a few repairs, but remains on daily display. You see, after all these years, Kathy and I have discovered that our happiness has never been found in using one another. It's found in using the resources and privileges God has given us to serve one another as Jesus served His disciples—and us!

When we exercise the sacrificial love of Christ, we deepen our understanding of God's care for us. And, as we discover and rediscover our own value to Him, we are made more able and willing to share His love! True happiness comes from giving ourselves to each other, as Christ modeled His care.

PRAYER: Jesus, I'm amazed that You, the Lord of Heaven, would stoop to wash earth from the feet of others. Help me today to find the joy of serving others with such care, and in doing so discover and rediscover the depth of Your care for me.

8

*The grace of God has appeared, bringing salvation for
all people, training us to renounce ungodliness
and worldly passions, and to live self-controlled, upright,
and godly lives in the present age. (Titus 2:11–12)*

I was just in my twenties when I concluded that I was a failure as a pastor. Every Sunday, I felt like I was just serving up shame and blame to get people to walk the straight and narrow like the Bible's heroes.

I thought I had to intimidate people into obeying God. I confessed to my wife, "I did not become a pastor to hurt people, but my preaching hurts people every Sunday—and I cannot do this anymore."

But then, the Lord exposed me to the ministry of a man who preached very differently. He specialized in displaying how flawed were all the "heroes" of the Bible—save One. The one true hero—Jesus—everyone else needed.

That perspective saved my ministry and revolutionized my preaching. I realized that if God could use people as messed up as those in the Bible, then He could still use me. And I could tell others He still has purpose for them despite their messes.

The grace of God did not release me from obeying God's calling; it fueled my passion for His purposes. That's what Paul says God's grace will do: it trains us to renounce ungodliness. When grace captures our hearts, we love to please the One who loved us and gave Himself for us.

Will some take advantage of God's grace? Of course. But those transformed by His grace love to love Him. Grace is the fuel of true godliness.

PRAYER: *Father, may the grace Jesus died to give captivate my heart more and more, so that I do what I most love to do: serve You with the passion of profound gratitude for Jesus.*

9

Do not repay evil for evil or reviling for reviling,
but on the contrary, bless, for to this you were called,
that you may obtain a blessing. (1 Peter 3:9)

We have a tendency to treat others the way they treat us. If they are nice to us, then we are nice to them. And if they are mean to us, then we either ignore them or find a way to "give as good as we got!"

But this tit-for-tat way of approaching relationships blinds us to Gospel realities. Relating to people solely on the basis of what they've done is not God's way. Scripture says our brothers and sisters in Christ are members of His family—indwelt by His Spirit and precious to Him despite their flaws.

Jesus intends for us to relate to other believers on the basis of our eternal relationship with Him and the identity He gives them by His grace.

There may be difficult things for us to work through, but Christians are called to approach one another on the basis of our status in Christ's family. So, we treat one another with the respect and love Christ provides, not simply on the basis of temporal tensions our fallen world produces.

You sense and share Gospel realities by looking past the inflamed eyes of those whose criticism or rage intends you harm to see Jesus indwelling them, claiming their hearts, and calling you to love them beyond their sin—and yours!

PRAYER: Lord, may I treat others the way You treat me, not repaying evil for evil but rather showing them the grace and love that I have received because of Christ in them and in me.

10

God chose what is foolish in the world to shame the wise;
God chose what is weak in the world to shame the strong;
God chose what is low and despised in the world ... to bring
to nothing things that are, so that no human being might
boast in the presence of God. (1 Corinthians 1:27–29)

There's an old story which goes something like this: When Jesus ascended into Heaven, He gathered His heavenly hosts around and explained what He would do next. He said He would take the weak, sinful, frail, and filthy people that He saved and use them as living stones to build the foundation of His Kingdom on Earth. *These* would be the ones to change the world!

The announcement was welcomed with an overwhelming silence. Then, after a long, agonizing pause, the angel Gabriel broke the silence by asking, "What's Plan B?"

There is no Plan B, because God's plan has always been to use people like us—weak, sinful, frail, and filthy—to show the wonders of His grace that are the foundation of hope for this world.

Be encouraged today, knowing that your flaws do not disqualify you from God's purposes. He is building hope for our world by pouring His glorious grace into and out of cracked earthen vessels like us! The broken pots of our lives are forming the foundation of a Kingdom that is hope for all.

PRAYER: *Heavenly Father, I am encouraged to know that You have chosen people like me to display Your grace in a fallen world for broken people. Grant me grace today to show Your mercy to those who doubt You could love them by telling them that You even love sinners like me.*

11

And as he was setting out on His journey, a man ran
up and knelt before him and asked him, "Good Teacher,
what must I do to inherit eternal life?" (Mark 10:17)

Remember this rich young ruler who wondered what *he should do* to gain Heaven? Jesus gives the young man an opportunity to understand the grace of the Gospel by first reminding him, "Only God is good."

The man is too intent on proving his own deserving to listen. He tells Jesus, "I have kept all of God's commandments since I was a child!"

Jesus had just said, "Only God is good," and moments later the spiritually deaf man gives himself that same distinction, as if he is as good as God.

God's Word teaches that none of us is completely righteous. All have sinned and fallen short of the glory of God (Romans 3:23).

That's why moral and doctrinal instructions that make no mention of the necessity of grace lead away from God—just as the young man who was so intent on touting his goodness ultimately walked away from Jesus.

We are most determined to live for God when we know He provides care despite our undeserving it, not because we have qualified for His love. After all, who needs God or His grace if you think you're already good enough without Him?

> **PRAYER:** Lord, help me to remember that I really am a sinful person who falls short of Your glory, so that I will live in thanksgiving for the grace and forgiveness You have offered to me through Jesus Christ.

12

*Let us consider how to stir up one another to love
and good works, not neglecting to meet together,
as is the habit of some, but encouraging one another,
and all the more as you see the Day
drawing near. (Hebrews 10:24–25)*

During a youth event, a group of teens gathered in a circle for devotions. But one girl sat alone, feeling dejected. Her life seemed unbearable, and she sobbed that nobody loved her. The other kids began to read encouraging Scripture verses to her, reminding her of God's love.

So, when she asked, "Why doesn't God really talk to me that way?" the youth pastor replied, "He does. He just did. God talked to you through the truths of Scripture as your friends encouraged you with His Word."

That's so helpful for us to remember: God can still speak to us from His Word, encouraging us with its truths. Sometimes God simply brings His Word to mind. Other times He comforts us by using understanding friends or family to bring His Word into our work, worship, and relationships.

Whether we are recipients of God's encouragement or dispensers of it, the eternal promises of His Word are always our greatest source of assurance in a broken world until the great day when Jesus returns to make all things right.

PRAYER: *Father, thank You for encouraging me through Your Word, as it echoes in my heart and as I receive it through brothers and sisters in Christ. Help me today to hear You and to be an instrument of sharing the comfort of Your Word with those around me.*

13

Truly, truly, I say to you, whatever you ask of the Father
in my name, he will give it to you. Until now you
have asked nothing in my name. Ask, and you will
receive, that your joy may be full. (John 16:23–24)

It's easy to pray to God in a moment of desperation, or politely tell someone, "I'll pray for you." We offer such prayers when we see no alternative or as a simple courtesy. But such habits can obscure the real purposes of prayer.

Prayers to God in Jesus's name are powerful instruments of divine blessing. When we pray in Jesus's name, we are asking God to do whatever is necessary in our lives to bring maximum glory to His Son and maximum good for His purposes.

A prayer in Jesus's name is not simply a prayer for our personal benefit—that would be a prayer in our name. Prayer in Jesus's name submits our finite understanding to God's infinitely good plan to show Christ's character and care. Whenever we pray in Jesus's name we are praying as Jesus did: "Yet, not My will, Father, but Your will be done."

So, the next time you pray, do so with confidence that God will always honor prayers truly offered in Jesus's name—even if the answer is according to His perfect will, rather than our human wisdom!

PRAYER: *Father, may my daily prayers be focused on Your good plan for Christ's name and not just my selfish desires. Thank You for the confidence I can have that, when I pray in Jesus's name, You hear and answer for infinite, eternal good!*

14

*Before they call, I will answer; while they are
yet speaking I will hear. (Isaiah 65:24)*

For many years, George Müeller never asked anyone for money to help fund his orphanage. He simply relied on prayer for the children's needs, and God had always provided. But on March 9, 1842, things took a turn, and resources the orphanage needed ran out.

Just when all had seemed lost, a special-delivery letter arrived. Inside that envelope was a sizeable gift that had been mailed several days earlier. Though originally misdirected, the timely arrival of the letter meant that the Lord had begun answering Müeller's prayers days before he asked.

God had interwoven the thoughts, events, and timing of all the details, so that the donation would arrive at the crucial moment it was needed.

The point of this is not that we should never ask for support from others—the Apostle Paul asked and taught us how (2 Corinthians 8). Rather, when we ask God for help, we do so with the confidence that the One who knows the end from the beginning will do precisely what is best. He is not guessing at outcomes. God is weaving everything together for good, even before we know what to ask. So ask!

PRAYER: *Father, thank You for always providing what is best for my greatest needs. Thank You for arranging all things so that Your blessings are being prepared even before I ask or know to. Help me to trust Your wisdom enough to ask for Your supply even when the wells of my wisdom run dry.*

No temptation has overtaken you that is not common to man. God is faithful, and he will not let you be tempted beyond your ability, but with the temptation he will also provide the way of escape, that you may be able to endure it. (1 Corinthians 10:13)

In my youth, I took comfort from my understanding that this verse taught that there was no struggle in my life that others somewhere in the world did not share. Misery loves company. But that poor-me view does not do justice to the verse.

The apostle's observation is far more comprehensive. He reminds us that there is no temptation in the world that is not common to us *all* (see also James 2:19). No, we have not all murdered or robbed others, but, "the seed of every sin is in every heart" (John Owen).

Jealousy, lust, pride, anger, self-righteousness, and greed have roots in all of us. Acknowledging our common vulnerability should stir us *all* to seek God's pardon, to sympathize with others' struggles, and to seek the path of escape God always promises.

Yes, next time you're feeling tempted, take comfort because you're not alone. But, the next time you face someone who has yielded to temptation, replace pride in your righteous resistance with proclamation of Christ's righteous provision for all who are vulnerable to temptation—including you.

Never will we find power against sin in our pride, but only in the humility that acknowledges our need for spiritual strength from daily grace.

> **PRAYER:** Lord, help me not to face the temptations of this day with the thought that I am invulnerable or alone. Please provide the way of escape that I need by turning my heart from pride to seeking You for the daily grace that I—and all others—need, and that You are faithful to supply.

16

*All Scripture is breathed out by God and profitable for
teaching, for reproof, for correction, and for training
in righteousness, that the man of God may be complete,
equipped for every good work. (2 Timothy 3:16–17)*

God's Word is perfectly inspired by the Holy Spirit to reveal His eternal truth and our daily purposes. But we can read the words and still miss the intentions of God's heart. For that reason, whenever we read a passage of Scripture, we need to put on our "Gospel glasses!"

We will read God's true intention by reading every biblical text through lenses formed by two key questions. The first is, "What does this passage tell me about the nature of the God who provides redemption?" And the second is, "What does this passage tell me about the nature of humanity that requires redemption?"

Or, more simply, "What does this text tell me about God?" And, "What does it tell me about myself?" The answers to those questions will ultimately reveal a gap between us and God that only the grace of God can span to cover our sin and enable us to love Him.

Anyone can read the words of the Bible, but to see God's heart, you have to *put on your Gospel glasses!*

> **PRAYER:** Lord, as I read the Bible, make the truths inspired by Your Holy Spirit be more than mere words on a page. Enable me to see the dimensions of Your heart by helping me consistently put on the Gospel glasses that reveal the grace You provide and I require.

17

My little children, I am writing you these things so that you may not sin. But if anyone does sin, we have an advocate with the Father—Jesus Christ the righteous one. He himself is the atoning sacrifice for our sins, and not only for ours, but also for those of the whole world. (1 John 2:1–2 CSB)

It's almost too pat to say, "If you get off God's *path*, the Bible will get you back on." But what exactly does that mean? What exactly is this *path*?

Scripture tells us that God's path is His instruction. He writes in His Word what is right and wrong so that we would not wander into sin and experience its miseries. But, if you don't understand the heart behind that instruction, then you may look at God's path through worried eyes. You become anxious that God is watching for any opportunity to punish you for straying from His path.

But that's not the message of the Bible. Yes, there is a path to walk but if we step off, we have an Advocate with the Father who paid the penalty for our sin. His sacrifice is sufficient to pay for the sins of the whole world, so we can be confident there will be enough grace for any of us who seek His provision.

The love that laid the path is from the heart that provides pardon for those who have Jesus as their Advocate. Knowing that His love does not depart when our steps do draws us back to the path that blesses all who walk according to His instruction!

PRAYER: Heavenly Father, thank You for instructing me daily through Your Word. And when I sin, help me to realize that Jesus paid the penalty for all my sins, so that I will have no fear of returning to You and to Your path of instruction!

18

*Every valley shall be lifted up, and every mountain
and hill be made low; and the uneven ground shall become
level, and the rough places a plain. And the glory of the* Lord
*shall be revealed, and all flesh shall see it together,
for the mouth of the* Lord *has spoken. (Isaiah 40:4–5)*

A family driving toward a Colorado vacation got excited as the mountains came into view. The father had been waiting for the moment. He took out a topographical map, showing his children how high the mountains rose and how deep were their valleys.

The display caused everyone to get even more excited about the natural wonders ahead, except the youngest daughter. Observing how high the mountains and how deep the valleys, she shrieked, "Oh daddy, we're going to fall off!"

The father quickly assured his child that someone had gone before them building bridges.

That's what Jesus did for us, too. Our holy God is high and lifted up, and we would only fall in our attempts to reach Him. So, He went ahead of us, bridging the gap between us and Himself.

The valleys of our sin have been filled with Christ's righteousness. Across the gap between God's holiness and our lowliness is Jesus's cross.

We need not build another bridge to God, only have faith to travel to Him on the One He has laid.

> **PRAYER:** Lord, thank You for bridging the gap between us and You through the cross of Christ. May my faith be in His work, not mine, so that I journey through this life with the confidence and joy of one who is eternally safe.

19

He sent from on high, he took me; he drew me out
of many waters. He rescued me from my strong
enemy and from those who hated me, for they
were too mighty for me. (Psalm 18:16–17)

Sometimes we think that we need a hero to drop from on high to save us from whatever calamity or evil we're facing! But however our rescue comes, the one who ultimately rescues is God.

We don't need to deny that a human person may physically rescue us, but we should understand that the presence and willingness to save came from the plan and provision of God.

Jesus said that apart from Him we could do nothing. That means all human resources, wisdom, courage, opportunities, and resolve ultimately come from our God. He is the ultimate rescuer, and His ultimate rescue was eternal, even though it was accomplished by sending His Son from on high to a cruel cross.

Because God sent Jesus to rescue us by taking the penalty of our sin on His cross, we do not have to suffer that penalty ourselves. But our blessings are not only spiritual. As those so loved by God, we are also protected from all that would damage our souls or endanger our eternity.

We were rescued from the eternal consequences of our sin, and are rescued daily from all that would jeopardize God's perfect plan for our earthly lives.

> **PRAYER:** Father, this world is filled with dangers, threats, and calamities. Thank You for rescuing me for eternity, and for assuring me now that nothing in Heaven or Earth can separate me from Your love. You are my daily hero!

20

He has said, "I will never leave you nor forsake you."
So we can confidently say, "The Lord is my helper;
I will not fear; what can man do to me?" (Hebrews 13:5–6)

Leaving home for the first time can be an exciting but overwhelming experience. My own trip to college was such. At first, I was bubbling with excitement as my father drove me to the school I had never visited, in a town I did not know. Then, anxiety crept over me.

As my bubbling conversation ceased, my father read the anxiety signaled by my silence. He pulled the car off the road, looked me in the eye, and said, "I don't know if you will do well or if you'll do poorly at this school, but you are my son, and that will never change. There's always a place for you in my home."

Such are the assurances of the Gospel of grace that God has given to you. His love will not be determined by what you do—but by Whose you are.

We are *children* of our Heavenly Father, and because we are His children, His love will never leave or forsake us. There will always be a place for us in His heart. That doesn't make all earthly challenges go away, but we face them without crippling anxiety, knowing nothing can sever us from His eternal care!

PRAYER: *Father, thank You for the promise that You will never leave me or forsake me! Give me courage to face every trial by remembering that earthly challenges are no match for my eternal security in Your heart.*

21

*"I will put enmity between you and the woman,
and between your offspring and hers; he will crush your
head, and you will strike his heel." (Genesis 3:15 NIV)*

There are not many places in the Bible where God addresses Satan, and this one is crucial. If we're going to understand how grace unfolds throughout Scripture to culminate in Christ's work, we must grasp the power of this first prophecy of Jesus. It is God's earliest war cry declaring Satan's ruin.

After Satan's temptation resulted in sin that corrupted our world, God immediately revealed His rescue plan. He promised to send an offspring of Eve who would ultimately crush the power of Satan. That offspring is Jesus!

God also tells us that the offspring of Eve will suffer injury from battling Satan, but Jesus's victory is sure. Satan will be destroyed, and many people will be made righteous (Isaiah 53:11). So, God tells us from the beginning, "You are not your Redeemer, but I will send Him to suffer and save you."

Not all subsequent texts teach this grace in the same way. Sometimes the Bible reveals aspects of grace through prophecies like this, but also through poetry, history, proverbs, and inspired letters.

As different as these Bible passages are, they have a common denominator: they show how God provides for those who cannot provide for themselves. The many facets of the diamond of grace are polished on every page of Scripture until we can see and treasure the jewel that Jesus is.

Through this jewel of grace, we not only understand how God's plan of salvation unfolds but how we should live in response to Christ's victory.

PRAYER: Father, thank You for promising the victorious grace of Jesus and revealing it with the divine patience needed for my heart. May the grace You unfold throughout Scripture capture my heart and change my life for His glory.

22

But you are a chosen race, a royal priesthood, a holy
nation, a people for His own possession, that you may
proclaim the excellencies of him who called you out of
darkness into His marvelous light. (1 Peter 2:9)

I have a friend who traverses the world helping corporations turn around their company culture. One day, he let me in on the secret of his success: to effect healthy transformation, the most important words you can say to another are *I am proud of you.*

It's often much easier to see flaws and point out messes when someone hasn't measured up to our standards. Honest critiques have their place but saying that you're proud and thankful for others is spiritual fuel without which positive energy dies.

The Apostle Peter knew that as he addressed oppressed and distressed Christians. Despite their struggles, he described them in precious terms made possible by the realities of God's grace toward them.

The apostle put on his Gospel glasses to tell people how he saw them through the lens of God's love. He could have cited many failures and shortcomings—and would offer correction in his letters—but affirmation came first.

After telling me his secret, my friend paused and then made his own confession: "I haven't told my struggling son that I am proud of him in years." The confession transformed his family relationships and helped change his son.

If you can withhold your criticism long enough to extend God's grace, then life-transforming power you've been given is yours to give to another.

PRAYER: Lord, I pray that You will enable me to look beyond human flaws and see people as you see them, extending to them such grace as You have lavished upon me.

23

Thanks be to God, that you who were once slaves of sin have become obedient from the heart to the standard of teaching to which you were committed, and, having been set free from sin, have become slaves of righteousness. (Romans 6:17–18)

There is a math of the mind that reasons, "If God will forgive all my sin, and substitute Christ's good work for my bad behavior, then I might as well keep sinning!" But that's not the only way our thoughts can function.

The Apostle Paul counters the shady math of such thinking with a leading question: "Are we to continue in sin so that grace may abound? By no means!"

Why? Because, as Paul explains, no one wants to be "enslaved to sin." Does anyone who has been "set free" from slavery really want to go back to it?

Paul makes clear the enslaving power of sin to caution us against any mental math that would try to take advantage of God's grace to subject our lives and loved ones to sin's ravages.

The apostle never waters down the Gospel of God's grace to turn us away from the horrors of sin. Nothing could be clearer than him saying, "Where sin increased, grace abounded all the more" (Romans 5:20).

Yet, as a preacher said long ago, "Grace is not sweet, if sin is not bitter." So, Paul makes us face the reality of enslavement to the guilt and power of sin so that we will treasure our freedom from its chains and embrace the life secured by the grace of Christ.

PRAYER: Father, thank You for freeing me from the slavery of sin and making me a servant of righteousness. May I never presume on Your grace but rather respond in gratitude and obedience to the life without chains secured by Your grace.

24

*By this we know love, that he laid down His life
for us, and we ought to lay down our lives for the
brothers.... Little children, let us not love with words
or talk but in deed and in truth (1 John 3:16, 18)*

Local news reported on two brothers who decided to play on mounded sandbanks formed by the dredging that keeps our local river channel clear. When the young boys were late for dinner, a search began.

Searchers found the younger brother unconscious—buried up to his shoulders in sand. He had stepped on a crust of sand hiding a large void formed by the dredging of wet sand from the river bottom. When the crust gave way, the boy fell in the void with its sand walls collapsing upon him.

When he was roused to consciousness, rescuers frantically asked, "Where is your brother? The child replied: "I'm standing on his shoulders."

With the sacrifice of his own life, the older brother had saved the life of the younger. With similar selflessness, Jesus, who is not ashamed to call Himself our brother, saved us. We were rescued from the pit of our sin by standing on the sacrifice of our elder Brother—who gave His life that we might live!

He now calls us to honor His love by sharing it with others, not just with words but with deeds as selfless as His own.

PRAYER: Lord, as I consider again what it means for You to have laid down Your life for me, give me a fresh appreciation of Your love. Then, fill my heart with Your love to give me a renewed desire to tell and show the world Your grace.

25

*You did not choose me, but I chose you and appointed
you so that you might go and bear fruit—fruit that
will last—and so that whatever you ask in my name
the Father will give you. (John 15:16 NIV)*

Why do we finish our prayers with the refrain "In Jesus's name?" Is this just a religious way of saying, *Roger wilco ... over and out?*

No, we pray in Jesus's name because of the assurance that the Father will give us whatever we ask that most honors Jesus's name. That is the secret to our fruitfulness as Christians. We submit ourselves and our prayers to the glory of our God more than to selfish gain.

You see, by God's grace and the goodness of the Son's and Spirit's work, believers were chosen for the glorious purpose of fulfilling aspects of God's eternal plan. We tend to see our lives only in the context of our daily goals and concerns, but God is weaving our lives—the good and the bad, the easy and the hard—into His infinitely good and lasting plan.

So, when we pray in Jesus's name, we are not coming to God to demand blessings based on our limited wisdom and merits, but we are confessing our need of God's wisdom and Christ's merits to bear fruit that is infinitely good and eternally blessed!

> **PRAYER:** Father, thank You for the assurance that anything I truly ask in Jesus's name and for His glory will be granted. Please help my prayers to bear the fruit that You intend because I am yielding my desires to Christ's purposes!

26

For if while we were enemies we were reconciled to God by the death of His Son, much more, now that we are reconciled, shall we be saved by His life. (Romans 5:10)

Many of us have heard a well-meaning Sunday school teacher or parent saying to children, "If you're a good little boy or girl, Jesus will love you." That may sound sweet, but it is *spiritual poison*. Telling children that Jesus loves them because of their behavior is totally contrary to the Gospel.

Jesus does not love any child, young or old, because the child is good. Jesus loves His children because *He* is good. The child trained to obey Jesus in order to secure His love will become the adult who doubts Jesus's love—especially when life's challenges make it clear that we are not always good little boys and girls.

Jesus really does love you, not because you are good but because *He* is good! Trust His goodness more than your own and teach your children to do the same.

PRAYER: *Jesus, thank You for loving me, not because I am a good person but because You are a good, gracious, and merciful God. Help me today to respond to Your grace by loving You more deeply and helping all of the children that You place in my life to do the same.*

27

Have this mind among yourselves, which is yours in Christ Jesus,
who, though he was in the form of God, did not count
equality with God a thing to be grasped,
but emptied himself, by taking the form of a servant,
being born in the likeness of men. (Philippians 2:5–7)

Hearts open to the message of Scripture soon recognize that God never commends nor commands selfishness. Instead, He uses the example of His Son's willingness to empty Himself of Heaven's glory to serve our needs as a way of calling us to serve others' needs sacrificially.

That can sound like a dreary calling and a sad life until we remember that Jesus also said, "Whoever finds his life will lose it, and whoever loses his life for my sake will find it" (Matthew 10:39).

Living a life with a willingness to serve to others frees us from the bondage of our self-serving appetites and selfish ambitions. In this new freedom, our lives become more fulfilling, less driven; more purposeful, less self-absorbed; more glorifying to the God we love, less a burden to those we love—and more a delight to live!

PRAYER: Lord, as Your glory was fulfilled and Your joy was made full when You were willing to become a servant to humanity, please help me to find the glory and joy of serving You by serving others.

28

The Spirit of the Lord GOD is upon me, because the LORD has anointed me to bring good news to the poor; he has sent me to bind up the brokenhearted, to proclaim liberty to the captives, and the opening of the prison to those who are bound. (Isaiah 61:1)

I magine a man in jail, sitting there with men who are far more hardened than he is. This man is middle-aged but mentally on the level of a frightened and confused eight-year-old.

And now imagine another man in that same cell who sees this man weeping in terror. So, he gets up, goes over, and quietly whispers to the one in tears: "I don't know what you are facing, but whatever it is, Jesus will help you through it if you trust Him."

Soon after, that middle-aged man with an eight-year-old mind comes to Christ and is changed forever. That man is my brother. He's still in jail for now, but his soul is free forever from God's condemnation—even as is the soul of the man who answered God's call to witness to him in that cell.

Prison bars did not keep God's grace from reaching my brother. They also will not keep him from freedom—from any impairment of mind, any limitation of body, or any guilt of sin in his ultimate heavenly home with Jesus.

Jesus promises the same freedoms to you, when you bind your heart to Him by faith, claiming the exhilarating liberty of His provisions for this life and the life to come. Trusting Jesus for pardon from our sins liberates our souls from guilt on Earth and liberates soul, mind, and body from all this world's pain in eternity!

> **PRAYER:** Lord, I know that I was in spiritual prison because of my sins, but You set me free! Now please help me to live in the freedoms that are mine forever and to tell others of how they can be free from their prisons of guilt and shame.

29

We have had earthly fathers who disciplined us and we respected them. Shall we not much more be subject to the Father of spirits and live? For they disciplined us for a short time as it seemed best to them, but he disciplines us for our good, that we may share His holiness. (Hebrews 12:9–10)

Obedience to God's standards is not a condition of His love for us, though it does affect our daily experience of His joy and peace. If we walk off His path of spiritual safety, we shouldn't be surprised that there are consequences. Those consequences are actually an indication of His love rather than the absence of it.

If God didn't love us, He would simply let us wander off and face even greater harm. In discipline, the divine hand is simply turning us back to the path designed by hands that will hold us eternally.

So, remember that even when we are in the throes of the harshest correction, God is showing His grace to us and turning us toward a great love that would shield us from the greater dangers and consequences of our sin!

PRAYER: *Heavenly Father, I know that You discipline me not out of arbitrary anger but rather out of love that only intends good and never damage to my soul. Help me today not to mistake a severe mercy for a capricious hand, and to grow in my desire and ability to follow Your loving will.*

30

Peace I leave with you; my peace I give to you.
Not as the world gives do I give to you. Let not your hearts
be troubled, neither let them be afraid. (John 14:27)

What is the peace that the world gives? It is a slice of time without pressure, problem, or threat. We can know such times but, in a fallen world, such peace never lasts. Knowing that, our hearts are never really at peace amidst the world's inevitable troubles.

Christ's peace can be distinguished from that of the world by paintings produced for an art competition. The prize was promised to the artist who best depicted *peace*.

One artist painted a pastoral scene: sheep in a rich pasture of green, a flowing stream, and a cloudless sky on a beautiful sunny day.

The other artist painted a storm at sea, with waves crashing, winds blowing, and the sea foaming. Yet, in the middle of the raging sea was a pelican calmly riding the waves through the storm.

Who won the competition? The one representing what Jesus wants us to understand: *Real peace is not the absence of trouble, but confidence in the midst of trouble.*

True peace in this world will never come through the perfection of our circumstances, but through confidence in the eternal security our Savior graciously provides.

PRAYER: *Father, when the storms of life surround me, may I experience the peace that passes understanding through confidence in my Savior's gracious provision of eternal care.*

31

What shall we say then? Are we to continue in sin
that grace may abound? By no means! How can we
who died to sin still live in it? (Romans 6:1–2)

Here, the Apostle Paul strongly cautions against using the grace of God to continue to sin by figuring, "All will be forgiven." This is not because there isn't enough of God's grace to forgive mounting sins.

Instead, Paul reminds believers that grace has destroyed the sinful life that once enslaved us. No one should want to go back to living in slavery. If we truly understand how powerful and profound is the grace of God that has made our slavery a thing of the past—an existence that is dead to us now—then we will never want to go back to that life.

Yes, God will always forgive those who confess their sin and need of Him. But, once we understand how incredibly gracious, generous, and loving is His pardon, then we increasingly desire to turn from the sin that grieves Him and enslaves us!

Resting on God's grace does not relieve our obligation to honor Him but powerfully stimulates our love to live for God's glory and in our freedom!

> PRAYER: Father, thank You for setting me free in Christ from the slavery of sin. Keep me today from returning to sin's slavery as I live to glorify You and to rejoice in the freedom from sin's guilt and power that Jesus provides!

32

I will betroth you to me forever. I will betroth you
to me in righteousness and in justice, in steadfast love
and in mercy. I will betroth you to me in faithfulness.
And you shall know the LORD. (Hosea 2:19–20)

From the outside their life seems ideal. The house is beautiful, the kids are sweet, and they are an attractive pair. But inside their home, things are far from ideal. The wife has an addiction, and nothing seems to help. Yet, her husband continues to love and help his wife, despite her failures.

Such love and care are not original. The biblical prophet Hosea was commissioned to show such love to his wayward wife to display God's covenant-keeping care for the habitually sinful people of Israel.

God loved, and kept loving, sinful people to show us that His grace is not dependent on our performance. Now, we who have received such grace are also called to show it—even to those who have damaged and disappointed us.

Hosea and this modern husband fulfill their biblical calling by turning a deaf ear to the voices of friends and family telling them to abandon their marriages and to move on to better wives. As a covenant-keeping God has loved us, we love.

PRAYER: Lord, even though I have been unfaithful to You in many ways, thank You for betrothing Yourself to me with covenant-keeping love. Help me so to respond in gratitude and obedience for those You call me to love.

33

You do not have, because you do not ask.
You ask and do not receive, because you ask wrongly,
to spend it on your passions. (James 4:2–3)

Faithful prayer hinges on how well we understand the meaning of *believing* prayer. We can get confused when well-meaning people bombard us with examples of praying for something they wanted to happen—displayed unwavering *belief* that it would happen—and then sat back and watched it happen.

Trouble looms whenever we make God subject to the wisdom and whims of our human desires. We need to reconsider any approach to prayer that requires God to provide all *our* wants, that allows us to sidle up to God with our finite wisdom and human desires in order to say, "Now, God, I *believe* that I have figured out what You need to do for me!"

Such prayer is not truly *believing* in God's infinite wisdom and perfect will, but in ours. Our confidence is to be that if we ask anything "according to God's will," He answers (1 John 5:14–15). Yes, we are to believe that God *always* answers biblical prayer, but such prayer trusts more in God's designs than our desires. We believe He is wise enough to answer yes, no, not yet, or above all that we would ask or even think.

PRAYER: *Heavenly Father, teach me to pray for the things You desire. Help me to trust You enough to ask for what I need and to believe that You know better than I what that is.*

34

Simon, behold, Satan demanded to have you, that he might sift you like wheat, but I have prayed for you that your faith may not fail. And when you have turned again, strengthen your brothers. (Luke 22:31–32)

We can make terrible decisions that damage us and those around us. A pastor friend went down such a path. It started as he began viewing the Bible as more a cultural document of human invention rather than as the inspired Word of God. That led him to question Christ's ministry just as Simon Peter did.

The questioning led him to honor only the parts of the Bible that he liked in the moment. The results destroyed his marriage, his ministry, and most that was dear to him in life.

He walked away from God, but the Lord was not done with him. On a "recreational trip" to the Holy Land, he confronted the realities of faith and began to "thirst again for God's Word." That Word led him back to the God in whose grace there was pardon, new life, and renewed ministry—a ministry even more committed to the necessities of grace.

If you've hit rock bottom, don't believe that means God is done with you! The darkness may be closing in, but you're not abandoned. The Lord who spells out unchanging truth in His Word is also saying, "Here's My heart for you." In that heart of grace is pardon and new life through Jesus Christ."

If such wandering from the Word marks you today, may God lead you back through His Word and back to His heart!

PRAYER: *Father, when I feel hopeless and far from You, please help me to find strength and comfort in Your Word that promises Your pardon, presence, and plan are never far.*

35

For even if I made you grieve with my letter, I do not regret it ... because you were grieved into repenting. For you felt a godly grief. (2 Corinthians 7:8–9)

The Apostle Paul tells us in 2 Corinthians 7:10 that godly grief produces a repentance that leads to salvation without regret, whereas worldly grief produces death. There is a difference between simply feeling bad for our sin and biblical repentance.

Mere remorse comes from experiencing the shame or consequence of our sin—we feel sad for our pain. True repentance feels sorry that we have pained our God, grieving the Holy Spirit and dishonoring our witness of the Son whose sacrifice fully paid the penalty for our sin.

Remorse and regret turn us inward, focusing on our pain. Repentance turns us away from sin and toward the joy of God's mercy, responding to His grace with renewed love for pleasing Him. Repentance does not purchase God's grace with our grief or renewed obedience, but turns us from sin to God with hearts melted and moved by His free grace, filled with new resolve to honor Him.

Our repentance for sin is complete when we grieve for God's grief, rejoice in His mercy, and live in gratitude for the grace we have received and in which we can forever rest. Repentant obedience is not our ticket to grace; it is our offering of thanksgiving for it.

PRAYER: *Heavenly Father, help me to express godly sorrow for my sin. Teach me to repent of the kind of repentance that tries to purchase Your grace with my sorrow, and help me to honor You with the joy that is my strength—the joy that comes from receiving and resting in Jesus's mercy for my sin.*

36

*The prayer of a righteous person has great power as it
is working. Elijah was a person with a nature like ours,
and he prayed fervently that it might not rain.,
and for three years and six months it did not rain
on the earth. Then he prayed again, and heaven gave
rain, and the earth bore its fruit. (James 5:16–18)*

One summer, our friend Joan took her disabled husband, Tom, for a
walk down the path of a nearby park. Tom, despite his wife's support,
floundered halfway through their walk. His strength evaporated, and he simply could go no further. With no other alternatives, Joan prepared to leave
him in order to get some help.

Despite her desperation, Joan paused to pray. When she lifted her head,
a police officer was coming down the path on a bicycle.

"What made you come down this way?" Joan later asked the officer. He
said that the city council had recently approved a greater police presence in
the park, and this was the first day for the new policy.

Joan knew that the policeman's presence had actually been approved by a
higher authority. Before she even asked, Heaven was answering as God knew
was best for His children. He always will do what is best, when His children
ask—and even before they do.

> **PRAYER:** Lord, throughout this day, help me to turn to You
> in prayer, knowing that You hear me and delight to answer my
> prayers in the way You know is absolutely best.

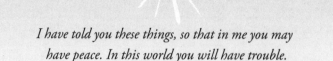

37

I have told you these things, so that in me you may
have peace. In this world you will have trouble.
But take heart! I have overcome the world. (John 16:33 NIV)

When English missionary Ann Judson accompanied her husband, Adoniram, to Burma, she could not have predicted how important she would be in reaching millions with the Gospel. Nor could she have anticipated the degree of sacrifice her usefulness would require.

When tensions arose between England and Burma, Adoniram was imprisoned as a suspected spy in horrible circumstances. Ann helped him survive with visits that were dangerous for her. She smuggled morsels of food and lifted her husband's spirits by whispering: "Do not give up. God will give us victory." When hope died in others, and Ann herself became deathly ill, the words kept Adoniram alive.

When Ann passed from this life into glory, Adoniram Judson took her words as a charge from God to keep sharing the good news of the Gospel of grace. His ministry and translation work ultimately reached millions. They were the spiritual children of Ann Judson who knew the peace and power of Jesus's words, "In this world you will have trouble. But take heart! I have overcome the world."

PRAYER: *Father, thank You for giving us the promise that Jesus's purposes will triumph despite the troubles of this world. Help me to live for Him, knowing that His purposes will prevail. Our trials will end but His triumph will not.*

38

The LORD, the LORD, a God merciful and gracious,
slow to anger, and abounding in steadfast love and
faithfulness, keeping steadfast love for thousands, forgiving
iniquity and transgression and sin. (Exodus 34:6–7)

Sometimes we use catch phrases to describe the grace we require for a relationship with our holy God. We describe grace as a "pardon," or "unmerited favor," or "it's not getting what you deserve." But such words seem rare in the Bible.

So, it's easy to draw a wrong conclusion—that grace is rare, or maybe the God of the larger Old Testament is very different from the Jesus we love in the New. The truth is that God is carefully developing our understanding of His grace through every phase and page of Scripture.

When God gives food to the hungry, rest to the weary, strength to the weak, warning to the wayward, mercy to the guilty, and hope to the hopeless—that's the message of grace steadily unfolding and becoming more clear.

Ultimately, God displays grace whenever He provides good for His people that they cannot provide for themselves. That's the grace fully revealed in Jesus, and always needed by us.

PRAYER: Lord, Your grace grows brighter and brighter until it shines perfectly in Jesus Christ. Help me to see that light when my weakness, waywardness, or difficulty makes my world seem dark—and help me to shine His light for others.

Our Father in heaven, hallowed be your name. Your kingdom come, your will be done, on earth as it is in heaven. Give us this day our daily bread, and forgive us our debts, as we also have forgiven our debtors. And lead us not into temptation, but deliver us from evil. (Matthew 6:9–13)

Have you heard the tale of the two monks and the horse? The first monk thought of a challenge for his companion. He offered him a horse if he could recite the Lord's Prayer even once without being distracted by worldly concerns.

The second monk took the bet and began to recite the prayer, but he stopped seconds later. "You win," he said. "Because even as I was praying, I began to wonder if the horse came with a saddle."

I know that kind of distraction, and I bet you do, too! Praise God for grace that He dispenses to imperfect and easily distracted people like us.

God knows my wayward thoughts and still teaches me (1) how to pray for His will to be done, (2) for my daily needs to be provided, (3) for His forgiveness to flow for me and others, and (4) for His hand to keep me from evil. Such a God I can trust to hear my imperfect prayers. The Lord's prayer reveals His heart to keep my heart riveted on Him.

> **PRAYER:** Lord, thank You for teaching me to pray! Help me not to let wayward thoughts keep me from praying. You knew me when You taught me to pray. So, help me to pray beyond my distractions for Your will to be done in me.

40

We know that for those who love God all things
work together for good, for those who are called
according to His purpose. (Romans 8:28)

Paul tells us in Romans 8:28 that God works all things together for the good of those who love Him. Paul knows we live in a fallen world. We're going to face hard things. Not all seems good or feels good or is what good people do, but God is orchestrating all for an eternal good.

The Good Shepherd promises to carry us through whatever we encounter, and to use it to deepen our faith, make us dependent on Him, and ultimately to defeat all that opposes our eternal welfare. He is always working the end game. He's more concerned about your spiritual eternity than making this temporary life easy.

We know that it is possible to draw a straight line with a crooked stick, and our sovereign, loving Lord is able to draw an eternal line of blessing with the corrupted features of this world.

When we love Him, He draws a line toward our eternity with everything we face on Earth. The corruptions of our world do not hinder the eternal plans of our gracious God but draw us to Him.

PRAYER: Father, please give me confidence in the eternal good You are accomplishing through all of life's circumstances. Help me to remember the divine love made certain through the cross of Jesus, so that I will keep believing that You love me and will use all things to accomplish Your good goals for my eternity. Help me to trust You no matter what I face today.

41

One will scarcely die for a righteous person—
though perhaps for a good person one would dare even
to die—but God shows His love for us in that while
we were still sinners, Christ died for us. (Romans 5:7–8)

Are you okay with God? Do you know God loves you? When we ask people if they are secure in God's love, we typically start an internal dialogue in their minds: *Am I okay with God? Well, how am I doing? Am I better than so-and-so? Was I good enough today?* and *What about yesterday?*

But none of these questions can get to the heart of the matter. They simply reveal someone's imperfect evaluation of their own imperfect performance or competence.

While we all should be concerned about whether our behaviors and thoughts please God, the Bible makes it clear that our qualifications don't determine His acceptance—His mercy does.

The question of whether I am okay with God cannot be answered by an assessment of anything about me, but only by acknowledging the sufficiency of Christ's provision.

His work alone can make us right with God. And, when we believe His work provided the pardon we need no matter how good our appearances or how great our sin, that's the good news of God's unlimited grace!

PRAYER: Lord, thank You for accepting me—not because of what I have done or avoided, but because of the mercy that Jesus made available on the cross. Help me to trust that His grace, rather than my qualifications, makes me okay with You—especially on the days that I know I do not qualify.

You have received the Spirit of adoption as sons, by whom
we cry, "Abba! Father!" The Spirit himself bears witness with
our spirit that we are children of God. (Romans 8:15–16)

L ong ago I read the account of a Christian who did not fully grasp the
meaning of this verse until visiting a busy market in Israel. There a lost
child ran through the crowd seeking his father by crying out, "Abba, Abba."

The account echoed sweetly for my own heart years later, as I followed
Jesus's route to the cross through the streets of Jerusalem. As the crowds
pressed upon our tour group, an Israeli child pushed past me at knee level
calling to the father who had gone ahead of us, "Abba, Abba."

The ancient endearment for "Daddy" is as used today as it was in Christ's
time, and still signals such love. When our hearts cry out with such longing
for our Heavenly Father, we not only signal our affection but witness the work
of the Holy Spirit in us.

Our love and longing for God is the evidence that He has gone before
us in life with the work of the Holy Spirit, transforming our affections. Our
seeking Him is the Spirit's witness that we are already the children of His care
and that He is ready to receive us.

God not only provides His Holy Spirit to align the desires of our thoughts
and prayers with His purposes, but also to confirm His love by our longing.
We can only love Him because He first loved us. Loving Him confirms His
love for us.

PRAYER: *Heavenly Father, confirm that I am a child of Yours*
by the love that I have for You as my Abba. May this love
granted me by the Holy Spirit be a powerful witness that I am
Your child whom Your heart is always ready to receive.

43

> *As he was setting out on His journey, a man ran up*
> *and knelt before him and asked him, "Good Teacher,*
> *what must I do to inherit eternal life?" (Mark 10:17)*

Duty and doctrine dispensed without grace can create only two possible human responses—human pride or despair. People will either think that they have checked off all the performance boxes that God requires or will despair that they never can.

Being good enough for God isn't the message of the Gospel. When the rich young ruler asked Jesus, "What must *I* do to inherit eternal life?" Jesus immediately understood the implication of the young man's question. He thought that he—a mere human—needed to *do* something good enough to inherit God's Kingdom.

Jesus quickly reminded the man (and us), "Only God is good." Thus, if our sole message to others (including our friends and families), is merely to be good or, at least, *be better* than you have been, we are ultimately teaching them to try to be God's equals.

Only by God's grace can we sinners stand before God without pride or despair, knowing that we are clothed in Jesus's righteousness before a holy God.

So, trust Christ's righteousness alone to make you good enough for God, and then show His goodness to others in how you love and live for Him.

> **PRAYER:** *Father, save me from pride or despair by rescuing me from the perspective that I have to be good enough to deserve Your love. Then, help me to teach others to trust Your grace by how I love and live for You.*

44

God, being rich in mercy, because of the great love with which he loved us, even when we were dead in our trespasses, made us alive together with Christ—by grace you have been saved—and raised us up with him and seated us with him in the heavenly places in Christ Jesus. (Ephesians 2:4–6)

There is a chemistry of the heart that is activated when we grasp the magnitude of God's love for us. It's that love that causes us to desire Him, and it's that desire that makes us *want* to walk with Him.

What sparks that "want to?" It's not faith in what we do, but in what Christ has done on our behalf.

The great Puritan writer John Bunyan was accused of encouraging disobedience by talking too much about the assurance of God's love. Accusers said, "If you keep assuring people of God's love, they will do whatever they want."

Bunyan wisely replied, "No. If we keep assuring *God's* people of God's love, they'll do what *He* wants."

We love because God first loved us (1 John 4:19), and such love is the chemistry of the Spirit that compels us to live for God (John 14:15). We need not fear that grace will always lead to license. The grace that stirs in the hearts of God's people will change their "want to" into what He wants!

PRAYER: *Father, Your Word tells us that we love You because You first loved us. May Your love stir in my heart so much that I want to walk with You and to live the kind of life that You want.*

45

Let marriage be held in honor among all,
and let the marriage bed be undefiled, for God will judge
the sexually immoral and adulterous. (Hebrews 13:4)

My wife, Kathy, and I witnessed the honor of long-lasting marital joy during a Valentine's Day social of a church filled with young couples. Despite the youth of the church, an older couple sang to entertain us.

The couple sang their own version of "Do You Love Me?" from the musical *Fiddler on the Roof.* The characters in the original musical sing, "After twenty-five years, it's nice to know you love me." But this couple looked into one another's eyes and sang, "After forty-eight years, it's nice to know...."

When they hit the last notes of the song, the room exploded in a standing ovation. The crowd of young couples cheered an enduring love that had so powerfully encouraged us all.

Kathy and I looked around the room with tears in our eyes, knowing the hopes and struggles of so many of the young people who were cheering. Their cheers for the long marriage were a longing and a prayer for similar grace in their own lives.

The reaction of the Valentine crowd echoed the words of the writer of Hebrews, who said, "Let marriage be held in honor among all." He also speaks of the beauty and purity of the marriage bed that blesses Christian marriage, reminding us that God's grace always blesses by leading us in the paths that honor Him and one another.

PRAYER: *Heavenly Father, thank You for the gift of marriage! May I honor Your blessing by honoring my spouse, and by honoring Your intention for others' marital purity also.*

46

I will instruct you and teach you in the way you should go;
I will counsel you with my eye upon you.
Be not like a horse or a mule, without understanding,
which must be curbed with bit and bridle,
or it will not stay near you. (Psalm 32:8–9)

God's precautions often come as practical advice that will keep us on the path of His blessing. And the principles of grace do not negate the importance of knowing how to avoid temptations.

Because we are human, we need practical instruction that helps us steer clear of dangers, avoiding moral pitfalls and heartache. Such guidance is not arbitrary legalism, but resistance to such guidance is self-sabotaging. Ignoring the instruction of an infinitely holy, loving, and wise God is like being a stubborn mule that needs a bit to keep it on a productive path—the Bible said that!

Why does God give such tough talk? Because we have wandering hearts that may need some stern guidance. Since God's love is not as fragile as our resolve to walk His path, He can be as practical and insistent as He needs to be: "Do not enter the path of the wicked…. Avoid it. Do not go on it. Turn away from it and pass on" (Proverbs 4:14–15).

When we know that God's love is behind such practical advice, our love for Him grows and our willingness to follow His advice strengthens. We learn to trust the divine arms that guide us, and to return to those outstretched arms when our stubbornness has taken us down a wicked path.

> **PRAYER:** Father, help me today to follow the practical advice and wise counsel You have given in Your Word. May Your truth guide me from, and enable me to overcome, whatever temptations are in my path.

47

*Though youths grow weary and tired, and vigorous young
men stumble badly, yet those who wait for the LORD will
gain new strength; they will mount up with wings like
eagles, they will run and not get tired, they will walk
and not become weary (Isaiah 40:30–31, NASB)*

This verse has never meant more to me than when ministering to a young man made an invalid by reckless driving.

Though raised a Christian, his life was wild and his heart hard to God. So, I expected his affliction would further harden him, and I dreaded speaking to him after he awoke from weeks in a coma.

For a while he fought his predicament with the rash pride that had gotten him into his trouble. He uttered vain predictions of "beating this thing" that would permanently confine him to a wheelchair. But, when arrogance did not get him on his feet or drive away those who loved him, his heart opened to God.

The young man who had stumbled so badly became a witness of the persevering love and eternal promises of God. His faith brought him joy that a wheelchair could not restrain. His witness to the promises of Christ soared above his afflictions and brought others to understanding of the Gospel.

Though he had stumbled badly in body and spirit, the Lord lifted his soul and revived his spirit for God's purposes that will be fulfilled in Heaven with a perfected body and the presence of others touched by his life.

PRAYER: *Lord, when I or those I love stumble badly, remind me not to give up on Your grace that can lift us up to soar on the eagle's wings of Your heavenly purposes.*

48

Delight yourself in the LORD, and he will give
you the desires of your heart. (Psalm 37:4)

In the Lord's Prayer, Jesus teaches us to pray, "Give us this day our daily bread" (Matthew 6:11). It's important to note that the Lord does not tell us to request strawberry shortcake or filet mignon, though He is certainly capable of providing such pleasures.

Praying for our daily bread is a request for God to provide our necessities, not every personal whim or fancy. But doesn't this contradict His promise to give us the desires of our hearts? No. God does not contradict Himself.

God's *promise* to give you the desires of your heart follows His *instruction* to delight yourself in Him. If He is our greatest delight, then delighting Him will be our greatest desire.

God will inevitably fulfill such desires when we pray for our daily bread. Jesus taught us that God's provision of such food is what enables us to do the will of the Father (John 4:34).

So, when we pray for daily bread, we are praying for whatever is necessary to fulfill God's purposes. He is certain to provide this bread, and certain to fulfill our deepest desires to delight Him in whom we most delight.

When we most desire whatever is necessary to fulfill God's will, then He not only gives what we most desire but more than we can ask or even imagine! That's better than cake or steak.

PRAYER: Lord, help me to delight more in Your purposes than anything else in this world, knowing when I ask You for the daily bread to live for You, then You are pleased to give me everything needed to fulfill these desires of my heart.

49

Your testimonies are wonderful; therefore my soul keeps them. The unfolding of your words gives light; it imparts understanding to the simple. (Psalm 119:129–130)

If our reason for reading our Bibles is to keep God from being mad at us, then we're reading to earn points that we can use to barter with God for His mercy. That's not what He desires.

God wants a relationship with us. He doesn't want us to read a few verses every day just to get them checked off our "to-do" list—or to keep Him off our backs.

Attempts to convert Bible reading (or prayer, or church attendance, etc.) into obedience nickels that we can plug into a celestial vending machine that dispenses Heaven's blessings always fall apart when we remember that our best works are filthy rags to God.

The only way we can have a loving relationship with Him is not to view any spiritual discipline as a holy bribe, but as bread—God's gracious provision to nourish and strengthen our faith in His heart.

So, the next time you're reading your Bible, let the message of His love satisfy you, rather than trying to barter with Him.

PRAYER: *Father, help me to relish my daily bread of Your care through Your Word. Make our relationship sweeter, richer and stronger by the grace You reveal in Scripture that nourishes my faith and binds my heart to Yours.*

50

*I received mercy for this reason, that in me, as the foremost, Jesus
Christ might display His perfect patience as an example to those
who were to believe in him for eternal life. (1 Timothy 1:16)*

If God shows mercy to people who have messed up as badly as the Apostle
Paul (and David and Abraham and Gideon and Peter and the whole host
of biblical "heroes"), then there is hope of for us—even when there are messes
in our background too.

One of the leaders of our church was shattered by a series of events that
destroyed his business, his children's security, his community's esteem, and
ultimately his health. As he left church one day, he paused at the door with
weary and watery eyes to say, "Pastor, now I'm just a zero."

Much of the man's status had been reduced to nothing in the world's eyes,
but our church was also watching. As this faithful man responded to his trials
without bitterness, his children awoke from the nominal faith of their former
affluence. Our church leadership also became attentive to his counsel when
economic hardship rocked our entire community.

Families fractured by loss were healed by the experienced care of this man
and his loving wife. The "zero" became such a hero of God's grace that this
pastor realizes he would not have been prepared for his own trials, or perhaps
have remained in ministry, without the grace displayed in one who thought
so little of himself.

Failure is never the final chapter of lives turned to hope by a greater grace!
God will patiently work His plan for eternal purposes. Wait patiently for Him,
trusting Jesus until His perfect will is done.

PRAYER: Father, thank You for Christ's patience with me.
Please give me patience for His perfect will to be done, trusting
that the love that sent Him will rescue me and use me for eternity.

51

*Here there is not Greek and Jew, circumcised
and uncircumcised, barbarian, Scythian, slave, free;
but Christ is all, and in all. (Colossians 3:11)*

When Billy Graham started refusing to segregate his crusades in the 1950s, and when Promise Keepers made racial reconciliation a priority for Christian men in the 1990s, they were applying the Apostle Paul's declaration of the first century: *We are all one in Christ.*

Throughout history, believers have been learning what it means to be united as one body in Jesus, our Savior. When we celebrate this unity, we are really celebrating what Jesus has done to form His family.

As our nation renews its struggle with racial injustice and ethnic prejudice, Christians have a special opportunity to testify to the transforming realities of God's grace by treating believers of different backgrounds as brothers and sisters in Christ. In fact, we betray the grace that gives each of us Christ's identity if we do not treat one another as family.

Ultimately this means that receiving one another in love is not just nice but necessary to fulfill God's purposes. We are not called merely to tolerate those unlike us in race or ethnicity but to recognize that without love for them we fail Him.

One day those from every tribe, language, people, and nation will sing praises to our Savior. To prepare for that day, we are called to love brothers and sisters united in Christ today. This means that we must not only appreciate and welcome the gifts and perspectives of those with different backgrounds but confess that we need them.

PRAYER: *Lord, thank You for making all believers one family in Christ! Help me share the beauty of my identity by loving all Christians and confessing my need of demonstrating such love for the sake of Jesus's witness in a hateful world.*

52

Each of you should use whatever gift you have received to serve others, as faithful stewards of God's grace. (1 Peter 4:10 NIV)

A new Wal-Mart opened in a rural community and quickly became the social center of town, drawing everyone who wanted to meet anyone. One of those drawn often was a dear, older woman named Florence, who practically made the store her second home, while her husband, Bill, made his second home his fishing lake.

When the time came that Florence could no longer drive, Bill sacrificed his time at the lake and took his wife to the store. Florence would walk the aisles, not so much to shop as to visit with friends.

Bill would follow her with a fold-up lawn chair under his arm. Whenever Florence's conversation lengthened in the aisle—which was often—Bill would unfold the lawn chair and contentedly take a seat until Florence moved on for the next conversation.

Everyone smiled as they passed the couple, knowing the man who loved the outdoors loved his wife more. He sacrificed his pleasures to serve her needs.

So, from his lawn chair in the middle of the superstore, Bill taught our community about the sacrificial love of Jesus, showing the grace we all long to receive—and did through the Christ who gave up His Heaven to provide ours.

PRAYER: Jesus, just as You served me by giving Your life for my salvation, may I also serve others sacrificially. Shine through me by how I live for others.

53

Our Father in heaven ... give us this day
our daily bread. (Matthew 6:9, 11)

To answer this prayer, God may sometimes deny the physical blessings of this life. In doing so, He never denies us the "daily bread" He taught us to seek in the Lord's Prayer.

Jesus taught the precise nature of prayers for daily bread when He said, "My food is to do the will of him who sent me" (John 4:34). The Christian who prays for daily bread asks God to supply the food necessary to further eternal purposes—God's will.

If sacrifice for the sake of others, or deprivation for the sake of deepening faith, is what is most needed to nurture a heart for God or make our witness of Him shine more brightly, then each is God's daily bread.

Do not believe that faithful Christians have never gone hungry or that God has ever failed to provide their daily bread (Hebrews 11:36–38). For the one whose spiritual food is doing God's will, there is no greater nourishment than the physical blessings or challenges that enable us most to glorify God.

Heaven's bread nourishes our desire and ability to please God. The prayer for daily bread is but another way of saying to the Lord, "May Your gracious will be done in my life."

PRAYER: *Father, may Your grace so stimulate my desire to please You that the daily bread that most nourishes my soul is whatever You provide that enables me to do Your will.*

54

From His fullness we have all received, grace upon grace.
For the law was given through Moses; grace
and truth came through Jesus Christ. (John 1:16–17)

Sometimes life feels like Monopoly. You land on Park Place and win the game or you draw the dreaded Do Not Pass Go card and head to jail. How well you do in life seems to hinge on how well you played the game.

But the reality is that playing the game of life well doesn't get you into Heaven or keep you out of Hell. Only the grace of God gives you hope that your eternity is secure. That truth should be a game changer for all of us, as we put our faith in the fullness of Christ's provision rather than our flawed human performance.

Does this mean that our behavior doesn't matter to God? Of course not. What it means is that our good behavior should be motivated by something more than avoiding Hell's consequence or earning God's affection. The life of faith is not motivated by mere dread of our guilt or desire for our gain, but by gratitude for God's grace that cancels our guilt and changes our desires.

The only One who wants you to serve God with a burden of guilt on your back or greed in your heart is Satan. Grace that is neither earned or deserved but received by faith produces the love that honors God's law and blesses our lives.

PRAYER: *Father, thank You for loving me so much that You sent Your Son to pay the full price for my sins. Help me to respond to this great grace—not with dread or greed—but by living the law of love that honors You and blesses me.*

55

Let your steadfast love come to me, O LORD, your salvation according to your promise; then shall I have an answer for him who taunts me, for I trust in your word. (Psalm 119:41–42)

When you open your Bible, what message comes to you? A record of sermons that is filled with duties and doctrines? A referee's whistle blowing a taunting disapproval of all your errors? No doubt the duty, doctrine, and disapproval can be found within the pages of Scripture—but there is something more.

The foundation beneath all the duty and doctrine—even the reason for the referee's whistle—is the steadfast love of the Lord. The rules and doctrines are there, sure, but the reason for them is pointing us toward a relationship—so that we will love the Lord with all that we are and have.

If we open our Bibles only expecting to see a bunch of regulations for how to perform or think in order to ensure a holy God's approval, where is the hope in that? After all, the Bible itself says that it's possible to get our duty and doctrine right and still have a heart far from God (Luke 17:10).

Personal pride in our behavior or belief is never a substitute for loving God with humility and gratitude.

So, if we are looking for a relationship with God that is the priority of His Word, then we will read every page to understand how it's crafted and how the steadfast love of the Lord never ceases.

That love will always come to us through God's promise, rather than our performance!

PRAYER: *Heavenly Father, help me to see Your love and care unfolding on every page of Scripture. Even when Your people struggle to understand or obey, help me see how You are using them to point me to the necessity of grace that culminates in Jesus. Use all to increase my love for Him.*

56

We are to God the pleasing aroma of Christ among those
who are being saved and those who are perishing.
To the one we are an aroma that brings death;
to the other, an aroma that brings life. And who is
equal to such a task? (2 Corinthians 2:15–16 NIV)

Some still recognize the name Bobby Richardson. Those who don't should know that he was a New York Yankees second baseman and an outspoken Christian. He played ball with the legendary Mickey Mantle, who derided Bobby's faith and mocked his life of obedience to Christ.

Many people thought the relationship between the two stunk. But, in one of Mickey's books he expressed respect for Bobby. Somehow he smelled something genuine in the man who consistently lived what he believed.

So, in his final days, it was Bobby and his wife, Betsy, that Mickey turned to for comfort. At his funeral, Bobby gave the eulogy, saying, "I believe what drew Mickey to me was my relationship with Christ."

Bobby was right. Mickey was searching for his Savior, and he turned to Jesus. As he lay dying, he urged the nation's young people, "Don't make me your role model." Instead, he pointed all to the Savior whom Bobby had helped him "smell" when the rest of life turned foul.

Bobby Richardson was the aroma of life to a man whose life stank despite his fame and riches. Praise God that the aroma of death was drowned out by the savor of the Savior.

PRAYER: *Lord, give me grace me to be a "pleasing aroma" to those who don't know You so that they may savor the Savior.*

57

*I entreat your favor with all my heart; be gracious to me
according to your promise. When I think on my ways,
I turn my feet to your testimonies; I hasten and do not
delay to keep your commandments. (Psalm 119:58–60)*

People often divide grace and law into two opposing ideas, and then give little thought as to how both reveal God's love. They're not polar opposites! Grace demonstrates the goodness of God's heart *and* the law shows the goodness of His path. Both reveal the beauty of God's character.

God's standards are never about what you have to do to make God love you. Rather God's law *reflects* a heart so loving that He has designed a good and safe path for every journey of His loved ones.

His grace *reveals* the path and provides pardon when we waver from it. He does not tell us to walk on the path so that He will love us. He provides the path and the pardon because He loves us.

Grace is not contrary to the law of God, but the reason it exists. By grace we know how to live and that God forgives so that we will walk on the path of His design *and* run back to Him when we wander.

PRAYER: *Heavenly Father, thank You for the law that provides a good and safe path for me to walk, and for grace that provides Your mercy when I stumble. Help me to remember the path that guides me in Your goodness, and the pardon that keeps me wanting to walk with You.*

58

*All things are yours, whether Paul or Apollos
or Cephas or the world or life or death or the present
or the future—all are yours, and you are Christ's,
and Christ is God's. (1 Corinthians 3:21–23)*

An old story goes something like this: A poor man spent years looking forward to a dream cruise. After finally saving enough money, he bought a ticket. But knowing he could not afford the luxurious food on board, the man packed some meager staples.

After a few days, his peanut butter crackers became stale and unappealing. So, the man begged the staff to let him work in exchange for food. "But sir," the concierge said, "the meals are included with your ticket. You may eat all you desire."

Sadly, this story can illustrate how many Christians live, believing that God has called them to a stale life of deprivation, instead of relishing the joy and fulfillment of accompanying the King of the Universe—with all His greatest blessings—on life's journey.

In Him are all the treasures of wisdom and knowledge (Colossians 2:3)— not simply matters of eating and drinking, but righteousness and peace and joy in the Holy Spirit (Romans 14:17). Everything we need for our heart's greatest fulfillment in this life or after has already been purchased for us by Jesus.

That's grace and a very good life—and eternity.

PRAYER: *Lord, help me to realize that in Christ You have provided to every believer all things most precious. Thank You for providing all by the grace of an eternal relationship with Jesus and with You!*

59

Your kingdom come, your will be done,
on earth as it is in heaven. (Matthew 6:10)

A childhood song teaches, "When it's hardest to pray, pray hardest." Jesus helped us follow that instruction by teaching us how to pray when life is so hard that we can hardly collect the words or thoughts to pray.

When I can hardly pray through my pain, I can still pray the words Jesus taught in the Lord's Prayer. Through years of resorting to, and resting in, the words of Jesus, I've learned that the petitions of this prayer are not a string of unrelated requests.

While each petition has a specific focus, the golden thread that knits these petitions together is found in asking God to do what best fulfills His Kingdom's purposes—asking that His will be done.

Behind this simple request in the Lord's Prayer is a profound truth: when we ask God to do what He knows is best, then we will be most blessed.

The petition for God's will to be done in and through our lives is the key to abiding in God's love and peace. Jesus prayed for God's Kingdom purposes even as the cross loomed before Him. When Jesus prayed, "Not my will, but yours be done," then he endured the challenge, rejoicing that He was fulfilling the gracious purposes of the Father He loved (Hebrews 12:2).

When pray this way, treasuring Kingdom purposes above earthly desires, then Jesus's peace, power, and joy are our daily blessing for eternity. We pray with assurance that our Heavenly Father will do as He knows is best for all.

PRAYER: *Heavenly Father, help me always to prioritize Your will in my prayers so that I may experience the power, peace, and joy that You intend for today and for eternity.*

60

Wait for the LORD; be strong, and let your heart take courage; wait for the LORD! (Psalm 27:14)

A few years ago, a young couple waited anxiously to hear if they were going to be the proud owners of their "dream home." But as one thing led to another, not only did the deal collapse but their faith took a tumble too.

Their disappointment was the soil into which some seeds of doubt about God's care began to sprout. They countered those sprouts of doubts by praying, and resolving to wait patiently to see what God was doing.

Only when the inspector called with news of serious but hidden flaws in the house did they understand God's plan. They had been spared the dangers of faulty wiring and pervasive mold.

They were trying to make a deal; God was protecting their lives. Remembering this experience helped the young family face more of life's inevitable disappointments with the courage and patience that comes from trusting God's hand and plan.

The family had been praying that God would provide them a house for a few years, but He gave them faith for every trial. They had prayed for the home they wanted; He provided the heart they needed.

PRAYER: *Lord, please give me courage to wait patiently and in faith for Your answers to my prayers. Make me strong by trusting Your hand and plan, as I thank You for providing more than I could ask or imagine!*

61

They said, "Come, let us build ourselves a city
and a tower with its top in the heavens, and let us
make a name for ourselves, lest we be dispersed
over the face of the whole earth." (Genesis 11:4)

What so special or unique about Christianity? Grace. All other religions teach that we must do something or reach some state of mind to climb up to God. But the Bible tells us that no amount of physical or mental effort can accomplish that. We can make no "stairway to Heaven!"

That's why the story of the Tower of Babel occurs early in the Bible. God graciously makes this unmistakable: creating your own stairway to Heaven is *not* the way to get to God. Instead, the beauty and uniqueness of the Christian message is that, when we could not climb up to God, He came down to us in the person of Jesus Christ.

Because we could never do anything by our personal strength or mental discipline to reach up to God, our gracious heavenly Father lowered His stairway down to us! When we believe that Jesus came to make a way for us to have a secure relationship with our God, then we are forever saved from our earthbound efforts and secured by His eternal mercy.

PRAYER: Lord, I know that I cannot reach up to You by my own efforts. Thank You for sending Jesus Christ down from Heaven to save me from my sin. I trust in Your mercy rather than anything in my might or mentality.

62

You formed my inward parts; you knitted me together in my mother's womb. I praise you, for I am fearfully and wonderfully made. (Psalm 139:13–14)

I love to watch the TV series *Antiques Roadshow*. And I'm convinced that one of these days I'm going to poke around in my attic and find a Van Gogh or a Rembrandt. While I may not be a good enough art critic to recognize a masterpiece by its features, I hope that I will at least recognize its preciousness by the artist's signature.

The Bible teaches us to recognize the signature of God's handiwork on another kind of masterpiece of His making. Scripture tells us that a child in the womb is formed by God, a wonder of His handiwork. From the very beginning of his or her life, a child is God's masterpiece. That child is not a Rembrandt or a Van Gogh but a *Jehovah*!

Every person is precious because, from the earliest stage of our creation, we bear God's signature. We each bear God's name because we are fearfully and wonderfully made by His amazing power and according to His eternal plan.

PRAYER: Lord, help me to realize that I am fearfully and wonderfully made by You and, therefore, am precious to You. And help me to see others the same way. As I encounter people today, may I treat them as priceless works of Your art.

63

He made known to us the mystery of his will according to his good
pleasure, which he purposed in Christ, to be put into effect when
the times reach their fulfillment—to bring unity to all things
in heaven and on earth under Christ. (Ephesians 1:9–10 NIV)

It's been said that "history is His Story." But how does the story of Jesus unfold across all the stages of time?

The Bible says that the big picture of God's dealing with humanity across history began with a good creation that was spoiled by Adam's fall. Now the redemption of all of creation (and persons) is made possible through the blessings Jesus made available through His death and resurrection.

Ultimately all things will be perfected under Christ's future and eternal rule, and all who have trusted Christ to remove the guilt of their sin will participate in the blessings of that rule.

In other words, God has a plan! He didn't give up on us or our world because of past sin. That means He won't give up on you either. Despite your sin, God provided a plan for your forgiveness and for an eternity that is free from sin's consequences.

We grieve that sin takes such a terrible toll on our lives, but we still take heart, knowing that our Lord had a plan from the beginning that was made possible by Christ's gracious rescue. Your history never blots out the blessings of His story.

PRAYER: *Heavenly Father, all of history unfolds Your great*
story of creation, fall, redemption, and eternal perfection.
Help me to live with confidence that this story is no mystery
to You. As I trust in my Redeemer, who gave Himself for me,
make my eternity no mystery to me either!

64

Does he [the master] thank the servant because he did
what he was commanded? So you also, when you have
done all that you were commanded, say "We are unworthy
servants; we have only done our duty." (Luke 17: 9–10)

The master doesn't say to his servant, "You have the privilege of sitting at my table because you've done the chores you were supposed to do." The master has every right to expect that his servant will fulfill his obligations without additional reward.

So, if the master says to the servant who merely fulfills his duties, "Sit at my table," that's not so much a sign of the servant's deserving as of the master's generosity.

Similarly, just because we've done the good works that we are supposed to do, that doesn't earn Heaven's privileges. What secures our place at our Master's heavenly table is the graciousness of His heart. That's the message of the Gospel of grace! His mercy, not our merit, assures us of God's eternal care.

When we perceive how generous is God's unmerited mercy, and how great is the privilege of sitting at His table in Heaven—even when we have not done all we were commanded—then we respond in loving service without expecting to earn the favor that is only granted by His grace!

> PRAYER: Jesus, I look forward to sitting with You at the great banquet in Heaven because of Your mercy, rather than my merit! May the sure hope that Your grace alone makes possible motivate my loving service to You today.

65

Now therefore go, and I will be with your mouth and teach you what you shall speak. (Exodus 4:12)

Deep in the beautiful countryside of western Kenya, there live some of the poorest people in the world. In this remote and impoverished region, Anglican Bishop Simon Oketch served faithfully the churches of the small Maseno North Diocese.

His position would seem unlikely to provide him any distinction, yet the Lord used him, as He used Moses long before, to be a faith leader for many through his simple faithfulness to God's Word.

Others have tried to shame Bishop Oketch for his devotion. But his courageous stand for God's Word has strengthened the resolve of Bible-believing Christians throughout Africa. Those of the remotest jungles and deserts of that continent, and other continents, have turned to God through a man who trusted Heaven's priorities over his own place.

There are no people or places too remote for God's grace or purposes! He who disregarded the shame and isolation of a cross to fulfill God's greatest plan can still use those from anywhere in the world and any station in life to advance God's Kingdom.

PRAYER: Lord, help me remember that You choose the weak things of the world to shame the strong, and the insignificant to accomplish what is most significant to You. When I doubt my place or significance, remind me of Your sufficient grace that makes Your children shine as stars everywhere You want.

66

By grace you have been saved through faith. And this is not your own doing; it is the gift of God, not a result of works, so that no one may boast. For we are his workmanship, created in Christ Jesus for good works, which God prepared beforehand, that we should walk in them. (Ephesians 2:8–9)

It's not possible for an imperfect person to become acceptable to a holy God by doing good but still imperfect works. So what hope do we imperfect people have?

The apostle says that we are made holy by relying on God's grace. That's necessary because unholy people can't make themselves righteous—just as it's impossible to clean a white shirt with muddy hands!

So how are we made holy? Paul says it's not by our imperfect works, but by faith in the perfect work that Christ has done for us. We trust His sacrificial mercy to wash away our sin so that He will accept us and we can live for Him.

Our good works do not make us right with a holy God, but because His grace makes us holy, we can do good works that honor Him and bless others.

He doesn't give grace because of our good works. We do good works because of His grace. The order never varies. We trust in the grace that fully cleanses us, so that we can now do what God long before prepared for His glory and our blessing.

> **PRAYER:** *Lord, I thank You for the grace that washes away my sin and enables me to please You with the good works that You created me to do. Please give me faith in Your grace to fulfill Your purposes for my life today and every day.*

67

*You, Lord, are a shield around me, my glory, the One
who lifts my head high. I call out to the Lord, and he
answers me from his holy mountain. (Psalm 3:3–4 NIV)*

The summer after his junior year of college, a young man I knew had an experience that left him reeling. Though he was planning to become a doctor, a racist slight caused him to drive away from an accident where he could have provided needed care.

The uncharacteristic moment of rage haunted him. The singular, unplanned act left him in agonizing despair. Deep down in his heart he believed his failure may have cost a life, betrayed his aspirations, and disqualified him from medicine.

He lost hope in his future, because he believed he could not be free of his past. His daily countenance changed as he hung his head in unrelenting guilt for his inexcusable sin.

Believers should understand the guilt but refuse to live in such despair. The Bible says that the Lord "is the One who lifts my head high." He takes no delight in bowing you before the regrets of your past.

You may feel guilty—and there are realistic consequences for sin—but remember that God is with you and Christ's grace frees you from condemnation. Jesus Christ paid the penalty for all your sins! Lift your head!

PRAYER: *Lord, I'm thankful that I don't have to despair over my past but rather can rejoice in Your forgiveness through Christ. Lift my head with the assurance of Your grace.*

68

Be subject for the Lord's sake to every human institution,
whether it be to the emperor as supreme, or to governors
as sent by him to punish those who do evil and to
praise those who do good. (1 Peter 2:13–14)

All Christians are to submit to those whom God has put in authority over their lives: citizens to governments, employees to employers, and God's people to church leaders.

We can be tempted to think the Bible must be speaking about other, better authorities than we have. But when the Holy Spirit gave these words to the Apostle Peter, his emperor was ungodly and cruel.

Our submission is never because of another person's deserving but for all persons' blessing. Without human authorities there would be no societal control—and chaos would keep the Gospel from spreading through cultures as God intends.

We are free to seek change according to just means, but our goal is always to advance God's Kingdom in God's ways. We offer our gifts, rights, and witness in service to others to build the Kingdom of God, as Jesus did.

PRAYER: Heavenly Father, help me to remember that everyone must submit to someone for Christ's purposes to flourish. I ask You to give me the resolve and humility to embrace Christ's values to promote His purposes.

69

This is the covenant that I will make with the house of Israel after those days, declares the Lord: I will put my laws into their minds, and write them on their hearts, and I will be their God, and they shall be my people. (Hebrews 8:10)

Today, many people speak about marriage like this: "We'll wed for as long as we both shall love; we'll stay together as long as we can keep each other happy."

Such sentiments suggest that marriage is a contract to be terminated if its terms are violated. Yet, contrary to common perception, Christian marriage is not a mere *contract*. A Christian bride and groom take vows to enter a marriage *covenant*.

A covenant is prior commitment to love even when present conditions are not what we desire. We commit to one another "for better or for worse, for richer or for poorer, in sickness and in health."

The marriage covenant is meant to reflect God's covenant with His people—His gracious promise to be their God, even when He knew they would fail and forsake Him in many ways.

Covenant love gives people security despite their sin, a foundation to start over again, and a willingness to forgive for the sake of another.

A covenant relationship says, "Just because we struggle, that doesn't mean we're done. I'm fully committed to you, and to working on what will heal us and make us better. My love is not based on your present performance but on my prior commitment."

That's the love God's covenant of grace establishes in our minds and hearts, and it is the grace He uses to secure the marriage of two sinners for their deepest joy and lasting love.

PRAYER: *Father, help me to reflect Your covenant love for me in my marriage. Thank You for the security that comes from knowing love without conditions and beyond faults.*

70

We have received not the spirit of the world,
but the Spirit who is from God, that we might understand
the things freely given us by God. (1 Corinthians 2:12)

Sometimes earthly things we consider solid and secure are anything but. C. S. Lewis expressed this idea in his book, *The Great Divorce*, where he writes of a fantasy bus ride that takes British tourists to Heaven. When these passengers step off the bus, they discover they're hollow and transparent, but everyone living in Heaven is solid and whole.

Lewis's fantasy is meant to picture this life as a mist—a shadow of what is to come. In contrast—and counter to our ordinary thoughts—Heaven is the more significant reality, the place where everything becomes solid, safe, and secure.

So counterintuitive are so many aspects of the Gospel—being saved by God's grace rather than our goodness, being secure in Heaven even when the earth is shaking, being loved even when we were God's enemies—that we require the work of the Holy Spirit to understand God's grace.

When by grace we are brought into God's holy presence, then this reality will become perfectly clear. But while we remain on Earth, we get brief glimpses of what Heaven will be that comes with this assurance from the Holy Spirit: "No eye has seen, nor ear heard, nor the heart of man imagined, what God has prepared for those who love him" (1 Corinthians 2:9).

PRAYER: *Lord, may Your Holy Spirit make Heaven's blessings so real to my heart that I am able to face the harsh realities of Earth with the assurances of Your grace.*

71

Do not repay evil for evil or reviling for reviling,
but on the contrary, bless, for to this you were called,
that you may obtain a blessing. (1 Peter 3:9)

As we live in this fallen world so full of imperfect people, much can frustrate and even anger us. As we consider the progress of political opponents, the slights of family members, or the betrayals of friends, the human impulse is always to respond in kind.

The grace that Jesus displayed toward His enemies and us who continue to betray Him sets a different pattern. To repay evil for evil is to become evil. Plotting how to revile those who have reviled us lets their sin control our words and thoughts.

Treating others with mercy and forgiveness is not merely for their good, but for our own blessing. Ruminating on how to pay others back for their evil, or how to answer insults, can preoccupy our thoughts and invade our sleep.

When we focus on our hurts more than our Help, we sour our joy by drinking from dregs of distilled rage. Every day tastes bitter because we lick our wounds until their poison fills our hearts. That's why bitterness is the acid that eats its own container.

It has been said that holding onto unforgiveness is like drinking poison to hurt someone else. Jesus provides different drink. As we bless those who curse us, we discover more of the heart of One who was cursed to bless us.

When we forgive as we have been forgiven, we radiate Christ's love and experience it. Forgiveness is not easy, but is blessed. It's not possible except by Jesus.

PRAYER: Lord, You call me to forgiveness that is beyond me to teach me more of the Savior who loves me. Fill me with His grace to forgive as I have been forgiven. And when I struggle to do as Jesus did, forgive me and give me more of Jesus.

*And I heard every creature in heaven and on earth
and under the earth and in the sea, and all that
is in them, saying, "To him who sits on the throne
and to the Lamb be blessing and honor and glory
and might forever and ever!" (Revelation 5:13)*

Dependence upon the grace of God does not make honoring Christ unnecessary or superfluous. Instead, our Lord's great mercy should make us want to honor Him even more, making His glory our heart's desire.

One day every created being will acknowledge His eternal glory, and even now, the hearts of those saved by His blood long to express that praise in what they say and how they live.

Knowing what pleases God and how we may honor Him provides us the ability to satisfy that desire. That's why studying God's Word, learning applications of it from other believers, and listening to the Holy Spirit as He prompts our hearts to careful obedience are important practices that will help us glorify God every day.

All of these paths of instruction bless us and help us to honor God. They are a sweet provision of His care for our hearts. So, today, take a moment to listen and learn the truth that God is speaking into your life by these means of grace so that you may bless His name in all you say and do.

PRAYER: *Dear Lord, as I study Your Word, learn from other believers, and listen to the promptings of Your Holy Spirit, please help me to join early in the praise that all creatures will one day give You by everything I do or say this day.*

73

My son, do not regard lightly the discipline of the Lord,
nor be weary when reproved by him.
For the Lord disciplines the one he loves, and chastises
every son whom he receives. (Hebrews 12:5–6)

When my children disobeyed, I would sometimes discipline or, other times, let consequences train them. I'm an imperfect parent, so I sometimes messed up by not doing these things selflessly—or making my children's welfare my first priority.

As a perfect parent, God always gets it right. He may discipline by direct means, or by allowing consequences to train us. But His gracious heart makes our good His priority in every divine action.

Without sacrificing one iota of His glory, God perfectly balances every measure of mercy and consequence. Though His approval may vary, His affection never does. Though His discipline may change, our relationship with Him does not!

Even when we are in the worst throes of discipline His parental sternness can issue, we are loved no less. Our need for discipline does not change His heart.

PRAYER: Father, thank You for loving me enough to discipline me when my good demands it. Help me to believe Your love is behind every consequence You allow, and that Your purpose is always to turn me from my sin's greater harm.

74

As for the one who is weak in faith, welcome
him, but not to quarrel over opinions. One person
believes he may eat anything, while the weak
person eats only vegetables. (Romans 14:1–2)

Many different experiences shape our opinions, and God's Word does not cover every detail of how to deal with these. We are given principles to guide our judgments and relationships, and then we are expected to apply these principles within the boundaries of God's commands.

Inevitably Christians will have some differences about matters that are not explicitly commanded. How do we handle those? We prioritize the good of others and do not delight in judging or quarreling.

Paul advises selfless care for the weak, but then strangely describes the weak as the most strict in their religious practices. Their weakness is not in their zeal but in their application of God's grace. How should we relate to them? By being gracious toward them.

We start by clearly distinguishing biblical commands from "good ideas." We can't *require* others to follow our good ideas. In fact, churches often fracture when some people decide their good idea should be a command for others.

We can only require what God commands, and among those commands is this: *Do not quarrel over disputable matters.* God's grace frees us from having to earn His acceptance by meeting others' expectations. It also frees us from the unholy pride or prejudice of judging others based merely on our preferences.

PRAYER: *Heavenly Father, enable me to avoid quarreling with other Christians over disputable matters—especially since they are Your servants, not mine! Help me to be gracious toward those I think are weak, lest I be.*

75

[Jesus said] "You know the way to where I am going."
Thomas said to him, "Lord, we do not know where you
are going. How can we know the way?" Jesus said
to him, "I am the way, and the truth, and the life. No one
comes to the Father except through me." (John 14:4–6)

What would you say is the most offensive word in the Bible? We could debate, but I'm going to suggest it's the word *the*. Just think about it. In John 14:6, if Jesus had said, "I am *a* way," our lives would be much easier at certain times. But He didn't. He tells us that He is *the* way, *the* truth, and *the* life. No one comes to the Father except through Jesus.

Our world perceives this proclamation as prejudice—the bigotry of exclusivity. And, indeed, it is—unless it's true!

If Jesus is one of many paths to God, and we are so arrogant as to exclude the other paths, then that's offensive pride. But, if Jesus is *the* path to God, and we proclaim it to friends, family, enemies, and everyone—then that is selfless love.

If there is only one safe exit from a burning theatre, then it is not unkind to point away from the other exits and say, "This is *the* way."

All other religious solutions tell people to get to God by measuring up to some standard of goodness or reaching some state of consciousness. Jesus alone taught that we could not reach to God, so He mercifully reached to us through His Son.

Since He is the way that God provides, love demands that we not pretend there are other ways but proclaim Him as the One to put your faith in.

PRAYER: *Lord, help me to love others enough to share Jesus as the way to God, confessing humbly that without Him I also would have no path to You and no hope of Heaven.*

76

His divine power has given us everything we need for
a godly life through our knowledge of him who called
us by his own glory and goodness. (2 Peter 1:3 NIV)

My wife, Kathy, was helping our daughter with an algebra problem, and by the sound of it … things were not going well. Our straight-A student had burst into tears, claimed she couldn't do it, and declared, "I'm just so stupid."

Kathy rarely speaks with an edge, but her stern response was sharp enough to cut through our daughter's tears. Said Kathy, "Don't you dare say that. You are a smart and capable young woman who has all the gifts to do this. Now do the work."

Kathy told my daughter what she *needed* to hear to do what was required. And what our daughter needed was a firm reminder of the knowledge and ability she had to handle her problems.

God may speak to us with a similar sternness from Scripture. When He hears our self-defeating cries, He lovingly but firmly corrects, saying, "My divine power has given you everything you need to deal with your problems and live for My glory and goodness. Do not give up. You can do this."

Even when we have reason to doubt our own abilities, we are called to faith in God. He promises to supply all that we need to accomplish all that He assigns for our witness and work. So, we trust His gracious supply and remain faithful to our calling.

PRAYER: Lord, help me to remain faithful to You by trusting Your promise to supply everything I need to live a godly life.

*As obedient children, do not be conformed to the passions
of your former ignorance, but as he who called you is holy,
you also be holy in all your conduct, since it is written,
"You shall be holy, for I am holy." (1 Peter 1:14–16)*

The Apostle Peter reminds us that God's command is plain, "You shall be holy, for I am holy." For the hot-tempered, rash-speaking, and thrice-denying-Jesus apostle those words could have been as scary to write as they are for us to read.

Without Christ's provision, those words should scare anyone! They should make us wonder, *How does God expect me to be* holy? *I know my faults of temper, speech, and courage. How can I ever meet this standard?*

The answer lies in the identity of those that Peter addresses. Yes, they are called to obedience, but they are also called *children*. The only way that you can really be God's child is if He is your Father. And, Jesus told us how we would really know our Heavenly Father: "No one knows ... who the Father is except the Son and anyone to whom the Son chooses to reveal Him" (Luke 10:22).

We know we are God's children, when we believe what Jesus revealed about Him: He sent His Son to save us. Jesus's sacrificial ministry reveals a Heavenly Father's care. If you believe this Father makes you holy by putting the penalty for all your sins on Jesus, then you are His child. The sins that would separate you from Him are forever forgiven.

When Peter calls us to be holy, he is not urging us to qualify for a relationship with our Heavenly Father; he is urging us to live for the Father who already provided Christ's holiness to make us His children by faith.

> **PRAYER:** *Father, I know that You have already made me Your holy child by my trust in the work of Your Son. Now help me each day to be more of what I am—a holy child, who loves and honors You in what I think, do, and say.*

*I know how to be brought low, and I know how to abound.
In any and every circumstance, I have learned the secret of
facing plenty and hunger, abundance and need. I can do all
things through him who strengthens me. (Philippians 4:12–13)*

There is an old story about a son who was tasked with removing some stones from his father's garden. Try as he might, the boy couldn't remove the boulders. He returned to his father, saying, "I can't do it."

The father told him to give it another try. Then, after a few more unsuccessful attempts, the boy said, "Father, I've tried with all I have, and I still don't have the strength to do what you require." At this, the boy's father replied, "You haven't tried with all your resources, because you haven't asked me to help."

That's a good reminder for us all. *We can do all that God requires of us through His strength!* Apart from Him we can do nothing (John 15:5), but through Him who strengthens us we can do all things (Philippians 4:13).

When the task seems impossible—when your strength is clearly inadequate for accomplishing God's will, do not forget to ask His help. We have not done all that we can for God until we have sought to be strong in the power of His might (Ephesians 6:10).

PRAYER: *Father, when I feel weak or inadequate, please remind me that "I can do all things through Him who strengthens me." Do not let me neglect to ask Your help.*

For this reason, because I have heard of your
faith in the Lord Jesus and your love toward all
the saints, I do not cease to give thanks for you,
remembering you in my prayers. (Ephesians 1:15–16)

In Ephesians, the Apostle Paul thanks God for people who are obviously flawed in many ways. They need his instruction for understanding God, worship, unity, forgiveness, family, and faith. They are people like you and me—broken, sinful, weak, and frayed. How can Paul give thanks for people like us?

Paul put on his Gospel glasses to see himself and others through the lens of grace. In doing so, he first reminds us all that our salvation and ongoing transformation are a gift of God, not a product of our works *so that no one can boast.*

Then Paul reminds all such boastless people that they have been loved eternally by God and will be the instruments of His eternal purposes. Through flawed people like us, God will bring all the world under the lordship of Jesus.

Paul gives thanks for people like you and me, knowing what God intends for all of us to be—transformed, transforming, and treasured witnesses of the necessity and power of God's grace.

Like any good pastor, parent, or boss, the apostle uses praise to help people see their potential, not merely their problems. He empowers those who struggle by sharing a perspective of them provided by the lens of grace. They may not think much of themselves, but Paul sees all believers clothed in the glory of the grace of God and gives thanks for them. So should we.

PRAYER: *Father, help me to put on Gospel glasses, so that I can see myself and others as You intend. Help me to help others by this perspective of grace and the power of praise.*

80

*Share in suffering for the Gospel by the power of God, who
saved us and called us to a holy calling, not because of our
works but because of his own purpose and grace, which he gave
us in Christ Jesus before the ages began. (2 Timothy 1:8–9)*

The Nike slogan, "Just Do It," can become a substitute for the Gospel in hearts accustomed to exchanging performance for reward.

We can even adopt the perspective that being a Christian simply means "just do more" than other people to please God. But how do you measure *more*? How much more will ever be enough to please a perfect God?

The answer, of course, is there will never be enough *more* in our performance to qualify us for an infinitely holy God's approval. We simply cannot lift ourselves to Heaven.

Instead, the Gospel assures us of that the infinitely holy and able God lifts us to Himself "because of His own purpose and grace."

Such "lifting love" so lifts our hearts that we become zealous for our Savior. We want to please Him. We are even willing to suffer for the One who gave us a holy calling before the ages began.

He loved us before we could qualify for His care, called us to His work before we knew Him, and empowers us by amazing grace for Heaven's purposes that will endure long after this world is done.

PRAYER: *Lord, You saved me, not because of my works but through Your grace. Help me to be gripped by an empowering love for the eternal purposes of this Gospel, even if I must suffer for its truth on Earth.*

81

God gave us a spirit not of fear but of power and love and self-control. Therefore do not be ashamed of the testimony about our Lord, nor of me his prisoner, but share in suffering for the Gospel by the power of God who saved us and called us to a holy calling, not because of our works but because of His own purpose and grace. (2 Timothy 1:7–9)

Missionary Myron Klaus spent many years in Costa Rica with the poorest of the poor. His mission focused on orphaned, urban children who took shelter and food from the country's garbage dumps.

Trying to educate these children to survive and flourish has been a monumental task. But one successful technique involved training them in public speaking and entering them in local competitions.

One boy did particularly well and won the national championship, which came with an invitation to speak to the president and his wife.

Meeting with the president caused some anxious thoughts, yet the child not only used his skills to speak boldly, but also to tell of his affection for his president—and his *Savior.*

Understanding that the grace that holds us is from the King of the Universe enables us to stand, despite any shame or flaws in our backgrounds, before presidents, employers, family, and friends with bold witness of the Savior who loves us. Knowing that we are held by the God whose love is unconditional and unending releases us from fear and for Jesus!

PRAYER: *Heavenly Father, may confidence in Your grace release me from a spirit of fear and enable me to speak for my Savior. Help me to remember the One who gave Himself for me is the King who also equips me for His eternal purposes.*

82

Then he said to them, "Go your way. Eat the fat and drink sweet wine and send portions to anyone who has nothing ready, for this day is holy to our Lord. And do not be grieved, for the joy of the LORD is your strength." (Nehemiah 8:10)

Nothing hinders our walk with Christ more than the two-headed monster known as *guilt* and *shame*! And oh, how Satan knows this! As your accuser, Satan wants nothing more than for you to try to serve God with a great burden of guilt and shame on your back.

Your Savior wants to lift your head and lighten your load with the assurance that He removes your sin as far as the east is from the west. This happens for us, as it did for God's people long ago, when we confess our sins with the strong confidence that His grace will provide the mercy we need.

There are Christians who believe the mark of true repentance is feeling as bad as we can for as long as we can. Such an attitude denies the power of the cross and substitutes our sadness for Jesus as the antidote for sin.

Yes, feel bad about your sin. Yes, grieve for the betrayal of Christ it reveals. But then, take all of that guilt and shame to the foot of the cross and *put it down*. If you continue to carry it, the burden will only sap your spiritual power and tell those around you that Jesus is only about frowning a lot. He is not!

The Bible celebrates, "The joy of the Lord is your strength!" We serve Christ best when we believe He has lifted our burden and we rejoice in His grace. Sadness is not what satisfies God. Jesus did.

PRAYER: *Father, though Satan tries to weigh me down with guilt and shame, help me to trust Your grace so that joy for the burdens You have lifted gives me strength to celebrate You in all You call me to do.*

83

Come now, let us reason together, says the LORD: though your sins are like scarlet, they shall be white as snow; though they are red like crimson, they shall become like wool. (Isaiah 1:18)

The call came from the airport. An unknown student had arrived from Africa, expecting to receive pastoral training. A kind teacher went to pick him up and found an old man with decaying teeth, rotting shoes, and a beaming smile.

Over time, we discovered he was the only pastor of a thriving congregation of a mere four thousand people. As his years were nearing their end, the people of his mud-floor, thatched-roof church combined meager resources to send their Pastor Augustin to seminary to receive training to prepare his successors.

We learned to love this gentle, humble, humorous man. He nearly fell from my car in laughter the first time he gave his food order to a microphone in the life-size Jack-in-the-Box at a drive-through.

The other time I remember him laughing to the point of tears was when this dear man from a tropical climate saw snow for the first time. He was standing without a jacket in the school parking lot, looking agape at the white flakes coating his shoulders.

When he saw me, he pointed skyward and shouted for joy: "Look, look. Though your sins be as scarlet, they shall be white as *this* snow."

The power and comfort of the Gospel come to our hearts when we retain the wonder and the joy of such a simple, profound truth. The grace of God is greater than all our sins. Though they be as scarlet, through Christ's pardon they shall be white as snow.

> **PRAYER:** Lord, when grief and guilt for sin threaten to overwhelm my heart, renew my joy with the promise of grace: though my sins be as scarlet, they shall be white as snow.

84

Those God foreknew he also predestined to be conformed to the image of his Son, that he might be the firstborn among many brothers and sisters. (Romans 8:29 NIV)

Perhaps the most-cited proof for God's persevering grace is Romans 8:29. The reason for citing this passage is how it continues. The apostle goes on, "Those whom [God] predestined he also called, and those whom he called he also justified, and those whom he justified he also glorified" (Romans 8:30).

In none of those phrases does Paul say, "*Some of* those...." When God tips the first domino in the process of our salvation, He makes all the dominoes fall without losing any of us in whom He began to work. Why is that so important and encouraging?

The assurance that God will finish the work He has begun reveals that—though we can have our ups and downs in the Christian life—He perseveres in His love for us. We may fail, but He is faithful. He who began a good work in us will bring it to completion.

So, if you have truly acknowledged that you are a sinner in need of a Savior, then God's wonderful grace has tipped the dominoes in your heart toward Him! You are Heaven-bound with all who love Him—there are no exceptions! Let this strong assurance crush all doubt and worry that would keep your heart from beating strongly for Jesus.

PRAYER: *Father God, thank You enabling me to confess my need and love of Jesus. Let those dominoes You have tipped in my heart join with biblical assurance of Your persevering love to keep me from spiritual defeat through anxious worry.*

85

*The Pharisee, standing by himself, prayed thus: "God,
I thank you that I am not like other men, extortioners,
unjust, adulterers, or even like this tax collector."... But
the tax collector, standing far off, would not even lift
up his eyes to heaven, but beat his breast, saying,
"God, be merciful to me, a sinner!" (Luke 18:11–13)*

"Guilty, as charged." Those are words we never want to hear, especially when it comes to our role in the horrific death of our Savior. We don't like to think we're guilty of sending Him to the cross. It's easier to point the finger at other key players: Judas, Pilate, and the Sanhedrin.

But it was for me my Savior died. My sins nailed Him to the cross. Such awareness of the true causes and culprits of Jesus's suffering should make us cry out, "God be merciful to me, a sinner."

Still, such words are hard to say, and harder to believe. Am I really such a sinner that Jesus had to die for me? Unless the answer is yes, we are saying the cross of Jesus was unnecessary for persons like us, and we line up with the Pharisee who prayed about himself, thanking God that he was not like others.

Why confess more than that? Because when we confess our need, we get Jesus—the King of the Universe and Savior of Sinners—to die for our sin, to advocate in Heaven for our needs, and to work all things together in Heaven and on Earth for our good.

Confession, we are told, is good for the soul—but it's actually much better than that. It's good for making all on Earth and in eternity God's blessing to us.

PRAYER: *Heavenly Father, I know that I am guilty of rebelling against You, but I don't tend to think that way. I confess my lack of confession. Help me again to sense deeply that it was for me my Savior died, so I long to live for Him.*

86

*To the praise of his glorious grace, which he has freely
given us in the One he loves...we have redemption
through his blood, the forgiveness of sins, in accordance
with the riches of God's grace. (Ephesians 1:6–7 NIV)*

Would you like to know the best summer traveling tip my family has found? Waffle House cheese grits for thirty-five cents! Now, I'm not talking about just a dab of grits, but a whole heaping, huge bowl of delicious grits. That's *almost* as good as free!

But don't miss the fine print on the menu: thirty-five cents *with any full entrée*. That *almost free* qualification got me thinking. Isn't this how many of us view God's grace? We hear the claims that it's *free*—but surely you must do something else to get it, right?

I mean, if God really offered grace freely, then it would be available to all no matter what they have done. Surely that can't be fair or right. Can it?

Well, it is not fair, but it is right. In fact, it's better than fair because it's a result of God's mercy. And, it is right because it is from God's heart.

God's grace is free because Jesus paid its price for all of us. Receiving His grace is not a consequence of qualifying for it, but of acknowledging that we could never qualify by our efforts or achievements.

Now anyone—regardless of things past or present—can receive grace by faith that God provided it entirely through the work of His Son and that it is really, entirely free. We don't receive grace by doing a little more or a lot more of anything.

We confess that we need God's rescue from sin and rest in our Heavenly Father's assurance that Jesus paid all that was necessary for our redemption.

PRAYER: Lord, thank You for offering redemption from my sin by the offer of entirely free grace received by faith alone in Christ alone.

87

Charm is deceptive, and beauty is fleeting; but a woman who fears the Lord is to be praised. Honor her for all that her hands have done, and let her works bring her praise at the city gate. (Proverbs 31:30–31 NIV)

The author of Proverbs 31 writes, "A wife of noble character who can find? She is worth far more than rubies. Her husband has full confidence in her and ... she brings him good, not harm, all the days of her life" (Proverbs 31: 10–12 NIV).

These verses remind us that love and respect are inextricably linked. The women the Bible presents as most desirable are those who are most respected by their husbands. This is simply because men are most relationally drawn to women they respect, even if they may be tempted to use those that they don't.

The Bible's emphasis on a woman's noble character does not deny the gift of beauty. But it makes clear that physical attraction alone, though powerful, will not maintain a relationship where mutual respect has died.

A Proverbs 31 wife loves and respects her husband, but she is also to be loved and respected by her husband, who praises her and calls her "blessed." Mutual respect rooted in God's grace toward each spouse forges the deepest bonds of biblical marriage!

PRAYER: *Heavenly Father, help me to see the connection between love and respect. Deepen love in my marriage by fostering respect in my heart for my spouse.*

88

*To this end we always pray for you, that our God may
make you worthy of his calling…so that the name
of our Lord Jesus may be glorified in you, and you
in him, according to the grace of our God and the
Lord Jesus Christ. (2 Thessalonians 1:11–12)*

Entering the yellow-tiled hospital room, I had no idea how powerful my
dying friend's ministry would be to me. When I entered, his wife left the
room briefly so that he would not be troubled by her tears.

My friend still knew why his wife had exited. So, he said to me with a
gentle whisper, "Please help my family not to hurt too much. I will see Jesus
soon, but all of you will have to wait. I feel sorry for you! I just pray that I can
glorify the Lord through this."

In his dying care, my friend showed me much of the beauty of eternal life
with Jesus. As though he was opening a treasure chest to reveal its jewels, my
friend's words showed me the gems of Christ's promises: life beyond disease,
hope beyond tragedy, presence with Jesus forever, and opportunity to bring
our Savior glory in every breath of life He grants.

I marveled at my friend's faith—and pray for the same. He ached for his
family, but he also wanted his life—even in his dying—to reveal Jesus's treasures to them. May God so use all of us to glorify Him who loved us enough
to give His own Son to die for us.

PRAYER: *Heavenly Father, thank You for giving Your own
Son on the cross for me. Help me to glorify Him in every
breath You grant so that I can share His treasures with my
loved ones and many more!*

89

By grace you have been saved through faith. And this is not your own doing; it is the gift of God, not a result of works, so that no one may boast. (Ephesians 2:8–9)

Long-ago preacher Phillips Brooks defined grace as *God's Riches At Christ's Expense*. That's not a bad definition, and it's a good way to remember what grace is.

We are saved through faith that what God has spent for us, rather than what we have done for ourselves, makes us right with Him. Our salvation is a gift of His mercy, not something we gain by merit.

As a result, no one may boast of their works before God, or claim that they are the reason God claims us. Instead, we live to show thanks to God for the salvation He provided at Christ's expense.

What was Jesus's expense of our salvation? He gave up Heaven's glory to come in humility, live in purity, suffer in agony, and rise in victory.

What are the riches we receive by faith in Christ's provision? The forgiveness of our sin, the clothing of His righteousness, our adoption by His Father, and assurance of the heavenly blessings of bodies and relationships made perfect forever with Him.

How do we respond to such GRACE? Not by boasting of our works, but by believing in Christ's work so that we live grateful and joyous lives for Him.

PRAYER: Heavenly Father, thank You for providing Your riches at Christ's expense. May I never boast, save in the provision of Christ, my Lord, so that faith in the gift of Jesus fills my life with the joy and power of Your amazing grace!

90

*The King will say to those on his right, "Come, you who are
blessed by my Father, inherit the kingdom prepared for you
from the foundation of the world. For I was hungry and you
gave me food, I was thirsty and you gave me drink,
I was a stranger and you welcomed me." (Matthew 25:34–35)*

A woman visiting our church told me a worn sofa was the reason she
entered the Kingdom of God.

An older woman in the church invited this visitor to her home. The house
was not fancy, and the furnishings were plain. Still, the two enjoyed a lovely
meal during which the guest noticed the worn couch.

The godly woman of meager means explained that she had welcomed so
many people into her home, the visits wore out the fabric! Simple hospitality
and a willingness to open a home to people she didn't know had given the
opportunity to share Jesus's love and grace with many!

This dear woman didn't invite others out of pride. She didn't fail to invite
them out of embarrassment. She simply shared and showed, from the means
that God had supplied, the message of His unconditional grace.

What a great example! A worn sofa represented the Gospel in action. It
was a glimpse of how we can let the world know that you don't have to be picture perfect to get into Jesus's house—or to share it. The grace that let us in is
the grace that others need to know, even if it is revealed by our imperfect lives.

PRAYER: *Lord, just as You have welcomed the mess of me
into Your Kingdom, so may I share Your love by welcoming
those who need Your grace, love, and forgiveness.*

*Blessed is the man who trusts in the LORD, whose trust
is the LORD. He is like a tree planted by water, that sends out
its roots by the stream, and does not fear when heat comes,
for its leaves remain green, and is not anxious in the year
of drought, for it does not cease to bear fruit. (Jeremiah 17:7–8)*

Many of us are encouraged by Bible verses that promise a reward for our faithful obedience to God. That's good. That's why such verses are in Scripture.

But there are two easy ways to mess up the encouragement. One way is to claim credit for the blessings; the other way is to claim nothing but blessings will come to those sufficiently obedient.

God's beautiful blessings should be viewed more as evidence of His *faithfulness* than of our deserving. The person who receives them "trusts in the Lord," not in his or her qualifications. We should never say, "God, I have earned my reward. So, pay up!"

Despite our undeserving it, God's tender care showers those who trust Him with kindness, grace, and mercy. In these ways the whole world can see His grace on display, and His people delight in His love.

But spiritual blessings do not always translate into material blessings. Family unity, personal well-being, and financial stability are often believers' *earthly* fruit, but not always. Heat and drought still come to trees once planted by water. If trials never came, we would not need to trust the Lord.

The trials of this world and the flaws of our heart ever turn us to our eternal Help. Through them we learn of God's sure blessings flowing beyond this world, not because we are good but because He is.

PRAYER: *Father, may Your eternal blessings for my heart strengthen me when earthly blessings seem few, and motivate me to bear fruit that pleases You and honors Your Son.*

92

Grace to you and peace from God our Father
and the Lord Jesus Christ, who gave himself for our
sins to rescue us from the present evil age, according
to the will of God our Father. (Galatians 1:3–4)

Has anyone ever sacrificed for you in a way that changed your life? Such provision happened for me during my senior year of college. I was undecided about a career path, facing college debt without a job, feeling the loneliness of singleness, and my parents' marriage was falling apart. This combo shook me to the core. I need spiritual rescue.

So, during my winter break from school, I met with a man I'd come to rely on. He was running a seminary and invited me to come study Scripture —just to help me get back on track.

It wasn't until about fifteen years later, when I became a leader at that same seminary, that I pulled up my old student file. I discovered not only had that man offered me a scholarship, but he also paid for it with his own money. He sacrificed so I could find the right path—a path that renewed my spirit, led me into ministry, and provided for my family.

Jesus's sacrifice does even more for us. He rescues us from our sin, transforms our hearts, and puts us on the path of eternal safety in His family.

Trust the One who gave Himself for you and walk the path His sacrifice proves was laid in love.

PRAYER: Father, thank You for rescuing me from evil and for putting me on the path of spiritual safety and blessing. Help me walk that path to honor the One who gave Himself for me.

93

*Let every person be subject to the governing authorities.
For there is no authority except from God, and those that
exist have been instituted by God. (Romans 13:1)*

Let's face it, some of God's rules are easier to follow than others. When God says, "You shall not murder," most of us rest easy, knowing we're probably not in danger of violating that one! But submitting to some of God's other rules can challenge us.

Consider how you feel about "pay to all what is owed," or "put away all anger, wrath, malice, slander, and obscene talk from your mouth," or "let every person be subject to the governing authorities."

Does the Bible really say that "prayers, petitions and thanksgivings [should] be made on behalf of all men, for kings and all who are in authority?" (1 Timothy 2:1–2 Paraphrase). Yes. The Bible says that. Advocating for a political cause does not excuse us from doing so God's way.

In our polarized culture, honoring temporal authorities who bring order to society so that the Gospel can spread isn't always easy—or even approved by other Christians. But we need to remember our ultimate citizenship is in Heaven and our ultimate ruler is the Lord. We never abandon His standards in advocating His purposes.

Our aim is to bring glory to Him in how we conduct ourselves, even in opposing wrong. We should not approve of evil; we must expose it. God will use righteous words and conduct toward those in authority for our witness to His greater glory.

PRAYER: Lord, I know You have appointed officials for the good of society. Help me rightly to honor their authority out of submission to You, as I trust You to accomplish Your purposes through Your people in Your timing.

94

*We all, with unveiled faces, are looking as in a mirror
at the glory of the Lord and are being transformed into
the same image from glory to glory; this is from the
Lord who is the Spirit. (2 Corinthians 3:18 CSB)*

If we're honest, we're all painfully aware of our faults and frailties. So, how is it possible for us to meet God's requirement for holiness? One answer is depicted in a children's version of John Bunyan's classic tale, *The Pilgrim's Progress.*

On his journey, Pilgrim discovers a wonderful mirror. There's nothing unusual about the front of the glass. It reveals the features, flaws, and blemishes of the one holding it.

However, the back of mirror displays the face of Jesus. Whoever looks at the person from the back of the mirror only sees Jesus.

When we honestly reflect on our lives, we see the flaws and blemishes that accompany all of our features. But, in His mercy, God chooses to look at us from the direction that reveals only His Son. We see our sin; God chooses to see His Son.

The pilgrim's wonderful mirror reveals how you can be holy in this life—not by your own merits but by the mercy of God that substitutes the goodness and glory of Jesus's image for yours, even as you are being transformed more into His likeness.

> **PRAYER:** *Father, thank You for looking at me through the image of Your Son. Now continue to transform me into that same image, so that the glory You have provided for me will become more and more reflected in me.*

95

The reason the Son of God appeared was to destroy the works of the devil. (1 John 3:8)

Immediately after Adam and Eve sinned, God said to the one who tempted them, "I will put enmity between you and the woman, and between your offspring and her offspring; he shall bruise your head; and you shall bruise his heel" (Genesis 3:15).

Bible scholars call this Genesis verse the "first Gospel." It is God's first promise to redeem a fallen world from the catastrophes of Adam's sin by an eventual Child of Eve.

God refused to give up on those who sinned against Him. Instead, He promised the divine provision of One who would come through the line of humans who had just betrayed Him to redeem them. That's a profound grace, but it was not the end of grace.

God's plan will continue to unfold until all the works of the devil are destroyed. No human conflict or natural disaster or family failure or personal sin has ever derailed God's plan—nor will it.

The Son of God appeared to destroy the works of the devil, even while experiencing an awful attack from him. Satan wounded Jesus on the cross—but our risen Savior crushed Satan, eternally devastating his influence.

We can take daily comfort from knowing God's grace is greater than all the evils of the world, including the failures of our hearts. Grace of that magnitude puts our problems in proper proportion.

When our God is so great, no difficulty is beyond His power. When His grace is so sure, no sin is beyond His pardon. God's grace triumphs!

PRAYER: *Lord, thank You for proclaiming the triumph of Jesus from the beginning of Your Word. Strengthen my heart to stand for You by remembering the greatness of Your grace.*

When they were come to the place, which is called Calvary,
there they crucified him, and the malefactors, one on the right hand,
and the other on the left. Then said Jesus, "Father, forgive them;
for they know not what they do." (Luke 23:33–34 KJV)

On Good Friday, we remember our Savior suffering and dying on our behalf. But His work did not start then. The seed of our salvation was planted at the dawn of humanity, blossomed in a manger in Bethlehem, matured in Nazareth, and lived through obscurity, poverty, persecution, and humiliation.

Jesus's journey eventually led Him into the jaws of prophecy, as the King of Glory took the hill of Calvary, dying there for you and me. On Calvary, our Savior descended to a hell of affliction, dishonor, and torment to save us from the hell we deserved.

Jesus did all of this not only for disciples who should have understood, but for those who heaped pain upon Him. For them, too, He prayed, "Father forgive them; they know not what they do."

That prayer would have been pitiably futile were Calvary the end of Jesus. But Good Friday is not the end of His story! Jesus now reigns as our Risen Lord, having rescued those who believe He suffered to pay for their sins and rose to save them from the pains of Hell forever.

If you think such grace could not possibly apply to you, remember the prayer He made for His tormenters: "Father, forgive them." He not only made the prayer; He gives the pardon for those who sin is as great—or greater—than yours. Believe the pardon is for you—it is!

> **PRAYER:** Lord, thank You for dying the death that I deserve to provide the grace I could not earn. When I doubt the sufficiency of Your grace, remind me of Your prayer for pardon and the heart that makes it available by my faith in You.

97

*All have sinned and fall short of the glory of God,
and are justified by his grace as a gift, through the
redemption that is in Christ Jesus. (Romans 3:23–24)*

If all we do is teach people to be good, they'll inevitably think that their relationship with God is a consequence of their behavior. But it's not. Our eternal relationship with God is a result of trusting in Jesus's death and resurrection—plus nothing else! There is nothing we can do to justify ourselves before God or to add to the perfect work already completed by Jesus Christ!

As important as our conduct can be for fully enjoying and honoring our relationship with God, neither our best behavior nor our finest expressions establish or sustain His love.

You do not become or remain God's child because of how good you are or how articulate is your religiosity. You are His child because of humble faith in the grace God extended to you through the loving sacrifice of His one and only Son.

When we grasp nothing but the empty cross as the basis of our standing before God, then those empty hands of faith are filled with nothing but the grace we require to love and live for Him.

PRAYER: *Lord, thank You for redeeming me from empty attempts to justify myself to You with claims of good behavior or refined religion. Please keep my hands empty of any claim upon Your love except through faith in my risen Lord. Fill my heart with the grace I need to love and live for You.*

98

Christ's love compels us, because we are convinced
that one died for all, and therefore all died. And he
died for all, that those who live should no longer live
for themselves but for him who died for them and
was raised again. (2 Corinthians 5:14–15 NIV)

What is the most powerful human motivation? Love! We shouldn't let that truth merely be a sentimental or romantic affirmation.

What drives a mother back into a burning building? More powerful than fear, or pain, or personal preservation is love.

Why does the Bible focus so much upon our need to love God—identifying such love as the greatest commandment (Matthew 22:36–38)? The answer is that there is no more powerful human motivation for God's purposes. When we love God above all things, even our own lives, then living for His highest priorities is our greatest compulsion.

What creates such love in us? The Bible is clear about that too: "We love because God first loved us" (1 John 4:19). When we are convinced that Christ died for us, then we desire to live for Him. His love makes us want to do His work, and His resurrection power in us makes that possible.

We may still get nervous when we try to tell others about Jesus, or stand for Him against opposition or temptation, but the love of God compels us—as it did the Apostle Paul—when we remember His grace.

PRAYER: *Lord, I confess my hesitation to live and speak for You. May the love You have shown me now compel me to show and tell others about the grace that is in Christ Jesus.*

99

Since we have been justified by faith, we have peace with God through our Lord Jesus Christ. Through him we have also obtained access by faith into this grace in which we stand, and we rejoice in hope of the glory of God. (Romans 5:1–2)

Somewhere in my attic I have a World War II-era newspaper given to me by my mother. She saved the paper when the war ended because the headline declared in six-inch tall letters, "PEACE."

My mother reported that when the news of peace spread through her small Tennessee town, people poured out of their homes and businesses to dance in the street! When peace came after so much suffering and dying, spontaneous joy overflowed and could not be stopped!

The Apostle Paul writes from the context of another war—a spiritual war, which can only be won through the gracious provision of God's Son. Because of Jesus's sacrifice to save us from the consequences of our sins, we can now have peace with God.

When you consider that the war with sin has been won for you by Jesus's victorious resurrection and your peace with God is secure forever, then you will know why you should rejoice in hope of the glory of God. His glory is revealed in the eternal peace that Jesus won. So even if you don't dance— REJOICE!

PRAYER: *Father, as I focus today on the peace Your grace has won through the sacrifice of Jesus and the victory of His resurrection, may I be filled with rejoicing! May the joy of the Lord be my strength.*

100

We do not want you to be uninformed, brothers, about
those who are asleep, that you may not grieve as others do
who have no hope. For since we believe that Jesus died and
rose again, even so, through Jesus, God will bring with him
those who have fallen asleep. (1 Thessalonians 4:13–14)

God's resurrection promises of loved ones' security in Heaven until our eternal reunion can provide profound comfort. My wife, Kathy, and I witnessed this vividly when visiting a grieving friend.

Days before our visit, our friend's daughter had been killed in a farming accident. The sweetness of the girl made the seeming senselessness of the tragedy all the more acute.

Still, with a deep faith in God's ultimate care, the girl's mother told us how she trusted God had already rescued her young daughter from the trials and temptations of an adult world.

After the funeral, the family gathered for a meal. A neglected TV in the room aired a public-service ad graphically warning of drug-infested streets. The ad caught the mother's attention. She shook her finger at the screen, declaring, "But you can't touch my baby. She's with Jesus."

Despite her heartache over being separated from her daughter for a time, the mother was comforted that her child was safe in Jesus's arms. She claimed the victory of grace that would reunite her with her child forever—a reunion that death itself could not deny.

PRAYER: Father, thank You for the confidence I will be reunited with loved ones who are "asleep" in Christ and that we will be together for eternity with Him.

101

Blessed be the God and Father of our Lord Jesus Christ!
According to his great mercy, he has caused us to be born again
to a living hope through the resurrection of Jesus Christ from
the dead, to an inheritance that is imperishable, undefiled,
and unfading, kept in heaven for you. (1 Peter 1:3–4)

A while back, I was invited to a *very* fancy party. I was feeling out of place amid the high-society crowd in their tuxedos and black ties when a young man in tattered jeans, flannel shirt, and hiking boots strolled over to me and struck up a conversation.

I enjoyed the opportunity to converse with someone who seemed more like me in social and economic status. Despite his apparent poverty and casual attire, he exuded a relaxed ease and personal confidence. Only later did I understand why.

Another friend asked me, "Do you know who you were talking to?" I had no idea. My friend said, "That is the heir to one of the largest chemical company fortunes in the world."

The man's father had insisted he live without the benefits of wealth for a time to learn the "real" world. But the young man was still confident of his inheritance. He was not bothered by his current challenges because his future status was sure.

In a similar way, we can face real, current challenges without crippling anxiety, because our relationship with Jesus assures us of an eternal inheritance that nothing in this world can deny.

PRAYER: *Father, thank You for the inheritance that awaits me in Heaven because of your gift of eternal life in Christ! Help me so to lay hold of Your assurance that I am an heir of Your Kingdom that I am not overwhelmed by any deprivation or discouragement that current circumstance may bring.*

102

If then you have been raised with Christ, seek the things that are above, where Christ is, seated at the right hand of God. Set your minds on things that are above, not on things that are on earth. For you have died, and your life is hidden with Christ in God. When Christ who is your life appears, then you also will appear with him in glory. (Colossians 3:1–4)

To be "raised with Christ" (which is resurrection language) requires that we first die. But how could the Apostle Paul write these words to believers still alive?

Their death was signaled by their baptism, when they identified with Jesus for a new life. We rarely think of baptism as a death certificate, but it certifies that the values and priorities of a previous life are past.

Those coming into the Christian faith from other religions know this is so. Their own families may say to them, "If you claim Jesus instead of our gods, or our way of life, then you are dead to us."

But that is not the end of each new believer's story. Our baptism also signals a new life spiritually united to Christ. Since He is raised, we are. Since He sits at God's right hand, we do. Since the wrath of God for sin was exhausted in Him, we are hidden from it. Because He will come in glory, we shall.

We do not yet fully experience all of these blessings, but by the grace of God we can already taste them. The Holy Spirit is the foretaste of these "things that are above" as He confirms them in our hearts.

Trials and temptations are still here, but they no longer determine your future or create your identity. As Paul proclaims, "Christ ... is your life!"

PRAYER: *Father, thank You for raising me from a dead way of life by uniting me to my Savior. Now when trials or temptations come, when failures or doubt oppress me, help me remember they are not my ultimate identity. Christ is my life!*

103

Like newborn infants, long for the pure spiritual milk,
that by it you may grow up into salvation—if indeed
you have tasted that the Lord is good. (1 Peter 2:2–3)

A minister friend from a tradition that only considered the Bible a human invention wandered from the faith. Still, when offered a free trip to the Holy Land, he jumped at the opportunity, only to discover that the tour was loaded with ministers.

He laid low, not participating in any of the worship duties until the final day of the trip. Then, he was asked to do his part by conducting a communion service at one of the sites commemorating Jesus's resurrection.

As he mouthed the familiar words about eating and drinking Christ's provision "until He comes again," the wayward minister's heart opened to real faith. He believed the truth of God's Word.

The rest of the ministers continued to walk the historical site, but my friend immediately returned to the bus. He could not wait to return to his hotel to read a Bible. "For the first time in my life," he said, "I was thirsty for the Word."

Too many people read God's Word as a religious ritual to bribe God to be nice to them. When we understand instead that it the bread of life, providing nourishment for our souls, then we long for it.

Like newborn infants longing for a mother's milk, those who have been born again by the Spirit of God thirst for the spiritual nourishment of Scripture. That's not a chore; it's the joy that strengthens.

PRAYER: *Father, as I read Your Word today, may You give me the nourishment I need to grow in Christ. Help me not to read to bribe You but to feast on the bread of life You offer.*

104

The Spirit of the Lord is upon me, because he has anointed
me to proclaim good news to the poor. He has sent me to
proclaim liberty to the captives and recovering of sight to the
blind, to set at liberty those who are oppressed. (Luke 4:18)

We see grace emerge on the pages of Scripture whenever God provides for those who cannot provide for themselves. Most often these reflections are not the full story of God's work of salvation but highlight aspects of His character and care that become fully revealed in Christ Jesus.

We hear early strains of the music of grace throughout the Old Testament as God provides food for the hungry, strength for the weary, freedom for slaves, a family for the fatherless, faithfulness to the faithless, and forgiveness for the undeserving.

The music rises to a crescendo in accounts of Jesus's ministry to the poor, blind, and oppressed, then climaxes in His death and resurrection, and continues reverberating through the ministry of the church that carries the music of grace to the world by His Spirit.

The difference this concert of grace makes comes on the days our sin or circumstances have made God seem silent. Then the bass drums, cymbals, and trumpets of Scripture announce Jesus afresh in a symphony of praise to stir weary or wandering hearts to beat in rhythm with the assurance of His grace and to live in harmony with His glory.

PRAYER: *Father, as Scripture's message of grace culminates in the ministry of Your Son, may my heart harmonize with His joy and beat for His glory.*

105

The disciples came to Jesus privately and said, "Why could we not cast it [a demon] out?" He said to them, "Because of your little faith. For truly, I say to you, if you have faith like a grain of mustard seed, you will say to this mountain, 'Move from here to there,' and it will move, and nothing will be impossible for you." (Matthew 17:19–21)

An old story tells of two widows living together in a cottage at the foot of a mountain. Soaking rains loosened the soil on the mountain's slope, and a huge boulder threatened to roll onto their home. So, the women prayed that God would anchor the stone.

But—the rain continued, the stone rolled, and crushed the house, prompting one of the women to say, "I knew prayer wouldn't work."

Well, of course, *doubting* prayer doesn't work, but what is *believing* prayer? Are we supposed to imagine that our desires are God's commands—that we are as wise as God about what should happen to shape His eternal plans?

True faith is never rooted in *our* designs, but in our God—His power, wisdom, and love. Nothing is impossible for Him, not even working beyond our prayers to fulfill His plans. Pray, believing that God can move mountains, anchor stones, and melt hearts of stone by Earth's blessings or trials.

Through such believing prayers, God will do even more than we can ask or imagine to accomplish His will on Earth as He intends in Heaven. When we pray, "Heavenly Father, I believe in Your wisdom, power, and love to accomplish what is absolutely best," then we will be most blessed. Trust the God of grace to be better than your prayers.

PRAYER: Lord, help me to pray, and to trust You more than my prayers. Do on Earth what is best for eternity.

Husbands, love your wives, as Christ loved the church
and gave himself up for her, that he might sanctify her,
having cleansed her by the washing of water with
the word, so that he might present the church to himself
in splendor, without spot or wrinkle or any such thing,
that she might be holy and without blemish. (Ephesians 5:25–27)

Have you wondered how husbands are supposed to live out God's command to sacrifice themselves for their wives? It's a tall order, for sure. We understand more of the obligation from its goal.

The Apostle Paul says, "Christ's sacrifice was to 'sanctify' His bride [the church] so that she would have 'splendor' to Him" (Paraphrase).

Giving oneself for the good and glory of another seemed far from the pattern of a friend whose idea of biblical headship meant his wife had to get his approval for everything she wore, to whom she spoke, and whenever she left the house.

So much did he use his authority to control and dominate his spouse that she was constantly fearful and depressed—and, consequently, less pleasing to him. His selfishness (driven by his own insecurities) deprived him of the splendor he wanted in her.

As Christ's glory was enhanced by the splendor of His bride, so also is the blessing of spouses whose goal is to give themselves for the splendor of another.

PRAYER: *Lord, help me draw understanding from how Your grace builds up and beautifies my heart to understand how I can love my spouse as Christ loves.*

107

*His name shall be called Wonderful Counselor, Mighty
God, Everlasting Father, Prince of Peace. (Isaiah 9:6)*

There are times when we all could use some good counsel—someone on our side who can understand our needs. In Scripture, Jesus is called *Wonderful Counselor*, but translators could just as easily have rendered it: "He will be a wonder of a counselor."

What does a wonder of a counselor do? We seek a counselor because we desire good advice. But that advice can only come when the counselor understands us (to better help us understand ourselves) and reveals a path to help and heal.

Our "wonder of a counselor" fulfills these responsibilities with greater insight and care than any human counselor. He knows us through and through. He created us. He listens to us. He watches over us. He sent His Son to be like us. He knows our hearts. He knows *your* heart. He knows the path to help and heal each broken life.

Because of God's great love for you, Jesus sympathizes with you. He has endured trials so that He can understand your pain, and He rose from awful loss so that He can reveal a path to help and heal your brokenness. If you need One who can truly understand, comfort, and guide you from pain and loss, then seek the Wonderful Counselor, Jesus.

PRAYER: Jesus, I'm grateful that You care for me and know me far better than I know myself. Reveal Your will in Your Word so that I will marvel at Your understanding, trust Your care, and honor Your counsel in my times of need.

108

We know that all things work together for the good of those
who love God, who are called according to his purpose.
For those he foreknew he also predestined to be
conformed to the image of his Son. (Romans 8:28–29 CSB)

We can throw the words of this verse around with casual ease, and not understand the richness or seriousness of its meaning.

Laura Story's song "Blessings" includes these lyrics:

> What if my greatest disappointments / Or the aching of this life / Is the revealing of a greater thirst / This world can't satisfy?
> What if the trials of this life— / The rain, the storms, the hardest nights— / Are Your mercies in disguise?[1]

When I hear these questions, I think of Joseph in Genesis, speaking to the brothers who sold him into slavery: "What you meant for evil, God has used for good" (Genesis 50:20).

Joseph was explaining to them, and to us, this profound truth: "God works all things together for the good of those who love Him, who are called according to His purpose." God was working Joseph's bitter circumstances for a sweet purpose that centuries later resulted in the provision of Jesus for you and me.

Even though we face difficulties and tears, God will weave all—from beginning to eternity—into His tapestry of salvation for us and those our lives touch.

PRAYER: *Father, help me to realize that You are using every-thing in my life—both bitter and sweet—to conform me to the image of Your Son and to help others know Him.*

109

Beloved, let us love one another: for love is of God;
and everyone that loveth is born of God and
knoweth God. He that loveth not knoweth
not God; for God is love. (1 John 4:7–8 KJV)

We all want to experience intimacy with God. We speak to Him in prayer, and we listen for His voice as we study His Word, hear sermons, and consider the counsel of fellow Christians.

But along with talking or listening to God, there's another component to spiritual intimacy: loving others. When we express Christ's love for those easy to love *and* for those hard to love, our hearts are experiencing the nature of His affection.

By expressing Christlike love, we get familiar with it and Christ's care becomes more meaningful and precious—moving us closer to Him.

So vital is loving others to intimacy with God that the Apostle John says we cannot really know God at all without loving relationships.

Sadly, we will meet those even in the church who do not realize this. They substitute doctrinal correctness and clever criticism for loving others, thinking they are honoring God with their razor-sharp defense of His truths when, in fact, they are cutting off themselves and others from Him.

If you really want to experience the love of God, love those easy to love, *and* those hard to love.

PRAYER: Lord, help me to know You more intimately by loving those easy to love and those hard to love. Make Christ's love dearer to me by how I love those dear to You.

*For the moment all discipline seems painful rather than
pleasant, but later it yields the peaceful fruit of righteousness
to those who have been trained by it. (Hebrews 12:11)*

I n his book, *The Great Divorce*, C. S. Lewis describes a man troubled by
a red lizard sitting on his shoulder. This lizard, representing sin and the
temptations with which we wrestle, constantly taunts the man.

One day, an angel offers his services, promising to rid the man of this
pesky tormentor, and the man is thrilled. But as the angel prepares to strike
the lizard, the man suddenly has second thoughts. What will life be like without this familiar creature that has given his life pattern and even occasional
pleasure?

The man's hesitation signals a willingness to endure the lizard rather than
risk a change. So, the angel prompts him: "This is the moment. You must
decide!"

The story reminds us how comfortable we can become with our sin. We
dream of being rid of the habits that hinder our relationship with God, but
also dread being without their familiar comforts.

So, in His Fatherly care, our God allows the consequences of sin to be
painful, while promising that there is a better life of peace and righteousness
beyond the lizard's lies.

So much of living without the burden and pain of sin is simply believing
that life could be better without it. God's gracious discipline accompanies the
promises of His Word so that our pain prods us to claim His blessings.

> **PRAYER:** Heavenly Father, help me to submit to Your discipline for my sin, so that I may be prodded by the pain to claim Your promises of the "peaceful fruit of righteousness" that blesses the life You design.

There is therefore now no condemnation for those who are in Christ Jesus. For the law of the Spirit of life has set you free in Christ Jesus from the law of sin and death. (Romans 8:1–2)

This beautiful phrase at the beginning of Romans 8 changes everything: "There is therefore now no condemnation for those who are in Christ Jesus." In this wonderful verse, the apostle lays bare the Gospel of what it means to be united to Christ.

Yes, we are sinful, and, yes, we have failed our God, but we are *in Christ Jesus*, and His grace covers our sin. A dear lady in our church gave me a Russian "nesting doll" to help illustrate. The doll contains others inside that look exactly like the doll on the outside.

By being "in" the larger doll, the smaller dolls are covered by its features and are also made to mirror them. So also, when we are united to Christ by faith, our past, present, and future are covered by Jesus, and God's heart views us as ones mirroring His holiness.

The personal sins and relational storms of our lives blow winds of self-rejection and self-doubt against our souls. Yet, our God does not condemn. As we unite our souls to Him by faith, we are *in Christ Jesus*, sheltered from wrath and granted grace.

All who confess their need of God's grace are united to Christ, beloved by God, and free of condemnation—that includes you, when you are in Christ Jesus.

PRAYER: Lord, thank You for grace that is greater than my sin because it places me in Christ Jesus, sheltered from condemnation and granted His righteousness over my sin.

*The Lord your God is in your midst, a mighty
one who will save; he will rejoice over you with
gladness; he will quiet you by his love; he will exult
over you with loud singing. (Zephaniah 3:17)*

A small statue at our door displays a Middle Eastern father with robe and turban, on his knees, holding a small child over his head. The child is "airplaning" over his father—arms out, feet back, and head forward, confident of his father's grasp.

What makes the statue so special to us is the look of rapturous joy on the face of the father and the child. The child delights in the father's care, and the father rejoices in the gladness of his child. When we first saw the statue, we knew the verse that had to go with it—Zephaniah 3:17.

In this portion of His Word, the Lord reminds us that the One who is mighty to save does not begrudge His care. He humbled Himself to lift us to Heaven and exults over us with singing. As a good Father, He rejoices with the gladness that He brings to our souls.

When I must seek His grace for my sin, I come burdened by grief to my Heavenly Father. But the One who humbled Himself to lift me from guilt does not delight in prolonging my shame. He who saves me from the consequences of my sin by a mighty hand holds me in love and delight no less strong.

I seek Him, return to Him, and daily depend upon Him knowing that He holds me and rejoices over me with gladness—which makes my heart glad and my life His.

PRAYER: *Heavenly Father, thank You for the mighty hand that saves me, lifts me from sin, and holds me forever. And thank You for the glad heart that exults over me, even me!*

113

Now may our Lord Jesus Christ himself, and God our Father,
who loved us and gave us eternal comfort and good hope
through grace, comfort your hearts and establish them in
every good work and word. (2 Thessalonians 2:16–17)

If you only measured yourself by the attitudes and actions of your life, would you be a *sinner* or a *saint*? If you use the Bible's standard that counts even our best works as "filthy rags" before God, the answer is pretty clear. There is so much humanity in our motives and deeds that no one is going to brag of earthly performance before a holy God in Heaven.

Since God's standard for our actions *and* attitudes is perfect holiness, Jesus said, "That even when we have done all that we should do, we are still unworthy servants" (Luke 17:10). Because God knows our thoughts as well as our deeds, honest reflection leads us to the Bible's conclusion, "All have sinned and fall short of the glory of God" (Romans 3:23).

That is bad news for everyone who hopes for a heavenly future—were it not for the grace of God. The Bible says that God our Father has loved us and given us eternal comfort and hope through the grace He has provided in Jesus Christ!

If you confess that *sinner* more than *saint* is your life's label, but you welcome Christ's grace, then you need not despair. Eternal comfort is yours!

Such comfort is a calling. It so changes the motives of our hearts that we desire to honor God with works and words that confirm to others—and our own hearts—the reality of His transforming grace.

PRAYER: *Father, thank You for granting the grace that is eternal comfort to a sinner like me. May that comfort be such encouragement to my heart that I have transformed desires to please You, and may my words and deeds confirm this change!*

*Do you presume on the riches of His kindness and
forbearance and patience, not knowing that God's kindness
is meant to lead you to repentance (Romans 2:4)*

One night in high school, I stayed out well past my curfew. I was having fun, and the time had gotten away from me. I was wrong, and no excuses would have made things right.

As I realized what was waiting for me at home—a set of angry parents with arms crossed and toes tapping—I lost all desire to hurry back. Why rush back to the wrath I deserved?!

When I finally did make it home, my parents hugged me instead of scolding me. Being so long overdue had worried them far more than I anticipated. Their joy at my return exceeded their anger at my absence.

My parents' reaction was so different than what I had anticipated that I immediately felt more chastened than if they had yelled at me. They were so happy I was safe that, even when they later corrected me, I had no doubt I was deeply loved. Their kindness sparked resolve in me not so to burden their hearts again.

Such is God's intention for us. His unswerving grace, even when mixed with parental discipline, is to convince us of His love so that we turn from the sin that hurts Him and us. The kindness of God leads to true repentance.

PRAYER: Lord, help me not to sin. And thank You that, when I do err, assurance of Your kindness turns me from sin to my Savior.

*I am sure of this, that he who began a good
work in you will bring it to completion at the
day of Jesus Christ. (Philippians 1:6)*

When an architect designs a building, he plans all the details. He draws in the spiral staircase, the dormer windows, and even the attic and basement. But while the structure is under construction, onlookers need some imagination to envision the final product. It can often look like a disorganized mess until final stages.

The Apostle Paul describes God as a divine builder, working for our good now, and also planning for our future glory. But day after day our human frailties remind us that we are still under construction. God is still framing our lives and installing proper supports, because He is working to bring us into conformity with His ultimate plan.

We can get discouraged that the construction takes time, and that we are not yet all we desire to be. So, the Apostle Paul encourages us to be patient with this assurance: "He who began a good work will bring it to completion at the day of Christ Jesus."

Until then, we are all "Christians under construction," thanking God that, though we are not all we should be, we are not all we once were or shall be. God's not done with us, yet, but He promises to bring us to completion according to His design.

PRAYER: Lord, thank You that I am forgiven, even though I am still under construction. Give me patience and encouragement as Your plan unfolds for my life, knowing You promise to bring everything to completion through Christ!

You have died, and your life is hidden with Christ in God. When Christ who is your life appears, then you also will appear with him in glory. (Colossians 3:3–4)

When all her older siblings had left home, my youngest daughter only had me to play with at the dinner table. One of our favorite games was "napkin war."

We would wait until the meal was mostly done. Then, one of us would ball up the paper napkin in our lap, wait for the other person to get distracted, and hurl the paper missile at the other's head.

Then, the war of the flying napkins was on—a war that I always won because I have a better aim than my daughter. But, whenever she began to lose, she knew exactly what to do. She would get up from her chair and hide behind her mother. Because I won't throw at her mother, my child was safe.

The game reveals and contrasts the grace of our Heavenly Father. He could have hurled His wrath upon sinners, but instead He poured it out on His Son. Now, when we are hidden in Christ, there is no wrath that touches us. We are safe.

PRAYER: Heavenly Father, I know that my life is hidden with Christ. When guilt causes me to doubt Your care, please help me to remember that I am safe in Your love because of Your assurance that Jesus took the wrath I deserve.

117

Though you have not seen him, you love him. Though you do not now see him, you believe in him and rejoice with joy that is inexpressible and filled with glory, obtaining the outcome of your faith, the salvation of your souls. (1 Peter 1:8–9)

The Gospel must be reflected in the attitudes as well as the actions of God's people. The reason? Those with whom we share Christ will reject righteousness that reflects His holiness but not His heart.

The good news of Christ never slights the seriousness of sin nor shades the wonder of God's pardon. Tears of confession must mingle with the joy that forgiveness brings to produce the gratitude that empowers a transformed life and to inspire the humility that reaches the most insecure.

When we truly perceive how great is the heart of the One who pardoned us, then our heart begins to beat in harmony with His. Though we have not seen Him, others should see Him in us. Though perfect righteousness is impossible, His cross should stimulate consistent thanksgiving. Though temporary setbacks are unavoidable, our joy should assure others that eternal salvation through Christ is unassailable.

So, we rejoice in the goodness of the Gospel that saves us from our sin, and others come to know our Savior because Jesus is our joy!

PRAYER: Lord, help me to remember and relish the wonder of my salvation, so that my joy drowns my disappointments and bitterness in the wonder of You. Then, may the beauty of my transformation be a signal of the glory of my Savior so that others may see and share my joy.

What then shall we say to these things? If God is for us,
who can be against us? He who did not spare his own
Son but gave him up for us all, how will he not also with
him graciously give us all things? (Romans 8:31–32)

When I began dating my professional flute-playing wife, Kathy, I didn't understand the relationship between a musician and her instrument.

I learned when picking her up after a concert. I opened the trunk of my car to store her flute for our date—only to have her recoil in horror! That flute was not going to ride in the trunk of my car, nor even in the backseat.

Kathy had worked and sacrificed for years to be able to purchase that high-priced instrument. So her flute had a place of honor in the front seat with us.

Remembering that experience helps me understand how precious and protective is God's care for me. When I sin or face a difficulty in life, I can be tempted to think that God would like to put me in the back seat of His plans or hide me from His view in the trunk of His purposes.

Instead, Scripture reminds me that He paid for my soul at too high a price ever to care so little for me. Because God did not spare the life of His Son to purchase my salvation, I am His treasured possession—and always will be.

PRAYER: *Father, thank You for purchasing my salvation with the precious blood of Jesus Christ. Help me to treasure the way You treasure me so that I do not sin against You!*

119

> *Lift your drooping hands and strengthen your weak knees,*
> *and make straight paths for your feet, so that what is lame may*
> *not be put out of joint but rather be healed. (Hebrews 12:12–13)*

God's discipline is an incredibly gracious display of His presence. Of course, no one wants to be disciplined, but when God acts in our lives to "put out of joint" the legs, knees, and ankles of our souls that are walking us into sin, we cannot deny He is here, He is real, and He really cares about our walk.

Discipline is evidence of God entering our world to rescue us from spiritual dangers we cannot handle or would not avoid without His intervention.

So, God's discipline is not contrary to His grace but is, in fact, *grace* itself. Just as we discipline our own children for their safety and maturity, God disciplines us to turn us from harm and to help us conform to the image of our Savior, Jesus Christ.

Yes, God sometimes allows difficult and painful paths, but His intention is always to lead us to the spiritual fruit of righteousness and peace.

As we partake of this fruit, we are healed from this world's trials and strengthened for our journeys by our Father's loving care. That is why His discipline not only confirms that He is here, but also that we are His.

PRAYER: *Father, when Your discipline is painful, help me to trust Your gracious plan for healing and strengthening me so that I treasure this confirmation of Your presence and care.*

120

We do not want you to be uninformed, brothers, about
those who are asleep, that you may not grieve as others do
who have no hope. For since we believe that Jesus died and
rose again, even so, through Jesus, God will bring with him
those who have fallen asleep. (1 Thessalonians 4:13–14)

The most powerful Christian testimonies don't usually come from "easy street" but are instead brought about by serious heartache. One such story came after the tragic passing of a young woman of faith. After she died, her aged father felt that there was little left in life for him.

But, then, this faithful woman's recent words of hope in a heavenly future with a reunion of loved ones began to fill his mind. Simple, unplanned conversations with her father about her understanding of God's promises replayed in his memories.

Though she was with the Lord, her ministry to him was still alive, echoing in the hope that her father began to share. He discovered profound comfort in the assurances of Heaven's promises. Faith in these truths that God had so graciously planted in his heart through those past conversations with his daughter restored hope and meaningful life for him—and for those his life now touches.

The beauty of our testimonies of grace can never be fully assessed until we are with the Lord. There we will see how the Lord uses us beyond all our expectations and, perhaps, beyond our lives to replace ashes of tragedy with new life and eternal hope.

PRAYER: *Heavenly Father, thank You that there is hope beyond the grave—restoration of our bodies, our hearts, and our relationships! May my life be a testimony to others of Heaven's promises so that they can share in this eternal hope.*

121

Clothe yourselves, all of you, with humility toward
one another, for "God opposes the proud but
gives grace to the humble." (1 Peter 5:5)

How can humility be a conduit of grace for us—and others? That depends on how you define humility. Humility is often not prized in our culture because it is confused with shyness or backing down, making it hard to understand as a powerful force for God.

Humility is a combination of two things: confessing our need of God and prioritizing the purposes of God. When people are willing to put the Lord's interests above their own and confess that they will need God's help to do that, then honoring God has become their focus.

God has no greater priority than His own glory—so that His will would be done and His goodness would be shared. So, when true humility is present, so is God. His attention, power, and grace flow through the conduit for His glory that our humility supplies.

Remember Jesus's greatest achievement was not done with pomp and circumstance, but with the humble offering of His life for us. His perfect humility was the greatest conduit for God's glory and grace the world has ever known.

Others have said that there is no limit to what God can do if it doesn't matter which of us gets the credit. There is no limit to the glory Christ can receive when we confess the grace we require to do His will—the same grace that provides His mercy when we don't.

PRAYER: Lord Jesus, thank You for demonstrating what it means to be humble through Your servant life and sacrificial death. Help me today to put Your interests above my own so that I may be a conduit of Your glory flowing into this world.

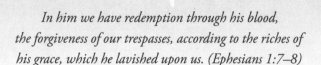

In him we have redemption through his blood,
the forgiveness of our trespasses, according to the riches of
his grace, which he lavished upon us. (Ephesians 1:7–8)

God forgives us for our trespasses by the blood of His Son. This great provision is a very precious truth to remember when we sense the magnitude of our sin. But we may miss some of the beauty of the concept by missing all the aspects of grace implicit in the Apostle Paul's terms.

In modern speech, we trespass when we cross into forbidden territory or onto someone else's property. That meaning is certainly included in the apostle's thought. But the biblical language means something more specific, *it means the notion of going outside a safe boundary.*

This makes sense when we understand that God's law marks the boundaries that His heart has marked for our safekeeping. His forgiveness of our trespasses focuses on extending mercy to those who have wandered outside God's loving protection.

Grace is on both sides of the fence of God's law. Grace lays the fence for us to stay within God's safekeeping, and grace extends beyond the fence for those who go outside His boundaries.

Jesus's blood does not only pay for our transgression of God's law, but also for our trespassing of His love. This means God's mercy is available not only for those who break His law, but for those who break His heart.

His grace is good enough for those who stay inside the fence of His care and great enough for those who have gone beyond it.

> **PRAYER:** Lord, help me to trust the caring heart that provided the safety of Your law. Please forgive my trespass when my willful heart wanders outside Your will, and may that kindness lead me to repent and return to Your care.

He drew me up from the pit of destruction, out of
the miry bog; and he set my feet upon a rock making
my steps secure. He put a new song in my mouth,
a song of praise to our God. Many will see and fear,
and put their trust in the LORD. (Psalm 40:2–3)

One of the men that I respect most in this world is my father-in-law, Bob. He is a real craftsman. Bob built the house in which my wife grew up with his own hands from foundation to roof. Seeing the fruit of his diligent labors stimulates great regard in my heart for the man.

But Bob's work was not always easy. The stairs of the house turned twice with tricky angles to reach the second story. After numerous efforts to get the stairs right, there came a moment when Bob walked out of the house into the yard, hung his head, and cried. He felt defeated and in a pit of despair, fearing he would never get things right.

But what if, in that moment, Bob could have known our regard for him these many years later? What if he had known that the difficulty of the task, and even the temporary failure, would not diminish our respect for him in the least? In fact, his endurance through the difficulty only increases our regard.

If Bob had known the end from the beginning, he would have been strengthened for his task despite temporary failure. For just such a reason, God assures us now of His regard forever, setting our feet on the rock that is Jesus, so that we have a song in our hearts to finish His work.

PRAYER: Father, thank You for lifting me from my pits of despair by reminding me of the solid rock on which I stand. That rock is Jesus. Help me always remember His grace so I have certainty of Your love and a song of praise in my heart.

124

Love is patient and kind; love does not envy or boast;
it is not arrogant or rude. It does not insist on its own way;
it is not irritable or resentful; it does not rejoice at wrongdoing,
but rejoices with the truth. Love bears all things, believes all things,
hopes all things, endures all things. (1 Corinthians 13:4–7)

Some men have used a misunderstanding of biblical headship to make servants of their spouses and slaves of their children. The goal of such wrongheaded headship is to get everyone to serve the interests of the husband and father.

But the Bible insists that men *love* their wives and children, and defines such love as not insisting on one's own way. Christ calls husbands to lead their families with the patience and kindness that requires daily sacrifice to reflect the heart and work of our Savior.

Such love is not envious, boastful, or proud. It seeks the good of others more than personal ease or gain. We are each called to love, as God in Christ loved us. Such love is the path to others' blessing and ours as well. Through such love Christ becomes real to us.

PRAYER: Lord, as I seek to serve You this day, help me also to serve my family. May the reality of You become a greater blessing to me, as I become a greater reflection of the blessing You are in the way I lead those I love.

125

Beloved, do not be surprised at the fiery trial when it comes upon you to test you, as though something strange were happening to you. But rejoice insofar as you share Christ's sufferings, that you may also rejoice and be glad when his glory is revealed. (1 Peter 4:12–13)

If every day of the Christian life were just a walk on easy street, we would have scant cause to lean on Him. That's why, odd as it may seem, God uses our suffering and trials to draw us closer to His heart.

The Apostle Peter says not to be surprised when we face a "fiery trial." Such a trial does not mean that we have done something wrong or that God is somewhere else. We should expect spiritual opposition in a fallen world, but that push back should push us into our Savior's arms.

After a couple of mistakes playing infield, my Little League baseball coach banished me to the right field desert. Then, the next batter got a hit that I misjudged and the ball sailed over my head. As I ran to retrieve the ball, I cried out to Heaven in my ten-year-old angst, "Oh God, what did I do wrong?"

I presumed that I was being punished for some unknown sin, not that I needed as-yet-unprescribed glasses. My trial ultimately resulted in a trip to the optometrist, then better ballgames, then better grades, then an improved confidence that God would use me for greater purposes than I could imagine.

Peter encourages such mature understanding, telling us not to think it strange that the world opposes Christians, but also not to waste our trials.

Through difficulty we can learn that God's presence is strength for trials, His promises are comfort in trouble, and His assurance of His sovereign care provides peace that passes understanding. Tears can be the spiritual lenses that give us sight of God's heart—and nearness to it.

PRAYER: *Heavenly Father, let me not be surprised by trials, but learn of You and lean on You through them. Help me trust that the heart that sent Jesus for me cares for me.*

126

In this the love of God was made manifest among us,
that God sent His only Son into the world,
so that we might live through him. (1 John 4:9)

God's love for us is the soil in which our love for Him grows. So, identifying His grace in all of Scripture is not simply a nice thing to do, nor is it a novel approach to reading the Bible. Regular exposure to grace ignites a consuming love for God, which is His greatest command.

We identify God's grace in all Scripture not to encourage license or laziness, but to fan into flame a compelling love for our Savior. Our goal is not merely gaining a correct interpretation of what Scripture says. We are also seeking to stimulate a profound love for God that embraces Him, abides in Him, and bears much fruit.

When love for God is our chief delight, then glorifying Him becomes the chief priority of our life! By His earthly life, we have eternal life. Because of His love we live, and because we live, we love to live for Him.

PRAYER: Father, as I reflect today on Your amazing grace by which I have eternal life through the Son You sent, please ignite such love for Him that my earthly life will glorify You every day in every way!

The Spirit helps us in our weakness. For we do not know what to pray for as we ought, but the Spirit himself intercedes for us with groanings too deep for words. And he who searches hearts knows what is the mind of the Spirit, because the Spirit intercedes for the saints according to the will of God. (Romans 8:26–27)

Here's an amazing promise: The God of all creation works through our prayers to do His will! That's not because we have all that wisdom and insight to tell God how to run His universe. Instead, we are assured that, even when we do not know how to pray, the Holy Spirit takes over our humble petitions, interceding for us.

I think of the Spirit's work when I watch my mother decorate a cake. She glops the icing into a piping funnel and presses it through a decorator tip to create beautiful designs.

With my limited wisdom and tainted desires, my prayers are often like the icing glopped into the funnel. The Holy Spirit is the decorator tip. So, as I offer my messy petitions, He transforms them into God's beautiful design—a design so perfect that all things work together for good.

Because the Holy Spirit is interceding for us, God answers our prayers better than we can ask them. So, you do not need to know all answers and outcomes to pray well. Instead, humbly come to God with your needs, trusting Him to deliver the answers that are best.

PRAYER: *Lord, I confess I don't always know how to pray or what to pray. But I thank You for the Holy Spirit, who intercedes for me with greater fervency that I can offer and transforms my humble petitions into Your perfect design.*

128

"I know the plans I have for you," declares the LORD, "plans to prosper you and not to harm you, plans to give you hope and a future." (Jeremiah 29:11 NIV)

We can be extremely grateful for the sacrifice of Jesus that paid for our sins, and still be extremely burdened by the guilt that required it. We are thankful that our debt was paid, but our consciences are still stricken that we accumulated the debt that required His death.

We wonder how God can really love those who required the suffering of His Son, even if we are saved by His grace. That is why God speaks so forcefully and repeatedly of His unwavering care.

The One who saved us did so for a purpose. He has plans for us—plans to prosper us and not to harm us. Our prosperity is not the stuff of worldly pleasures that charm us for the moment and leave us after a season. Rather, God promises hope and a future.

Our hope is the firm confidence that our future is secured by One who loved us enough to send His Son to claim us for His eternal home. His love does not hold the past against us. So we can let it go, too.

Today rest in the sure hope God has graciously given you through His risen Son, Jesus Christ, so that you can fulfill the plan He has for your future!

PRAYER: *Heavenly Father, thank You for loving me enough to claim me by the life of Your Son. Help me to find joy in the blessed hope and future You have given me by His sacrifice— and keep me from living in the guilt You have removed forever.*

129

His master said to him, "Well done, good and faithful
servant. You have been faithful over a little; I will set you over
much. Enter into the joy of your master." (Matthew 25:23)

My wife, Kathy, came across a news story about a woman from her child-hood named Ruth. According to the article, Ruth was hesitant to talk about her sixty years of teaching Sunday school. She told the reporter, "You can talk about me when I'm gone."

Ruth only agreed to the interview on the condition that the story would run after her death. Then, she insisted that everything she had done in her life of influencing generations of children was only possible through the strength and abilities graciously given by God. "The credit is His, not mine," Ruth said.

Ruth never heard the acclaim of her community for her faithful teaching. But I have confidence that on the day she stood before the Lord in glory, she heard, "Well done, My good and faithful servant,"

Sixty years of teaching little children is no small feat, but it may have been a greater feat to do it so well *and* acknowledge that the grace of God enabled it.

By Ruth's faithfulness, blessings will reverberate in children's lives for eternity, and acclaim will echo in the halls of Heaven for just as long. But no "well done" will ring louder that the Lord's blessing on the one who points God's children to His enabling grace.

The highest honor desired of those claimed by grace is to know God takes joy from the ways we have used His resources to share His heart.

PRAYER: Heavenly Father, help me to be faithful in the duties You give by depending on the grace You offer so that I may someday hear the words, "Well done, good and faithful servant." May Your grace make Your approval my joy.

130

You formed my inward parts; you knitted me together
in my mother's womb. I praise you, for I am fearfully
and wonderfully made. (Psalm 139:13–14)

God has applied beautiful creativity in knitting each child according to His specific design and wonderful purpose. So, the uniqueness of our children shouldn't frustrate or bewilder us.

God's creativity encourages parents to tune their hearts to respond to each child in accord with the Lord's handiwork. We shouldn't ask our sumo wrestlers to move like ballerinas, nor fail to treasure the talents of artists and athletes, musicians and mathematicians.

Helping children discover God's unique gifting for their lives is no easy task. That's why a loving relationship with God is essential to parenting.

As we discern God's special gifting for our lives, we grow in appreciation for our uniqueness and for how it enables us to parent unique children. We discover why, out of all the parents in the world, God especially chose us for our children.

As Christian parents, our goals are both to reflect our Savior and to help our children do the same. Each time we control our anger, endure being misunderstood, take time for needed attention, absorb an insult, love patiently, discipline firmly, forgive gently, and choose which approach is best for each child and situation, we're reflecting our personal love for Christ as it is needed for this particular child.

We train children best when we treasure how they were made for God, and how we were made for them!

PRAYER: *Heavenly Father, thank You for Your beautiful creativity! Help me to celebrate the uniqueness of my children in how I reflect Your special love and grace for them.*

131

Flee youthful passions and pursue righteousness,
faith, love, and peace, along with those who call on
the Lord from a pure heart. (2 Timothy 2:22)

The air war over Bosnia in the late 1990s made Scott O'Grady famous. For days, the downed American flier had evaded capture in enemy territory. When the rescue helicopter finally landed in the clearing near where O'Grady was hiding, he didn't hesitate. He shook off his fatigue, prepared his weapons, split the bushes, and with all the strength he could muster, ran to his rescue.

His actions parallel those of believers who engage in the spiritual warfare of this world. We should not assume that because God promises to provide a way out of temptation, we can just relax with nothing to do. God expects us to use every weapon of His provision to fight our spiritual opposition and claim the rescue He promises.

As long as you're in this world, you are spiritually in enemy territory. So run to the rescue God provides by diligently employing every resource of Scripture, prayer, godly counsel, and spiritual resolve that is yours by Christ's grace!

PRAYER: *Lord, I know that I live in enemy territory and face many temptations. Please help me not to use the promises of Your mercy to be lax about sin's threats. Instead, help me use the spiritual resources graciously provided for my rescue!*

132

While we were living in the flesh, our sinful passions, aroused by
the law, were at work in our members to bear fruit for death.
But now we are released from the law, having died to that which
held us captive, so that we serve in the new way of the Spirit
and not in the old way of the written code. (Romans 7:5–6)

Before we were saved by the power of the Holy Spirit, we were living in the power of the flesh. We desired what God's law reveals as harmful to us because we were controlled by earthly passions rather than any desire to honor God.

In that sense, the law became a meter of our wrongdoing and a measure of the condemned life to which we were chained by our sinful passions. Praise God those chains are broken!

Since believers are indwelt by the Holy Spirit, our passions are being transformed and we have power to resist sinful impulses. So, the Bible not only teaches us how to live according to God's love, but also assures us that we are not slaves to sin.

At times, we may yield to temptation and even surrender to Satan's lie that we cannot help it. In such moments we must respond with the assurances of the Gospel: we have been released from the guilt *and* power of sin.

We act with that power, when we replace our love of sin with a greater love—the supreme love of Jesus Christ! The grace that God reveals in every passage of Scripture stirs us not to dodge our obligations but to fulfill them out of love for the One who loved us and gave Himself for us!

PRAYER: *Jesus, now that You have freed me from the chains of sin's guilt and power, convince me daily of the Spirit's power in me to fulfill Your will for my life by following the standards You have lovingly revealed in Your Word.*

I pray that you, being rooted and established in love,
may have power, together with all the Lord's holy
people, to grasp how wide and long and high and deep
is the love of Christ. (Ephesians 3:17–18 NIV)

MOM ON STRIKE. Those words appeared on a sign planted in the front yard of a home near us. A young mother, who had tired of her children's whining and back-talk, moved high into the family's backyard treehouse and declared herself *on strike.*

A local television station interviewed her husband. The dad, frantic to get his wife to come down from the tree, urged his kids to quit whining, promise obedience, and make amends.

We understand the mom, but it's important to know that our God is different. He doesn't go on strike because we haven't made amends or cleaned up our act. Because we could never do enough to climb to God in His heavenly house, He came to us in the person of His Son.

Because we could never make amends for our sins, Jesus made atonement for us. He paid the price for our sins before our good behavior lasted long enough, or we grieved for our sins deeply enough, or we opened our arms wide enough to Him. While we were yet sinners, Christ died for us (Romans 5:9).

Our relationship with God never depends on the sufficiency of our goodness, but on grace we cannot earn and do not deserve. He is never on strike but always available to those who call out in faith to the One who made amends for us.

PRAYER: Lord, I'm grateful that You never go on strike because of my sins, or wait until I've made sufficient amends to help me. Thank You for extending Your grace to me in Christ before I ever earned it or could deserve it!

His intent was that now, through the church,
the manifold wisdom of God should be made known
to the rulers and authorities in the heavenly realms,
according to his eternal purpose that he accomplished
in Christ Jesus our Lord. (Ephesians 3:10–11 NIV)

Most people have heard the story of Joseph's multicolored coat, but don't know the story receives special attention as the Apostle Paul describes God's purpose for His Church.

The word ancient translators used to describe Joseph's multicolored coat is the same term used to describe God's "manifold wisdom" as He builds His Church from every nation, tribe, people, and language.

The Gospel of grace is not a one-colored story. It's a multicolored mission that embraces diverse personalities, ethnicities, and generations. So that all the world would be reached with the grace of Christ, He calls different kinds of people from throughout the nations into His church to reach all nations.

Sometimes we think it is very "nice" of us to welcome those unlike us into our fellowship. The Bible actually says that it is *necessary* for us to do so in order to fulfill Christ's mission for our churches.

When Jesus changes us so that we receive others despite differences, antipathies, and prejudices, even spiritual powers in the heavenly realms are awed by the wisdom and might of God's transforming grace. Even the angels marvel and say, "What a God!"

PRAYER: *Father, thank You for the multicolored story of Your redeeming love in Christ that claimed me when I was not of Your original chosen people. Help me now to welcome all into Your mission of spreading the good news of grace to all.*

135

We are afflicted in every way, but not crushed; perplexed,
but not driven to despair; persecuted, but not forsaken;
struck down, but not destroyed; always carrying in the
body the death of Jesus, so that the life of Jesus may also
be manifested in our bodies. (2 Corinthians 4:8–10)

I was graduating later that day and met our graduation speaker, Rev. Ian Tait, coming down a set of stairs. He asked about my plans, then gave a brief word of advice that I have needed many times.

"Just remember, Bryan," he said, "there will always be blessings and battles—never all one or the other."

I have recited Tait's words many times amid blessings and battles. In times of blessing, I remember that I am being bolstered for work to come. In times of battle, I remember that they are not necessarily punishment for wrong or signs of mistakes.

Until the Lord returns, there will be battles for His servants to fight in a fallen world of sinners like us. There will also be blessings to prepare and strengthen us for the battles.

If we know there are always blessings and battles, we won't be distracted by one or destroyed by the other. Blessings don't mean we deserve nothing else, and battles don't mean we failed. We aren't necessarily more righteous because we have blessings, nor ever abandoned because we face battles.

Sunshine and rain are needed for the harvest that God intends to reap from our lives. Knowing that weather forecast prepares us to face every day's events and people with confidence in God's grace.

PRAYER: *Lord, thank You for showing others Jesus through me. Equip me for the blessings and battles I need to face for that purpose without being distracted or destroyed by either.*

136

We do not lose heart. Though our outer self is wasting away,
our inner self is being renewed day by day. For this light
momentary affliction is preparing for us an eternal weight
of glory beyond all comparison. (2 Corinthians 4:16–17)

The uncontrollable grunts and grimaces of Tourette's Syndrome can be hard on families, even when doing routine things like eating out. It was during one such outing that Justin's mother had to rush her symptomatic young son and his sisters out the restaurant door.

As the family escaped the harsh whispers and stares from people around the room, Justin's sister asked, "Mommy, will Justin always be this way?" The mother, too stressed to give an answer at the time, later recounted the question to her husband.

He asked, "How did you answer?" The mom sighed, "I didn't have any answer."

Then, Justin's father lovingly reminded his family, "The answer is no. Justin will not always be this way. When we are with Jesus, all will be made right, and our afflictions will be far outweighed by His glory. Justin will not always be this way!"

Trials come in many forms, but they all will come to a heavenly end for God's people. Then, the glory we experience in Christ's Kingdom will include perfect health, healed relationships, and eternal joys that far outweigh the passing trials of this earth. You can endure this earth by trusting in that eternity.

PRAYER: *Father, help me each day to remember the coming day when You will make everything right. Help me now to "look not to the things that are seen but to the things that are unseen. For the things that are seen are transient, but the things that are unseen are eternal" (2 Corinthians 4:18).*

137

The law of the LORD is perfect, reviving the soul; the testimony of the LORD is sure, making wise the simple; the precepts of the LORD are right, rejoicing the heart. (Psalm 19:7–8)

Why do people, even Christian people, think that God's grace is a license to sin or to ignore the needs of others?

Nowhere does the Bible say that if we love God, we can abuse His grace, trample on Christ's blood, disregard His Word, and neglect those who are poor, hurting, or disadvantaged. To the contrary, Jesus tells us, "If you love Me you will keep My commandments."

Our obedience does not qualify us for His mercy, and our disobedience does not disqualify us from it. So, why is God concerned for our behavior?

The answer is the heart that dispenses God's grace is the same that designed God's law. God does not save His children from sin's disease, then encourage them to play in its traffic. His standards revive the soul, make wise the simple, and bring joy to hearts by the relationships they protect.

Those who have been trapped in legalistic observance of God's law—thinking that they are earning His love by their behavior—sometimes swing the pendulum of obedience into license when coming into an understanding of grace. They assume that because grace grants freedom from legalism, Christ has no standards at all.

The reality is that God has established His commands in order to care for those His grace secures. Out of love for us, He calls us to walk in paths that are perfect for experiencing His love.

PRAYER: *Father, as I seek Your will in Your Word, give me the grateful heart to walk the paths perfectly designed by Your gracious heart.*

138

Do you remember those old Western television shows that showed a small town being terrorized by an evil gunslinger? The story always changed when the townspeople finally realized that, if they just stuck together, the gunslinger wouldn't hold any more power over them.

That's true for us as Christians also. The Apostle Paul says that, when we stand together without fear against cultural evils or societal pressures, Christ will triumph through us. But what will create such fearlessness?

Christian courage in the face of evil is the fruit of resolute faith that our God will prevail. Battles are real and may be fierce, but confidence in God's triumph in God's time is the source of our strength. Even if we lose earthly life or gain, redeemed bodies and souls are secure forever with the One who will overcome all evil.

Remember the testimony of missionary Jim Elliot, who gave his life for the eternal reward of others' salvation with this confidence: "He is no fool who gives what he cannot keep to gain that which he cannot lose."

The promise of our eternal security grants the assurance that all spiritual foes will ultimately be destroyed. So, we can now stand firm and stand together knowing that God's purposes and people will triumph. We may not be ahead in every inning, but we are on the winning team!

PRAYER: Lord, fill me and my fellow believers with confidence in Your salvation so that we will stand together and unafraid when confronted by enemies of the Gospel.

*Be imitators of God, as beloved children. And walk
in love, as Christ loved us and gave himself up for us,
a fragrant offering and sacrifice to God. (Ephesians 5:1–2)*

My ministry began with the privilege of leading an historic church. I soon discovered that I was not prepared for the problems and pain of the position.

The church was in a mining and farming community being ravaged by economic woes. The mines were closing, the farms were dying, but the sins were not. As jobs and incomes crashed, family problems skyrocketed.

I thought I knew what to do. With clear explanations of biblical texts, I would thunder to those trying to medicate their pain with addictions, abuse, and adultery, "Stop it!" After a while, I had said, "Stop it" so often, I couldn't stand myself! I said to my wife, "I didn't go into ministry to hurt people, but I stand in the pulpit every Sunday and do just that."

Only when I was also despairing did I become open to a mature minister teaching me to read the Bible not as a simple rulebook, but as a revelation of God's redemption of the hopeless. Grace beacons from every page, if we will see how God is working to rescue those who cannot rescue themselves.

When I began to see grace, the Lord gave me hope to share with desperate people—and with my own despairing soul. Such hope resurrects desire to live each new day trusting in Christ's love, and is available to you this day through faith in Jesus.

PRAYER: Lord, as I read my Bible today, save me from despair by showing me Your heart in the ways You have worked to rescue those who cannot rescue themselves. Then conform my desires to the designs of Your heart for lasting joy.

140

Truly, truly, I say to you, it was not Moses who gave you the bread from heaven, but my Father gives you the true bread from heaven. For the bread of God is he who comes down from heaven and gives life to the world. (John 6:32–33)

In the Old Testament, we see God providing manna for food, water from a rock, and hope in a promised Messiah. In the New Testament, we see Jesus heal the sick, give strength to the weak, provide victory to the defeated, food for the hungry, and rest for the weary. And throughout the Scriptures, we read about the Holy Spirit interceding for our prayers, guiding our steps, and sealing our future in Heaven.

By these accounts—and many more like them—God is explaining the essential nature of His grace. Grace is God providing for His people what they cannot provide for themselves.

The message in the manna is the nature of the Messiah. As God sent bread from Heaven to provide for His people's physical needs, He also sent Jesus to provide for our spiritual needs. In both cases, the provision was beyond the capability of the people.

By coming to the rescue over and over in Scripture, God demonstrates that His salvation is not man-made but God-made. His solution to our sin was to send Jesus Christ to suffer and die in our place, exchanging His righteousness for our sin.

God provided the solution to sin that we could not. Jesus came to our rescue. That's grace we could never ourselves provide but can believe and receive. Believe and receive this Bread of Heaven today.

PRAYER: *Father, You provided the Bread of Heaven for me. I could not earn it, make it, or bake it, but You provided Him. Nourish my heart by this Bread so that I might live for the One who came to rescue me from my sin.*

141

Two are better than one, because they have
a good reward for their toil. For if they fall,
one will lift up his fellow. (Ecclesiastes 4:9–10)

There are no shortcuts to spiritual victory, but thankfully there is no mystery either. Seeking prayerful associations and accountability with others is one key. As we support one another in such healthy Christian relationships we grow in understanding others, ourselves, and our Savior.

Ours is not a magic religion full of mysterious incantations, secret handshakes, and arcane codes. Instead, we gain strength and understanding from the encouragement, counsel, correction, and worship of fellow Christians. As we participate in loving practices and patterns with others, they help us and we help them to persevere and grow as God intends.

No Christian flourishes as an island. So, come alongside someone today, because "two are better than one.... For if they fall, one will lift up his fellow." And do not worry, or object, that God has designed you to thrive spiritually when others come alongside you, too.

PRAYER: Lord, just as You come alongside me to comfort and strengthen by the help of the Holy Spirit, help me to support another today—and not object to the help I, too, have been designed to receive.

142

When the goodness and loving kindness of God our Savior appeared, he saved us, not because of works done by us in righteousness, but according to His own mercy. (Titus 3:4–5)

Raising his family in the rural South, my father taught all his sons how to use a cross-cut saw. One brisk fall morning, we began sawing through a log that we didn't know was rotten inside.

The log unexpectedly split, fell off the frame, and hit the ground hard. A piece that broke off looked to my childhood imagination like a horse's head.

Later, I used that rotten piece of horse-head-looking wood to construct a rickety tie rack for my father's birthday. He carefully removed my clumsy wrapping, examined the gift, and tactfully said, "That's wonderful. What is it?"

After I explained, he used it as his tie rack for years. Yet, as I matured, I recognized more and more my "work of art," was not nearly as well-crafted as my boasting ego claimed. My father used my work not because of *its* goodness but because of *his*.

In a similar way, our heavenly Father receives our works, not because they deserve His love, but because He *is* love. His goodness causes us to delight to offer Him our works, even if we know they still need His gracious acceptance and fatherly understanding.

PRAYER: *Father, I present myself and the work I do today as a gift to You. Thank You for lovingly accepting it more out of Your goodness than mine—which makes me even more desirous of serving You with my best rather than my boasting.*

143

Oh how I love your law! It is my meditation all the day. Your commandment makes me wiser than my enemies, for it is ever with me. I have more understanding than all my teachers, for your testimonies are my meditation. (Psalm 119:97–99)

The power to obey the Lord requires that we know what honors Him. This knowledge of God's law is power. After all, we cannot do God's will if we don't know what He wants.

So we need to study God's Word and learn what pleases Him. Then we are able to display God's character in such a way that we and others understand how His care touches every area of our lives.

The psalmist wrote: "Oh, how I love your law!" So he meditated on its application for the situations of the whole day. The motivation of such meditation was not an attempt to make God love the psalmist.

Rather the psalmist's delight came from understanding that God's law was already a sweet indication of His care for His people. The law provided a spiritually good and safe path for God's children. If He did not already love them, He would not have provided such care for them.

The law was not the culmination of that care—Jesus was—but the law was confirmation of God's care! Knowing the heart that laid the path, the Psalmist delighted to walk it, relishing the vistas that would ultimately reveal the need for and heart of Jesus.

PRAYER: Lord, may I be like the psalmist and delight in Your Word—from Genesis to Revelation. Help me to see clearly Your provision for my safekeeping and understanding so that I will always trust the love that designed it—and that culminates in Christ.

144

*I have been crucified with Christ. It is no longer I who
live, but Christ who lives in me. And the life I now
live in the flesh I live by faith in the Son of God, who
loved me and gave himself for me. (Galatians 2:20).*

An old car commercial boasts, "You are what you drive." I don't know how others reacted to the ad's character analysis, but I found it *insulting.*

Perhaps the reason I was so concerned was that, at the time, I was driving a dented Ford Pinto that had over 100,000 miles on it and needed new tires and a paint job.

Of course, I really shouldn't have been upset. The good news that our Savior makes possible is that our identity before God is not based on what we drive but in Whom we trust.

The Apostle Paul reminds us that our past faults and failures—the dents in our lives that we would love to paint over—are dead to us and to God. The sins that once identified us were nailed to the cross of Christ, crucified with Him when we trusted that He died for us. Our sinful identify died with Jesus.

But Jesus did not die forever on that cross. He lives! And by the Holy Spirit's work that same Jesus lives in us by faith. So if your sinful identity is dead, and Jesus is alive in you, whose identity do you have now? His!

Jesus bore your sins by dying on the cross and shares His identity by living in you through the Holy Spirit. That means when you unite your heart to His by faith, you have the status of a child of God—which is what you really are (1 John 3:1)!

God loves you as much as He loves Jesus because you are united to Him by faith.

PRAYER: *Heavenly Father, help me to realize that my worth is not determined by my failures or successes, but by my union with Christ. Because I trust that Jesus loved me and gave Himself for me, I am Your child no matter what others think of me. Thank You for loving me as You do Jesus.*

145

I want you to understand that the head of every man is Christ,
the head of a wife is her husband,
and the head of Christ is God. (1 Corinthians 11:3)

Only by having a close relationship with the Savior and regular exposure to the mind of God in Scripture will a man know what it means to be the head of a home. Christ must be his head before a man can be the biblical head of his home.

Always we must be in submission to Christ in order to know how He wants us to lead others and what to expect in their submission. That is why Christ Himself submitted to His Father in order to teach us what biblical submission is.

The submission taught by Christ's example was never mindless or whimpering surrender of His gifts, but full expression of His privileges and resources on behalf of others. He did not abandon His wisdom, power, or authority, but humbly applied them to accomplishing the will of His Father for the benefit of loved ones.

Only when a man truly humbles himself in this way can he give a proper account of his headship to God. Such a man prays for his family, works for their welfare, places the needs of others above his own, and asks God to help him be the man *God* desires.

The head of a home stands before God on behalf of his family, and he lives before his family on behalf of God. This is the only headship God honors!

PRAYER: Father, please give me the desire to serve more than to be served, to consider the needs of others above my own, and to trust that You will bless my family when I courageously and consistently submit to Christ in this way. Help the head of my home to lead with Christ's character and priorities.

146

Whoever brings back a sinner from his wandering
will save his soul from death and will cover
a multitude of sins. (James 5:20)

We may hardly dare to consider the consequence of sharing our faith—or not doing so. James, the brother of Jesus, minces no words. When we bring a sinner back from wandering away from God, we save a soul from death. If no one shares Jesus, eternal death is certain.

In our town, TV crews captured a man breaking the fall of multiple family members from the upper floor of a two-story home. The multiple blows to his body sent the rescuer to the hospital. Why did he absorb those injuries? Because without his heroic efforts the family members would have died.

What made the man's deeds even more heroic, as the story unfolded, was an old dispute he had with the family over neighborhood issues. The hero chose to look past those issues because lives were at stake. The magnitude of potential loss made it important to minimize past tensions with the family.

Saving souls from death may well require the same from us. The ones that we are most likely to influence for Christ are those closest to us. And if they are not walking with Christ, they are the ones most likely to have sinned against us.

The magnitude of their loss to Satan requires that we minimize—even cover—a multitude of sins against us. Why should we do this for those who have sinned against us? Because the Savior we love loves them, and because He purchases their souls with the same blood that purchased us.

PRAYER: *Heavenly Father, help me to share the hope of the Gospel to save wandering souls from death, and to be willing to cover a multitude of sins to do so.*

147

He was despised and rejected by men, a man of sorrows and acquainted with grief; and as one from whom men hide their faces he was despised, and we esteemed him not. (Isaiah 53:3)

When we face the pressures of finances, when illnesses ravage our families, when trusted friends and colleagues become our sharpest critics, when governments act unfairly, and when those we count on turn their faces away, there is still cause for joy.

Whether we suffer under the weight of circumstances or because of the wrong of others, our suffering teaches us more of what Christ endured for us. Through our afflictions, which cannot match our Savior's suffering for a sinful world, we come to know a measure of His care at a depth mere contemplation could never achieve.

The Bible says Jesus became like us to sympathize with our condition, but the reverse is true as well. When we become like Him in our suffering, we understand His heart better.

His suffering included poverty, humiliation, betrayal, pain, and death—all of which demonstrate how tender and tenacious is God's grace for us. We don't fully understand such grace until we have experienced a measure of the suffering that it cost.

By our pain we gain understanding of the dimensions of Christ's grace that is needed to outweigh our suffering.

PRAYER: *Jesus, thank You for suffering for me. May I grasp more fully the depth and breadth of Your grace by earthly afflictions that I realize are spare measure of its cost!*

148

Being found in human form, he humbled himself by
becoming obedient to the point of death, even death on
a cross. Therefore, God has highly exalted him and bestowed on
him the name that is above every name. (Philippians 2:8–11)

In 1987, Northwest Airlines flight 255 crashed just after takeoff. One hundred fifty-six people died while only one survived—a four-year-old named Cecilia. At first, rescuers did not believe she had been on the plane but in a car onto which the plane crashed.

But as investigators pieced together details, they confirmed Cecilia's presence on the plane and discerned her mother's heroic care.

Cecilia survived because, as the plane was falling from the sky, her mother got down on her knees in front of her child's seat, covered the little girl, and refused to let go. Nothing could separate the girl from her mother's love—neither height nor depth, nor life nor death. Such is the love of our Savior for us.

Jesus left His place in Heaven, lowered Himself to us, and saved us by the covering sacrifice of His own body. Jesus would not let go of us no matter how great the danger to Him. Even death would not separate His love from us.

Our assurance of Jesus's sacrificial, inseparable, and undying love inspires our love for Him, and stirs our hearts to honor Him.

PRAYER: Lord, help me today to experience the assurance
of knowing that the One who came from Heaven to cover me
with His love will never let me go!

149

*I am the vine; you are the branches. Whoever abides
in me and I in him, he it is that bears much fruit,
for apart from me you can do nothing. (John 15:5)*

A friend's independent daughter had a car accident. Because she had no means of paying for the damage or the traffic ticket, her parents agreed to loan her the money.

They hoped the arrangement would teach lessons she needed to mature, but their daughter struggled with the diligence and discipline required to pay her parents back.

Reminding her of her responsibility resulted in an angry, "Mom and Dad, this is *my* problem. I just wish you would leave me alone so that I can figure out a way to fix this!"

Said her father, "Sweetie, what we really want you to know is that, without us, you can't fix it."

Our independent spirit sometimes leads us to try to solve life's challenges and our sin problems in our own way. Yet God teaches that "we can do nothing apart from Him" that truly satisfies our hearts or solves our problems.

We need His grace to mop up our messes and fix our problems. Amazingly, He delights to do so to bring us to spiritual maturity. He provides His grace to turn us from our own resources, receive His forgiveness, and live the future of His heart's design.

PRAYER: Jesus, I naturally turn to my own resources, devices, and amends to address my problems and sins. Please help me to turn to You and to abide in Jesus by realizing I can do nothing to satisfy You or repair my soul apart from You.

150

When you pass through the waters, I will be with you;
and through the rivers, they shall not overwhelm you;
when you walk through fire you shall not be burned,
and the flame shall not consume you. (Isaiah 43:2)

Is it really true that the trials of this world will not overwhelm God's children? The answer requires us to face a real world and acknowledge that God does not promise that troubled waters are not in our path, that rivers will not rise, nor that flames will not threaten.

God promises that the waters shall not overwhelm and the flames shall not consume. These are *not* assurances that no believer ever drowns, nor that no saint has ever died at the stake.

But God has lost no soul. No trial has triumphed over His purposes. No tragedy has the final word. The truest you, "the soul that on Jesus has leaned for repose," He will never—no, never—abandon or desert to His foes.

As children of God, believers are assured of fatherly help *when* we face any difficulty, rather than the absence of all difficulties. God's care is never lacking. Earthly trials lead to the advance of God's purposes and our maturity until our earthly path is done. Then we are securely in God's hands for eternity, safe forever.

God passionately protects the ultimate welfare of His children and promises what the centuries-old hymn teaches: "When through the deep waters I call you to go, the rivers of sorrow shall not overflow; for I will be with you, your troubles to bless, and sanctify to you your deepest distress."

PRAYER: Lord, give me the grace I need to endure the difficulties I face today with the confidence that You are with me and no trial will overwhelm Your purposes or my security.

151

*One thing have I asked of the LORD, that will I seek
after: that I may dwell in the house of the LORD all
the days of my life, to gaze upon the beauty of the
LORD and to inquire in his temple. (Psalm 27:4)*

I'll never forget my first "date" with my wife. I was on an outing with her
family. As the new, single minister of their little country church, I had been
invited to her family's picnic, which was held in the restored Victorian village
of Elsah, Illinois.

When the beautiful blonde with the lovely green eyes asked me if I wanted
to take a walk with her, my immediate response was: "You bet!" Her beauty
made me delight to walk with her—as I have now for more than four decades.

In a similar fashion, Jesus reveals the beauty of His love to us throughout
Scripture, more and more demonstrating the wonder of His grace. So when
Jesus calls us to walk with Him, our heart's response to the beauty of the Savior
is to do just that.

The Christian life is not dreaded drudgery. We delight to walk with Jesus
because we are drawn to the beauty of the One whose grace has shown Him
to be altogether lovely.

PRAYER: Lord Jesus, thank You for the beauty and glory of
the grace You have revealed throughout Scripture. Help me
so to delight in Your heart that my heart will desire to walk with
You this day and all my days.

152

Let us continually offer up a sacrifice of praise to God,
that is, the fruit of lips that acknowledge his name.
Do not neglect to do good and to share what you have,
for such sacrifices are pleasing to God. (Hebrews 13:15–16)

Because our holy God knows our thoughts and motives, as well as our actions, doing the right thing for the wrong reasons *is still wrong.*

An example of this is found in the Old Testament, when God declared that sacrifices offered by His people were a stench in His nostrils. That seems wrong. God ordered the sacrifices, and the people offered them. So why did He take offense?

God's people were offering the sacrifices as a way of placating the Almighty while ignoring His commands. The people were trying to bribe God to approve of—or at least to ignore—their sin. Sacrifices that mark true devotion please God. Sacrifices that try to buy Him off are sin.

We, too, should consider whether our sacrifices are for praise or for personal gain. Do we read Scripture, give offerings, or even pray in order to bribe God to be nice to us, or in order to honor His grace toward us? Sacrifices of praise please God. Sacrifices intended to manipulate Him to please us fool only us.

Serving the God we love by acts of devotion and service is a wonderful way of growing in grace, but serving God to make Him love us will stunt our growth and stink to God. Offer praise because you love Him, not to make Him love you—He will love the praise more and so will you.

PRAYER: Lord, thank You for offering the only sacrifice that makes me acceptable to You—Jesus. Help me offer my sacrifices of praise to honor His grace, not to cover my sin or serve my selfishness!

153

I give them eternal life, and they will never perish, and no one will snatch them out of my hand. My Father, who has given them to me, is greater than all, and no one is able to snatch them out of the Father's hand. (John 10:28–29)

No one acts as righteously as God requires or loves as fully as He desires. Because of our weaknesses we cannot hold onto God. He must hold onto us!

How does that work? I think of what theologian Francis Schaeffer once called the "empty hands of faith." We come to God holding to no claim of our goodness or ability. We reach for Him with empty hands, in humility and thankfulness, acknowledging our need of the power of Jesus's work on the cross.

Why does that work? My answer brings to mind the way I played with our children when they were small. I would lie on the top bunk of their bed and lower my hand so that they could hold on as I lifted them skyward.

But as their feet would get only inches off the floor, they would call out in panic, "Daddy, I can't hold onto you. Hold onto me." Then, I would close my hand over theirs, and hold them safely on the heavenward trip.

So also God holds onto us when we confess that we cannot hold onto Him. His grip is sure and no one is able to snatch us from His hand.

PRAYER: *Heavenly Father, thank You for the assurance that no one can snatch me from Your hand. Please keep my hand empty of any claim of merit so that all that holds me for Heaven is You!*

154

The love of Christ controls us, because we have concluded this: that one has died for all ... and he died for all, that those who live might no longer live for themselves but for him who for their sake died and was raised. (2 Corinthians 5:14–15)

Why do sins tempt us? Because we love them. Consider this: if a sin did not attract you, then it would have absolutely no power in your life. Our sins control us by our love for them.

What can displace such controlling love for sin? The answer: a greater love.

When our love for Christ is the top priority in our lives, it drives out our love for sin and encourages our devotion to Him. Scottish preacher Thomas Chalmers once described this process as the "expulsive power of new affection." He understood that our behaviors change as our affections change. We will most do as we most love.

We conquer sinful passions when our greatest desire is to please the One who died and was raised for us. This doesn't mean that battling sin will never require intense spiritual warfare, but victory lies in intense affection for our Lord.

That is why Paul wrote to believers, "The love of Christ controls us." We no longer live for our sinful desires when Christ is our greatest desire. He fuels that desire by filling us with love for Him through the grace He provides for our sin.

PRAYER: *Heavenly Father, work in my heart—convicting of sin and convincing of grace—so the love of Christ controls me. Help me so to treasure His sacrificial love that my greatest desire is to honor Him.*

155

He has said, "I will never leave you nor forsake you."
So we can confidently say, "The LORD is my helper;
I will not fear; what can man do to me?" (Hebrews 13:5–6)

In a primitive tradition, tribal people throw ashes at the moon and beg their god to leave them alone. The practice may seem far distant from us until tragedy enters our life. Then we too may look to Heaven and say to God, "If You really loved me, then You would leave me alone. You wouldn't allow this pain, or bother me, or make such demands on me."

Asking God to keep His distance is understandable when we are hurting, but we still need to consider what such prayer requests. We are asking God to act against His nature—which He cannot do.

God has promised never to leave or forsake us, and God cannot break His own word. He will not leave—but neither will He forsake. Nothing that we experience is a result of His absence or abandonment.

The commands He gives are an expression of His character and care for us. His discipline intends only to turn us from greater harms and into His arms. No failure is final, and no tragedy is His ultimate truth.

Hymnist William Cowper, who knew much of this world's pain, sang through his tears, "Behind a frowning providence, God hides a smiling face."

When God says He will not leave us alone, He may intend a holy confrontation, but never does He confront without care. He cannot and does not.

PRAYER: *Father, thank You for always being with me, and never forsaking me. Help me to understand that a holy confrontation signals no lack of Your love, but rather divine dedication to my soul's security.*

*Train up a child in the way he should go; even when
he is old he will not depart from it. (Proverbs 22:6)*

The apostles and prophets tell us that God is our Father, encouraging us to use His divine parenting as the model for our own.

Sadly, in light of that perfect model, Christian parents may struggle to deal with their shortcomings. We may read parenting proverbs (wise words to guide wise people) as promises (divine guarantees for perfect outcomes) they were never intended to be.

Proverbs give us fatherly wisdom for what tends to be helpful in a fallen world, and wise people take them to heart—but a proverb is not promise. Families don't function like math equations.

No one can bear the pressure of proverbs mistaken as promises or meet the standard of perfection such a reading requires. As a result, the misreading of Scripture's proverbs about rearing children creates anxious, insecure parents who either give up on God or on their children.

God's intention in His proverbs is to give us the counsel that our imperfect parenting requires, and also to remind us that He doesn't give up on us because of our failures. His enduring and encouraging counsel frees us to parent our children wisely—not to give up on them or forget the grace that we too need!

The relationship with God that He secures gives us the security to love and discipline our children as God intends—reflecting His wisdom and remembering His grace!

PRAYER: Father, thank You for parenting me with love that disciplines for my good, and does not walk away when I need more grace. Please help me to be so secure in Your parental care that I can reflect it wisely with my own children.

We have this treasure in jars of clay, to show that the surpassing power belongs to God and not to us. We are afflicted in every way, but not crushed; perplexed, but not driven to despair; persecuted, but not forsaken; struck down, but not destroyed; always carrying in the body the death of Jesus, so that the life of Jesus may also be manifested in our bodies. (2 Corinthians 4:7–10)

Some years ago, a college friend spoke of a beloved daughter with Goldenhar Syndrome, a condition that causes some children to be born without facial bones.

His daughter had no facial bones on her left side. In the early years of loving and raising his precious girl, my friend said that he and his family were often buffeted by waves of worry that required them to cling to a rock with two sides.

One side of the rock was the testimony of Scripture that our God is *very great.* The other side of the rock was the proof of the cross that God is *very good.* My friend said, "In our time of trial, we needed to hold firmly to both sides of that rock named Jesus."

In every life there come the waves that will require us to cling to the Rock with two sides. When our trials and disappointments seem more than we can bear, we must hold to the One who holds us because He is very great *and* He is very good. Hold to the Rock with two sides through your waves today.

PRAYER: *Father, this fallen world is full of pain and suffering— some afflict me and my loved ones. When the waves roar, still help me to cling to the Rock with two sides. When I am desperately in need, keep me trusting in the One who is very great and very good until His work in me is done.*

158

Wives, submit to your own husbands, as to the Lord.
For the husband is the head of the wife even as Christ
is the head of the church, His body, and is Himself its Savior.
Now as the church submits to Christ, so also wives should
submit in everything to their husbands. (Ephesians 5:22–24)

Today, from palaces to campuses, and from churches to our own homes, the question of how a wife is supposed to love, honor, and obey her husband is debated more than ever. Pat explanations that do not consider the challenges of our times, the dignity of each person, and the authority of God will not do.

So how is a Christian wife to live? The plain answer in Ephesians is clear: a wife is to *submit*. But simply repeating the word does not explain its meaning. The word *submit* in the Bible combines the Greek terms for "arrange" and "under." Those who submit in this context *arrange* their gifts and resources *under* purposes that are best for another.

Christ submitted His glory and power to the needs of salvation we had. A wife who submits biblically does not throw away her brain or her talents but arranges them in support of her husband.

Husbands are commanded to love sacrificially, as Christ loved the church! Wives are commanded to love submissively *as the church honors Christ.* No such honor occurs if the church dispenses with its gifts, but only as it arranges them with excellence devoted to Christ's purposes.

So also wives truly honor husbands not by suppressing gifts but expressing them fully and selflessly for the good of a loved one.

PRAYER: *Lord, please help me to follow the instruction and the example of Jesus as I honor Him and my spouse. It can be against my human reflexes to live for another, but grant me the heart of Christ to find the beauty of loving as He did.*

159

*We all, with unveiled face, beholding the glory of the
Lord, are being transformed into the same image from
one degree of glory to another. For this comes from
the Lord who is the Spirit. (2 Corinthians 3:18)*

French mathematical genius Blaise Pascal spent years running from God—
like so many people today. Then Pascal encountered God's life-changing
grace.

How did a life of pride in intellectual achievement become a life of joy
in Jesus? Eight years after his death, a parchment note was found sewn into
Pascal's coat that recorded his powerful conversion.

The note read in part:

> Year of grace 1654, Monday 23 of November ... from about half
> past ten at night to about half an hour after midnight, FIRE. God
> of Abraham, God of Isaac, God of Jacob, not of philosophers and
> scholars. Certitude. Heartfelt joy, peace. God of Jesus Christ. God
> of Jesus Christ. 'My God and your God.' ... Joy, joy, joy, tears of joy
> ... Jesus Christ. Jesus Christ. May I never be separated from Him.

Pascal discovered in the Scriptures a joy and peace that was like fire in
his heart, surging into joy beyond words. The years of prideful striving for
recognition could not compare to the Spirit's revelation that the God of all
history had reached down in a moment of time to love him.

This newfound faith provided a joy from which he never wanted to be
separated, and is yours to share through Jesus Christ. Just like Pascal, you can
trust Jesus Christ to be your Savior for joy, joy, joy!

PRAYER: Father, as I behold Your glory in the face of my
Savior, Jesus Christ, may I be transformed by Your grace from
whatever pride has enslaved me into the life of inseparable
love and irrepressible joy You offer!

160

I tell you the truth: it is to your advantage that I go away, for if I do not go away, the Helper will not come to you. But if I go, I will send him to you. And when he comes, he will convict the world concerning sin and righteousness and judgment. (John 16:7–8)

Sometimes people believe it's a pastor's job to make others feel guilty. I gently remind them that's not *my* job. The Holy Spirit convicts hearts of sin and righteousness and judgment.

That actually sounds like a terrible job, except that Jesus told us the reason the Holy Spirit would convict hearts. His purpose is in His name: *Helper.*

The Holy Spirit helps us by convicting our hearts of the sin that is in us, the righteousness that is of God, and the judgment that is to come. When these realities grip our consciences, they bend our knees before God and turn our hearts to Jesus.

Jesus said that the ultimate job of the Holy Spirit was not only to tell the truth about us, but to "testify of Me" (John 15:26). The Spirit helps us by revealing our sin *and* our Savior—doing one without the other would be no help. So, yes, it is my job as a preacher to convict of sin, but my job is not done until I have convinced of grace.

Grace is not sweet if sin is not bitter. So the Holy Spirit convicts us of our sin, God's standards, and judgment to come. But that is not the end goal. Our failings are made known to us so that our Savior's necessity would be confessed and His grace claimed.

PRAYER: Lord, help me be sensitive to the promptings of Your Holy Spirit, so that I will confess my sin, claim Your grace, and live for You—helped by the Spirit who revealed You.

161

Which one of you, if his son asks him for bread, will give
him a stone? Or if he asks for a fish, will give him a serpent?
If you then, who are evil, know how to give good gifts to your
children, how much more will your Father who is in heaven
give good things to those who ask him! (Matthew 7:9–11)

Isn't it wonderful how God tells us to bring our requests to Him—big or small? This truth hit home for me during a difficult season. From his prison cell, my newly believing younger brother with mental limitations prayed that God would help my parents find his runaway dog.

I have to admit that I thought, "God has got bigger problems to deal with!" But my father, who still wanted to find ways to show love to his wayward son, went to the parking lot where "ol' Red" had run away the week before.

After he'd called out Red's name several times with no response, my father said, "This is silly. What am I doing?" Then, as he turned to walk back to the car, there was ol' Red, wagging his tail!

Jesus promised, "Your Father who is in Heaven [will] give good things to those who ask Him." That's not a promise to answer every whim but to give what is best for our souls. And there is no qualification on the significance of the gift—or of the requester. God will simply provide what is best for our eternal care, even to wayward children who ask. So, make *your* requests known to God. He cares. He's listening.

PRAYER: *Father, as I come to You in prayer today, help me to realize that You delight in giving good gifts to Your children. Help me not to put limits on what You can do or how much You care because of my wayward heart.*

162

I will give you a new heart, and a new spirit I will put within you. And I will remove the heart of stone from your flesh and give you a heart of flesh. And I will put my Spirit within you, and cause you to walk in my statutes and be careful to obey my rules. (Ezekiel 36:26–27)

We've all seen a newborn baby stretch and yawn as though life is no more challenging than a summer afternoon in the shade. But when a child nicknamed "Baby John" was still in his mother's womb, doctors discerned that his heart was defective, and without treatment he would soon die. His life was challenging.

In an amazing operation, surgeons performed a heart repair before the child was even born. Where once death was certain, new life was made possible by skills and knowledge far beyond what the child possessed.

As believers we can identify with this helpless child. Before we were born again, God discerned our hearts to be defective, damaged by sin. Then, with His divine power and knowledge, He gave us new hearts to love and live for Jesus. Where once only spiritual death was possible, now there is new life in Christ.

Now God calls us to live the life that He desires with the power and desires of our new hearts that His grace and love made possible. Live for Him as the heart He gave you beats with love for Jesus.

PRAYER: Father God, thank You for sending the Great Physician who, by the work of the Holy Spirit, gave me a new heart that beats with love for my Savior. Help me today to be strengthened by that heart for Your service.

163

Those who live according to the Spirit set their minds on the things
of the Spirit.... To set the mind on the Spirit is life and peace.
For the mind that is set on the flesh is hostile to God.... You,
however, are not in the flesh but in the Spirit. (Romans 8:5–7, 9)

The Bible makes it clear that only by the grace of God can we become holy. And only by the blood of Jesus Christ are we washed white as snow— freed of sin's ugly stain and guilt. That is good news!

But there's more. God's Spirit then creates in us righteous desires, setting our minds on the things that please God and unsettling our hearts about anything that does not.

We are not ultimately called to do what we do *not* desire, but to do what our Spirit-renewed affections *actually* desire. God does not merely tell us what to do, He changes our *want to*. By His Spirit's work in our hearts, we want more and more to do as He desires.

Once our minds were only hostile to God, but when they were captivated by the sacrificial love of Jesus for us, we began to love pleasing and honoring Him. In fact, we now find our greatest fulfillment and peace in loving what and whom He loves.

This change of affections is not complete when we are saved, but it is progressive as we more and more perceive the grace of Christ toward us that increases our love for Him.

Once I believed the job of the preacher was to get people to do what they don't want to do. That's a horrible job! I no longer believe that. I believe it is my job to help God's people love Jesus more and more, so that His will is their desire. That's a great job!

PRAYER: *Father, help me continue to yield my heart to Your Holy Spirit so that my affections are transformed, and pleasing You is what provides my greatest joy.*

164

Far be it from me to boast except in the cross of our Lord Jesus Christ, by which the world has been crucified to me, and I to the world. For neither circumcision counts for anything, nor uncircumcision, but a new creation. (Galatians 6:14–15)

We can acknowledge the truth of God's free grace without applying it to how we approach God for forgiveness.

We *say* that we are forgiven on the basis of grace alone and not through any merit of ours. But then we *act* as though God grants forgiveness only if we qualify for it by being sad enough for sin long enough to make God happy. We turn repentance into a merit badge that earns God's grace by the depth or sincerity of our grief.

We need to be careful what we are trusting. Yes, we are to grieve for our sin and, yes, we are to be sincere about our repentance. But repentance depends upon the sufficiency of grace, not the adequacy of our remorse.

True repentance humbly receives God's mercy; it does not strive to leverage grace from His heart by increasing the weight of our grief. Repentance is more a depending than a doing—more a leaning on our Savior than a measuring of our tears. Sincere grief for sin delights God; manufactured grief denies grace.

If we would know the blessings of grace, we do not point to our tears, but to Christ's blood; not to our spiritual discipline, but to Christ's provision; and not to the sufficiency of our sorrow, but to the sufficiency of our Savior.

Repentance isn't a good work to offer God to broker your pardon. It is sorrowfully confessing your sin and the inadequacy of your merits to satisfy God; then, turning entirely, humbly, and—ultimately—with joy to grace for the pardon and power to love and live for Jesus.

PRAYER: *Father, may I never boast except in the cross of Christ! May I trust Your mercy more than my merits, living in the joyous freedom and sweet devotion that comes from depending more on Christ's sacrifice than my sorrow.*

By this we shall know that we are of the truth and reassure our heart before him; for whenever our heart condemns us, God is greater than our heart, and he knows everything. (1 John 3:19–20)

If our hearts continue to condemn us after genuine confession, this is not of God. Holding onto guilt denies the sufficiency and power of Jesus's pardon.

A friend told me that he and his wife had gone for marriage counseling. The counselor asked each to write down concerns about the other. My friend said his wife began to write furiously, making a long list of offenses. He knew he was in trouble.

When their lists were complete, the counselor first asked the husband what was on his list. He said, "I have no right to say anything. I have been a burden to my wife and she has been a saint to stay with me."

Then, the counselor asked the wife for her list. She paused, then said, "I don't have anything either." Had the husband begun to argue with her about that, it would have dishonored her mercy.

The account reminded me that receiving another's forgiveness honors them. If we refuse to receive God's forgiveness—substituting gloom for grace—that is not holiness; it is rejection of God's provision.

God sent His Son to die for our sin, not to keep our guilt alive. Only Satan wants you to try to serve God with a burden of guilt on your back. Receive and rest in the grace that is in Christ Jesus.

PRAYER: Heavenly Father, when the adversary tries to burden me with guilt, help me not to trample on Jesus's blood by denying its power and substituting gloom for grace. Enable me to receive grace as an act of worship that honors You.

166

God has done what the law, weakened by the flesh, could not do. By sending his own Son in the likeness of sinful flesh and for sin, he condemned sin in the flesh, in order that the righteous requirement of the law might be fulfilled in us, who walk not according to the flesh but according to the Spirit. (Romans 8:3–4)

The Apostle Paul passionately argues here that while God requires righteous conduct for our well-being, our conduct doesn't earn our salvation. God alone provides our right standing with Him. He did this by sending His own Son in our likeness to die for our sin.

This clearly demonstrates that God has no tolerance for our sin, and at the same time, it demonstrates His unswerving love for us. That love allowed for the requirements of the law to be met by Jesus on behalf of all who believe in Him. That same love revealed what God requires to experience the blessings of His Spirit as we walk through life.

We wrestle and argue to make sense of it all, but as Jesus explained, even a child can make sense of the basics. A mother puts herself at risk to bear a child (John 16:21–22). Nothing the infant has done, or could do, caused it to deserve such love. The mother's love that gave life was sacrificial and unconditional. And from the same heart of love will come instructions to the growing child about what is safe to do.

Love provided the life and love provides the instruction. Following the instruction does not make the child a son or daughter, but a child who believes in the love of the mother, and wants to experience more of it, will follow the instruction. We follow God's law not to earn His love but because of it.

PRAYER: *Heavenly Father, I believe You sent Jesus because You loved me before I loved You. Now help me live for Him who loved me and gave Himself for me.*

167

*My frame was not hidden from you when I was made
in the secret place, when I was woven together in the depths
of the earth. Your eyes saw my unformed body;
all the days ordained for me were written in your book
before one of them came to be. (Psalm 139:15–16 NIV)*

No matter what's happening in our lives right now, we have assurance that our Heavenly Father is intimately involved in the details.

In detailed and dramatic Old Testament prophecies of Christ's coming and our future, we have the assurance that God knows the big picture of world events. He knows all that is to come. More than that, He is sovereignly working throughout creation for eternal good through all circumstances!

But our God is not only engaged in world-scale events. The psalmist reveals that God was engaged in our lives even before our birth. He saw us in our mothers' wombs. He has been with us through every year and wept for every tear.

Our Heavenly Father has been with us on every journey, and will be with us for eternity. No turn is unknown to Him; no twist is a surprise to Him. The psalmist writes, "All the days ordained for me were written in your [God's] book before one of them came to be." When you don't know what the future holds, trust the God who says: *I know, and I've got this.*

PRAYER: Lord, help me to trust in Your sovereign grace at all times and in all circumstances. You who hold the world in Your hands know every detail of me and what's coming. Nothing is hidden from You, and You've got me.

168

Count it all joy, my brothers, when you meet trials
of various kinds, for you know that the testing of your
faith produces steadfastness. And let steadfastness
have its full effect, that you may be perfect and
complete, lacking in nothing. (James 1:2–4)

You may remember Brit Hume as a national news anchor, but may not have known that he became a committed Christian during one of the hardest times in his life.

Challenges drive some people away from faith; others see the necessity of Jesus through them and are drawn closer to Him. Hume's greatest challenge came from the suicide of his son, Sandy.

Despite having been a nominal Christian most of his life, Hume said the one thing he recognized almost immediately after the tragedy was that he truly believed God could help.

The death was not something anyone expected, but somewhere in the middle of all his grief, questioning, and searching for peace, Hume said that he felt closer to Christ than ever before.

These are not easy truths but are lifelines to God's care when we are clinging to faith from the ragged edges of life. When all else is stripped away, we can still find meaning, and hope, and reason to carry on in the comfort of a God whose love continues beyond life's regrets and Earth's boundaries.

We do not rejoice *for* earthly trials but find joy in a sovereign God whose eternal love and unending care provide the steadfastness that is needed for this world's inevitable storms.

PRAYER: *Father, when I experience life's inevitable trage-dies, help me to draw comfort and strength from assurances of Your abiding presence and eternal care.*

169

You have received the Spirit of adoption as sons,
by whom we cry, "Abba! Father!" The Spirit himself
bears witness with our spirit that we are children
of God, and if children, then heirs—heirs of God
and fellow heirs with Christ. (Romans 8:15–17)

Here the Apostle Paul puts us into the middle of a court hearing in which he asks two important questions: Who are the heirs of God's inheritance, and how can they prove they are heirs?

Before we dismiss the inquiries as irrelevant to us, Paul explains that we are the heirs in question, and that our status is established by the testimony of two witnesses—the standard for a Jewish court.

We are heirs of the promises of God based on (1) the testimony of our spirit (as we love the Father) and (2) the testimony of the Holy Spirit (as He confirms the Father's love for us in Scripture and in our hearts).

Without the Holy Spirit's work in us, we could not love God as our Abba (Daddy). Our hearts would be hostile to Him, and we would be convinced of His hostility toward us. So our love of the Father along with the Spirit's testimony of His love for us combine to witness that we are God's children.

So if we ever doubt God's love for us, we need honestly to answer one simple question: "Do you love God?" If you really love Him, that is the testimony of the Holy Spirit that you are God's child and a co-heir of Heaven with Jesus.

PRAYER: Lord, thank You that I can love You as my Abba, and for assuring me that such love can only be generated by the Holy Spirit. By this love in my heart, I know You are assuring me that I am Your child. Thank You for such grace.

170

*My son, do not forget my teaching, but let your heart
keep my commandments, for length of days and years of
life and peace they will add to you. (Proverbs 3:1–2)*

When we love God, pleasing Him pleases us. Loving God and loving ourselves are not competing motivations. When we please the One we love the most, we find our own greatest pleasure. Satisfying the One we most love satisfies us most fully.

So we do not need to see pleasing God as an onerous burden that we assume simply to make Him happy. As a loving Father, He teaches us to follow paths that are good and safe, thereby adding to the length and peace of our days that extend into eternity.

Those who find true happiness in the Christian life do not see their service to God as begrudging duty to an arbitrary master. We come to understand obedience as a means of pleasing a loving Father who is guiding us to the best of this life's blessing every day. Service to Him both satisfies our souls and blesses our lives.

In a fallen world, trials and tragedy will come into every life, but there is no better, safer, or more satisfying path for God's eternal blessings and earthly joys than one He prepares for us and walks with us.

When love for God is our highest priority, then honoring Him is our greatest joy! Such joy is not denied by trials but is often discovered through them. Serving God through our challenges becomes the ultimate expression of His honor and our satisfaction.

By honoring Him most we love ourselves best!

PRAYER: Father, help me long to please You in everything I do today, knowing that by honoring You out of love I will find my greatest fulfillment.

171

You do not stay angry forever but delight to show
mercy. You will again have compassion on us; you will
tread our sins underfoot and hurl all our iniquities
into the depths of the sea. (Micah 7:18–19 NIV)

Minister and church leader Alexander Whyte told the story of an older saint who was nearly destroyed by guilt and shame.

After a church meeting, the older man had lingered in idle conversation. Then, in what was meant to sound like a jest, the man said, "Now, Dr. Whyte, what word of comfort do you have for an old sinner like me?"

Beneath the pasted-on smile, Dr. Whyte perceived the man's deep agony and later wrote how the question took his breath away. This dear saint was old in the faith, but he did not have the peace of knowing God's forgiveness.

Dr. Whyte said that he was unsure what to say, but crossed the room to where the man was seated, took his hand, and quoted from the prophet Micah: "Our God will *delight to show mercy.*"

Not much more was said between the two, but the next day a note came from the older man to Dr. Whyte. It said, "Those words you quoted were comfort to my soul. I will never doubt my God again. When Satan comes to convince me that I am unworthy of the mercy of God, I will say, 'You are right, and you know not the half of it, but I have to deal with the One who will delight to show mercy.'"

So do you!

PRAYER: *Father, thank You for hurling all my sins into the depths of the sea! I do not claim my worthiness; only that I have to deal with the One who delights to show mercy.*

172

*Wives, submit to your husbands, as is fitting in
the Lord. Husbands, love your wives, and do not
be harsh with them. (Colossians 3:18–19)*

Scripture never justifies dictatorial rule by one spouse, nor does it require the abandonment of personal dignity by another. Despite the controversies of our age over Scripture's instruction, the Bible's marital instructions are rooted in its core message—we are to embrace Christ's grace and extend it to others.

Hearts open to that core message will recognize that God neither commends nor commands selfishness. When the prince of Heaven gave His life to rescue us from our sin, He taught the glory of selfless sacrifice.

Wives who submit their personal gifts to the support of their husbands and husbands who sacrifice personal gain for the benefit of their wives are living the grace that Jesus died to reveal.

The Bible never defines love as using another for personal benefit, but as using one's blessings to bless another despite their undeserving or past offense.

When we discover the grace that the God of all power and authority sacrificially extended to His loved ones, then we begin to discern our mission to reflect that same heart to our loved ones.

PRAYER: *Father, thank You for Your gracious care through Your Son, Jesus Christ. Help me today to turn away from selfishness, or from holding onto past offense, in order to display Jesus to my loved ones. Help me love as He loves me.*

173

Beloved, we are God's children now, and what we will be has not yet appeared; but we know that when he appears we shall be like him, because we shall see him as he is. And everyone who thus hopes in him purifies himself as he is pure. (1 John 3:2–3)

A sign recently appeared along the path where I jog. It announced that a piece of land was going to be subdivided into eighteen new home sites. The proposal for the rough plot of ground seemed preposterous, and everyone who saw the sign concluded the building plan was *crazy*.

We weren't looking at the scene with the eyes of the architect. What made the land valuable to *him* was not its current condition, but what could be done with it. He understood the ditches could be filled, the hills leveled, and the bare ground freshly planted.

In a similar way, God is never limited by our current condition. The Master Architect has a beautiful plan for what He wants to do in us and through us so we shall ultimately be as He designs.

God does not value us on the basis of our past or our present, but on the basis of what we shall be by the work of His loving hand. So remember, your value is not fixed by what is or what has been, but by what will be by the grace of God.

PRAYER: *Lord, thank You for encouraging me with the plan of the Master Architect. You see my value based on what You will do, not what I have done. May that hope motivate me to let the past go and live for Your tomorrow.*

174

The Father loves me, because I lay down my life that
I may take it up again. No one takes it from me,
but I lay it down of my own accord. (John 10:17–18)

Christ came to Earth with His death in mind. The cross wasn't a surprise ending. His heart of all-consuming love did not deprive Him of sovereign knowledge of His sacrificial death for our sins.

The One who gave the prophets vision of His provision knowingly fulfilled His own prophecies. He became *the Lamb of God who takes away the sins of the world* not simply because of His enemies' plots but because of His own eternal plan.

Our Lord Jesus knew the whole story before it ever began, and still He came to Earth and willingly laid down His life. He knew what was coming and kept on coming!

This is true of your life, too. Jesus knows your sins—past, present, and future—and still He comes to you by the truth of Scripture and the witness of the Holy Spirit in your heart.

He did not turn from offering Himself for a sinful world, and He will not turn from offering Himself to you. You may not know how much you will need Him, but He does—and still He offers Himself to you.

By offering Himself as a sacrifice for a sinful world, Jesus bore witness to His all-surpassing love and grace. He is the relentless Savior who knew the worst about this world and came to save its sinners. He also knows the worst about you and graciously offered Himself for your soul.

The One who knew what was coming and came anyway comes to you now. Come to Him!

PRAYER: Jesus, thank You for coming to the cross to take away the sins of the world. Assure me that a love great enough for the world is gracious enough for me so that I come to You now by believing You are my Savior.

What then shall we say to these things? If God is for us,
who can be against us? He who did not spare His own
Son but gave him up for us all, how will he not also with
him graciously give us all things? (Romans 8:31–32)

One of my pastorates was in a rugged coal mining region. There I was taught much of how faith could survive and thrive through the difficulties of life.

The story was told of an old man made an invalid by a mining injury early in life. A lifetime of struggle did not steal his faith, and a younger man came to ask, "Why?"

The old man smiled at the question and responded. "Yes, sometimes Satan comes to my bedside. He points out my window to friends with fine homes, growing families, and healthy bodies. Then he taunts me by asking, 'Does God love you?'"

The younger man gasped at the honesty of the invalid, and asked, "What do you say to Satan when he asks you that?"

Said the old man in the bed, "I take Satan by the hand to a hill called Calvary. There, I point to the thorns on Jesus's brow and to the nails in hands and feet, and I say to Satan, 'Doesn't God love me!'"

If we try to prove God's love by pointing to our circumstances in a fallen world, we will fail. But, if we point to His character revealed at the Cross, then we need never doubt His eternal love. When God did not spare His own Son, but gave Him up for us all, He proved for all time and circumstances His love for us.

PRAYER: Father, help me not to look to my circumstances but to Your character for the assurance of Your love that I need every day until Jesus returns to this fallen world for me.

176

When Daniel knew that the document had been signed,
he went to his house where he had windows in his upper
chamber open toward Jerusalem. He got down on his
knees three times a day and prayed and gave thanks before
his God, as he had done previously. (Daniel 6:10)

How would you define *courage*? According to the Merriam-Webster Dictionary, courage is "mental or moral strength to venture, persevere, and withstand danger, fear, or difficulty."

Right next to that definition of courage you might expect to see a picture of Daniel, the prophet who was taken into captivity as a young man, was made to serve pagan kings and, in his old age, was thrown into the lion's den!

Despite fearsome struggles, Daniel was the epitome of courage, persevering in his faith through *prayer, obedience,* and *integrity*. But there came a time when his visions of the future frightened him to fainting (Daniel 8, 10). Then he did not deny his fears but faithfully confessed his and his people's sin to affirm God's provision for the battles to come.

Daniel's faithfulness to God was rooted in God's faithfulness to him. Confidence in God's persevering grace was the fuel for persevering courage and, even when that grew faint, Daniel humbly prayed and turned to his ever-gracious God for more fuel.

Daniel's story is not so much about how we muster human courage as about how God's persevering grace fuels it. May we, like Daniel, grasp the daily power of an ever-faithful and forgiving God as we seek courage for our modern-day trials.

PRAYER: *Father, before I would dare to be a Daniel, take my heart to the gracious God in whom he trusted. Instill confidence in Your grace to enable me to persevere in my trials.*

177

We rejoice in our sufferings, knowing that suffering produces endurance, and endurance produces character, and character produces hope, and hope does not put us to shame, because God's love has been poured into our hearts through the Holy Spirit who has been given to us. (Romans 5:3–5)

When we're facing a challenge, our tendency is to wonder if God has abandoned us. Why doesn't God make our lives *easy*? One reason is that adversity prepares us for spiritual battles that lie ahead.

The Apostle Paul explains that one reason God allows suffering is to prepare us for future work. He exercises our faith muscles to prepare us for spiritual battles that would otherwise overwhelm us.

After a very difficult year in my early ministry, I overheard a godly woman in our church say, "I wonder what the Lord is preparing Bryan to do that requires him to go through so much testing?"

I wondered, too. But since that time, I have often considered how strengthened I was by the godly woman's words. She helped me realize present trials were not purposeless. So when greater trials came, I believed that God had prepared me. I was strengthened *in* the immediate trial *for* the later work.

Our sufferings produce the endurance we need, the character our situations require, the confident hope that our trials will end, and the spiritual dependence that keeps our love strong enough to see it all through for Christ's sake.

PRAYER: Lord, when I'm facing life's challenges, help me to realize that they help me to grow stronger in Christ and prepare me for greater fruitfulness.

178

The LORD of hosts has sworn:
"As I have planned,
so shall it be,
and as I have purposed,
so shall it stand." (Isaiah 14:24)

The nightly news can discourage us with accounts of violent crime, social injustice, natural calamity, viral disease, global terrorism, and human foolishness.

Evil is real, but it never thwarts God's ultimate purpose. Despite earthly wrongs, our God reigns. Time and again in Scripture, evil appears to prevail from a human perspective, but God is not dismayed. He is never surprised. He never says, "Oops."

Never was this more clear than at Christ's crucifixion. Had you or I stood at the foot of the cross, we would have cried, "God stop this. It is wrong!" It was evil, but it was not wrong. It was God's intention to offer His Son in sacrifice for our sin (Isaiah 53:10).

Evil required the work of Jesus but did not negate it—not even for a moment. Though evil persists, this is still our Father's world. As Maltbie D. Babcock wrote, "That though the wrong seems oft so strong, God is the ruler yet."

He weans us from the temporal with the consequences of evil, even as He woos us to the eternal with the assurances of Jesus. We would desire no rescue without the world's evil; we would have no rescue without Jesus.

God's purposes are never derailed. The proof is the cross. Trust the wisdom, power, and love of the heart that gave Jesus there for us, according to plan.

PRAYER: Father, help me to trust in Your sovereign plan as I live through a fallen world. When the evil threatens to overwhelm my soul, show me Jesus. When I am losing hope, show me Jesus. Every day and for every trial, show me Jesus.

179

*Let us be grateful for receiving a kingdom that cannot
be shaken, and thus let us offer to God acceptable
worship, with reverence and awe. (Hebrews 12:28)*

Tony Snow was fifty-three when he died. Snow, a Christian, had terminal cancer while serving as the press secretary for President George W. Bush. Despite his affliction, Snow was eloquent about how God works in a fallen world.

He wrote,

> We want our lives to be a simple, smooth trail as far as the eye can see, but God likes to venture off-road. He provokes us with twists and turns, and He places predicaments in our lives that seem to defy our endurance and comprehension. Yet, we do not deny Him.[2]

Why not? According to Snow, it's not because God makes life easy. A life of belief teems with thrills, dangers, shocks, reversals, and triumphs. The reason we endure is not that God promises us endless earthly tomorrows; rather, He promises an eternity filled with love and life beyond anything we can comprehend.

Our God will do (or allow) whatever shaking is needed in our lives on Earth for us clasp the hand that will hold us securely for His eternal Kingdom that cannot be shaken.

PRAYER: *Jesus, when I encounter difficulties and hardships that shake me, help me to cling to the hand that will hold me securely for the unshakable Kingdom You promise.*

180

You know how, like a father with his children, we exhorted
each one of you and encouraged you and charged you
to walk in a manner worthy of God, who calls you into
his own kingdom and glory. (1 Thessalonians 2:11–12)

The Marlboro Man represents the manhood of a biblical father about as well as a five-year-old in a cowboy hat resembles John Wayne. The strength of character required to be the head of a home is not displayed through outward appearances, but developed through a heart of daily sacrifice.

As a young man, I witnessed the example of such true manhood through my father. His job often required him to be on the road, and his travel allowance could have made his hotel stays quite pleasant.

But rather than take advantage of the perks, my father would drive through the night to be with his children at breakfast. He walked (and drove) in a manner worthy of the God who had traveled from Heaven to Earth to bless His family.

My father's example made clear that a biblical family head selflessly reflects the One who gave of Himself so we would be blessed as His family!

PRAYER: *Heavenly Father, You have not only saved me but also made me a member of Your eternal family! Please help me to live and love selflessly for the sake of the family You are grooming me for Heaven through my earthly care.*

*The kingdom of heaven may be compared to a man
who sowed good seed in his field, but while his men
were sleeping, his enemy came and sowed weeds among
the wheat and went away. (Matthew 13:24–25)*

Jesus paints a picture of a beautiful wheat field which was spoiled by an enemy. Coming into the field, the enemy planted another kind of seed—weeds.

Now, if you're a farmer and weeds are sprouting up in the middle of your maturing crop, you know you can't just go and jerk out all the weeds. The weeds' roots are entwined with the wheat's. If you pull up the weeds, you'll destroy your harvest!

Jesus tells us this same thing happened in our world. At creation, God planted all that was needed for a good Earth, but the evil one sowed seeds of corruption through Adam's sin.

When we question why God doesn't just eradicate all sin from the earth *now*, Jesus's response is that His harvest of souls is not ready. If all corruption were suddenly uprooted, there would be no sorrow for sin and no desperation of soul to turn us to our Savior. Additionally, if God were to weed the world now of all sin, then there would be no sinners like you and me left for God's eternal harvest.

God is good. He allows the weeds among the spiritual wheat of the world until His harvest of souls is ready. Then He will redeem all those who have turned to Him by confessing they need Him. In His divine timing and by His patient grace, God cultivates the earthly fields in which our hearts mature to secure our souls for His heavenly storehouse.

PRAYER: *Heavenly Father, help me to avoid judging You by the evil that is in the world. Jesus explained what You allow to turn my heart and others' to You. May His love guide my heart to You.*

182

I will bless the LORD at all times; his praise shall continually be in my mouth. My soul makes its boast in the LORD; let the humble hear and be glad. Oh, magnify the LORD with me, and let us exalt his name forever! (Psalm 34:1–3)

Have you ever tried praising God when you are in a trial? It's not the natural thing to do. It's also not a fake spirituality that denies real pain. Yet praise helps us measure and meet trials by reminding us how God sovereignly uses them to help us treasure Him.

When God's greatness and goodness fill our thoughts, fears drain from our hearts. As others have said, "When our God is small, our troubles are large; but when our God is large, our troubles are small."

Praise focuses our minds on the greatness of God, so we sense afresh how wise, powerful, and loving He is—more than a match for any trial. Such praise does not require that we believe our troubles are small, only that we remember our God is greater.

Praise doesn't erase trials but equips us for them. Praise does not dry all tears but helps us see beyond them. Praise renews the resources we need to endure. There will be nothing lacking that we need to stand for God when we utter the praises that make Him present and powerful in our hearts (Psalm 22:3).

The testing of our faith, when it stirs us to praise God for His greatness and goodness, produces steadfastness in us because we become focused on the One who is steadfast (James 1:2–4). Since He will never fail, our trials cannot prevail.

PRAYER: Father, I don't enjoy the temporary trials and painful difficulties in my life, but I praise You that they help me to become more steadfast for the One who is always steadfast. Let my praise focus my heart on Your greatness.

Be strong in the Lord and in the strength of His might.
Put on the whole armor of God, that you may be able
to stand against the schemes of the devil. (Ephesians 6:10–11)

When my daughter was five, she decided to play soccer with her older siblings and cousins at a family gathering. Very quickly in the game, she accidentally tripped and was trampled by the larger kids.

She ran off in tears, determined never again to enter the family fray. But once I scooped her up in my arms, hugged her to my chest, and reentered the game, she begged to play more.

She shrieked with laughter as we ran *together*. And with confidence in her security restored, she became our most zealous team member—held in my arms for the rest of the game.

Similarly, we gain strength and zeal for life's spiritual battles when we know we are securely held in the Lord's arms. Our strength is in His might.

Knowing we are secure in the grasp of the One who is Lord over all gives us the will to fight for Him, and even to reenter the fray after taking a fall, because we are in the embrace of great grace.

PRAYER: Lord, I know that life is full of spiritual battles. May the power of Your might enable me to stand firm and fight for You, knowing I'm secure in Your sovereign care.

The LORD is my light and my salvation; whom shall I fear?
The LORD is the stronghold of my life; of whom
shall I be afraid? When evildoers assail me to eat
up my flesh, my adversaries and foes, it is they
who stumble and fall. (Psalm 27:1–2)

We all face life crises. They may be large-scale: the result of misguided governments, natural disasters, or even terrorists. Or they may be very personal: a health scare, a financial hurdle, a career setback, or a difficult relationship. Whatever your circumstances today, remember that God's purposes for you cannot fail.

David's psalm reminds us of that truth with an image all Israel would know. Their "stronghold" was a mountain of rock with steep sides, but also with a level top where God's people could live in safety. More than once David fled to such a stronghold to find safety from his enemies.

But what gave David greater confidence than the natural fortress to which he could flee was the supernatural Savior who was always with him. David did not have to flee to find this safety because he knew that this fortress was never far away. Wherever he was and whatever he faced, David was always in the stronghold of God's protection.

Crises would still come and enemies would still threaten, but David knew he did not need to be afraid that they could ever overcome God's purposes for his life. The same is true for us because the same God is for us. You and I can say, "The Lord is the stronghold of my life; of whom shall I be afraid?"

PRAYER: *Heavenly Father, I need You in my own crises. Help me to trust that You are my stronghold, that I am eternally secure in Your care, and that Your purposes cannot fail for me, so that I am not afraid.*

185

The share of the one who goes into battle is to be the same as the share of the one who remains with the supplies. They will share equally. (1 Samuel 30:24 CSB)

Janette Alexander, wife of the great nineteenth-century theologian Archibald Alexander, was treasured by her family for her scriptural insights.

Although she lacked the formal training of her husband, her son—who also became a famous Bible teacher—often sought her insights. He said his mother's heart, tuned by walking closely with God, granted understanding worth more than all the commentaries in the world.

In this wonderful compliment, we can glimpse God's perfect perspective that treasures every person according to His purposes. Jannette Alexander was not a seminary professor. But as a wife and mother, she steadied and deepened the faith all family members would need to fulfill God's plan for their lives that would touch millions.

The world may only recognize the gifts of "a Billy Graham" or "a Charles Spurgeon" or "a John Knox," but we should understand the honor due the mother, or Sunday school teacher, or camp counselor who nurtured faith in such a person.

Because our lives are so interwoven in God's divine plan, one who enables another to fight for God is just as important as the one on the battlefield— both are needed for the battle. God uses and treasures both!

PRAYER: Lord, help me to serve You with the gifts you have given by believing You treasure my role in Your plan. Weave my gifts into the tapestry of Your purpose to build up those who are needed for Your battles.

186

My son, do not despise the LORD'S discipline or be weary
of his reproof, for the LORD reproves him whom he loves,
as a father the son in whom he delights. (Proverbs 3:11–12)

We may create some shock by asserting, "The Lord will never punish His children," but that is actually the truth. We understand this truth when we see how God's Word distinguishes discipline and punishment.

Punishment is designed to inflict a penalty in response for a wrong. God will not punish His children because the penalty for all our past, present, and future sin was placed on Jesus. Jesus paid it all!

Discipline is a different matter. The goal of discipline is not to inflict a penalty but to promote maturity. Punishment and discipline may feel similar (both hurt) but their goals are very different. Punishment imposes harm for past misdeeds, but discipline intends help for future blessing.

Punishment is for criminals. Discipline is for children. Punishment follows condemnation. There is no condemnation for those who are in Christ Jesus.

Punishment is for those of whom society disapproves. Discipline is for those in whom God delights. Punishment is administered with a scowl. Discipline is administered with tears. Punishment pours out wrath for a wrong. God's discipline comes out of the heart of a Father.

So even when we are in the throes of the worst discipline Heaven can bring, we are loved no less. God only disciplines those He loves to turn us from sin and to Him. Let God's discipline turn you to the One who loves you enough to harm Himself to help you.

PRAYER: *Father, thank You for the love that disciplines me, so that I turn from the harm of sin and receive the blessings of my Savior. Help my heart to receive this love as You intend.*

187

Walk in a manner worthy of the Lord, fully pleasing
to him: bearing fruit in every good work and increasing
in the knowledge of God; being strengthened with all
power, according to his glorious might, for all endurance
and patience with joy. (Colossians 1:10–11)

Watching those who compete in Ironman competitions makes me dream of what I might have done if I only had been given the opportunity—and *a different body!*

My dreams of Ironman victories were revealed for their vanity when I watched the father-and-son team of Dick and Ricky Hoyt. The two participated in more than eight hundred races together.

What makes their story so special is that Ricky was born with cerebral palsy, and to compete he had to be pulled, pushed, or carried by his father.

Dick provided what was necessary for his son to race even as Ricky competed with determination and fervor that exhausted him. He endured and finished because he depended on his father's power!

We should similarly engage in the race of faith our Heavenly Father puts before us, trusting that we will be strengthened by the power of His might. The desire to run with Him still must be in us, but we *can* run with and for Him because of the power in Him.

The grace we need from our Father in Heaven is not only for the end of our days, but for every day. Depend upon Him through obedience and prayer, confident that you will be strengthened by His might.

PRAYER: Father, I often tremble at the race of faith before me. Give me strength to run the race, confident in the power of Your grace carrying me—all the way to the finish line!

188

Husbands, in the same way be considerate as you live with your wives, and treat them with respect as the weaker partner and as heirs with you of the gracious gift of life. (1 Peter 3:7 NIV)

The Bible commands wives to respect their husbands and for husbands to treat their wives with respect. The respect is to be mutual, but not the same. The Apostle Peter reminded husbands to be considerate of their wives' physical weakness *and* eternal worth.

Though most wives are not as physically strong as their husbands, this should provide no excuse for a man to be domineering or abusive. Why must he not simply "throw his weight around" as the head of the home? Because his wife is an heir with him of Christ's grace in this life and eternally.

Ultimately the love and regard spouses give to one another is not a consequence of the things they do, but the treasure each is to our Savior. If we love Jesus, then we will love what and whom He loves. We are blessed if our spouses live so as to be treasured by us, but even if they do not, we are to treasure those whom Christ purchased at the cost of His own blood.

A husband should respect his wife for the tenderness she brings to the home and for the support she offers him. In such ways she blesses him and their home. Still, his ultimate regard for her resides in grasping the treasure she is to Jesus.

Why does the apostle remind us of these truths? Because love and honor are intimately linked in God's design. The more you honor your spouse, the more you are able to love and the more blessed will be your marriage with a joint heir of Christ's grace.

PRAYER: *Heavenly Father, help me to treat my spouse with love and respect, because You have treasured us both as joint heirs of Your gracious gift of life.*

189

*I pray that you, being rooted and established in love,
may have power, together with all the Lord's holy
people, to grasp how wide and long and high and deep
is the love of Christ, and to know this love that surpasses
knowledge—that you may be filled to the measure of
all the fullness of God. (Ephesians 3:17–19 NIV)*

My family enjoys vacationing at a remote cabin. As we prepare to vacate the cabin for winter, we drain all the plumbing. We open valves, releasing all the water to keep pipes from bursting in the coming freeze.

In the springtime, we reverse the process, closing valves and turning the water back on. But there is one valve we leave open until new water fills the system: the valve at the top of the hot-water tank.

We allow the incoming water to drive out the air in the tank that would otherwise keep it from fulfilling its purpose.

Similarly, when love for Christ fills our hearts, it drives out the love for sin that is the air in which temptations thrive. What fills our hearts with such love for Christ? Grasping how wide and long and high and deep is His love for us.

PRAYER: Father, help me to grasp the greatness of Christ's love for me so that I will be filled with the love for Him that is power for resisting sin.

I am sure that neither death nor life, nor angels nor rulers, nor things present nor things to come, nor powers, nor height nor depth, nor anything else in all creation, will be able to separate us from the love of God in Christ Jesus our Lord. (Romans 8:38–39)

The Apostle Paul provides a wonderfully long list of things that will never be able to separate us from God's love in Christ Jesus our Lord.

However, some readers fear that there is something missing from that list—*sin*. Should that worry us? No.

We should realize that while it's true sin is not mentioned in Paul's list, he has just finished telling us that God will work all things together for the good of those who love Him.

If God knew there was something in your path—life or death, things present or things to come, evil powers, or anything in creation—that would separate you from Christ, then His perfect plan for you would require Him to take you to Heaven before that spiritual calamity hit you. He would have to do this in order to work all things for your eternal good.

God will not allow anything in your life that would cause your separation from His heart. He will not allow you to proceed into sin or unbelief that would destroy His love. That's why there is nothing that can separate us from Him, not even our sin.

So when there is sin or failure in your life, do not fear to seek the Savior who has bound Himself to you with love that nothing can sever. If it could, He would already have taken you to Himself.

PRAYER: Lord, You give me great comfort and hope by promising that nothing can separate me from Your love. May that inseparable love make me run to You when I need to repent and run for You in every day's race to represent Jesus.

191

The righteous will never be moved;
he will be remembered forever. (Psalm 112:6)

Elaine Pereira is author of *I Will Never Forget*, a story about a woman caring for her aging mother through the stages of dementia. The way Pereira describes her mother's deterioration is not noble or sentimental. The loss of memory creates many embarrassments.

Yet, as the story unfolds, we ultimately understand that the mother's dignity is restored, not by a return of her memory but by her daughter's memories. Pereira remembers her mother for who she was—and still is—a beloved person made in the image of God.

In an even more profound way, God maintains our dignity and preciousness to Him by remembering His provision for us. Even when our lives are not as they should be, God treats us with the dignity and care reserved for His beloved.

The One who covers our sin with His blood also covers our shame with His righteousness. God remembers that we are His precious children.

The world, our country, our community, even our family may forget us. God will not. He will always say, "You are Mine and precious to Me. I remember you!"

PRAYER: *Heavenly Father, thank You that You will not forget me. May the dignity of the memory You maintain for me also stir me to see others through Your memory of them.*

192

*Stand therefore, having fastened on the belt of truth,
and having put on the breastplate of
righteousness ... and the sword of the Spirit,
which is the word of God. (Ephesians 6:14, 17)*

Spiritual warfare is real. We can make two mistakes concerning its nature. The first is to ignore its reality; the second is to exaggerate its power.

We are ill-equipped to engage struggles against wickedness and injustice without recognizing that evil truly affects our material world. The Apostle Paul said, "Our struggle is not against flesh and blood, but against the rulers, against the authorities, against the powers of this dark world and against the spiritual forces of evil in the heavenly realms" (Ephesians 6:12).

The world available to our physical senses is not the only reality. Spiritual forces are vying for power and influence in every area of our lives. That understanding, however, can twist our perceptions into imagining ghouls behind every bush. Satan is not as silly as that, nor is his influence so pervasive.

Our Sovereign God yet rules this world, restraining and conquering evil to accomplish His will. We should never doubt His influence or fail to engage it. Already we have an Advocate with the Heavenly Father who has equipped us with the armor and weaponry needed for spiritual victory.

The battles may be intense, but we have God's truth, Christ's righteousness, and the Spirit's Word for every fight. Claim them, cling to them, and use them. God will grant the victory of eternity's purposes. The battle belongs to the Lord, so stand firm with Him!

PRAYER: Lord, remind me to call upon You in my time of need so that I will face spiritual reality with spiritual weaponry and prevail in Your strength.

You will call upon me and come and pray to me,
and I will hear you. You will seek me and find me,
when you seek me with all your heart. (Jeremiah 29:12–13)

In 2014, French atheist-turned-evangelical-theologian Guillaume Bignon shared how the light of God's grace penetrated the dark places of his soul.

Bignon's journey began after a whirlwind romance with a girl. Because the girl was a Christian and did not want a deep relationship with someone who did not share her love for Jesus, Bignon began to explore her faith.

He read the Bible to learn about her beliefs. The accounts of Jesus were impressive, but Bignon remained unsure. Then he thought, *I'm a scientist; there's an experiment I can carry out to test the truth of Jesus. I'll pray and ask God, "If You're real, reveal Yourself to me."* And God did in a special way!

Here's how: Consideration of Jesus's character revealed to Bignon that his real motive for reading the Bible was to have an affair with the girl. He was willing to sacrifice her faith to satisfy his lust—and that was an evil in Bignon that he had never before faced. Such sin in him revealed not only the truth of why Jesus came but also Bignon's need of Him!

If God has revealed your sin to you, believe that His purpose is to show you the truth of your need and of your Savior. Call out to the Lord today and ask Him to cover you with the grace that has revealed your sin and your Savior!

PRAYER: Lord, I ask You to reveal Yourself to me more and more each day. I am willing to ask, knowing that the more You show Yourself, the more sin I will see in myself. But the more I see my sin, the more I will cherish Christ's cross. Where sin increases, grace will increase all the more. Praise God!

194

*Even though I walk through the valley of the shadow
of death, I will fear no evil, for you are with me; your
rod and your staff, they comfort me. (Psalm 23:4)*

As Christians, we're not given a pass on suffering. God promises to provide His comfort, but we need it because the valleys of shadow are real. Believers are not promised the absence of valleys but the presence of God. What difference does that make?

The Psalm writer says he will not fear the darkness of the valleys because God is present with His rod and staff.

What are a shepherd's rod and staff all about? The specifics can get a little murky, but what is clear is that a good shepherd has the tools both to *protect* and to *guide* His sheep—a rod and staff. Each is needed to care for the sheep the shepherd loves.

Sheep need to be protected from predators, from aggressors (yes, even among sheep), and from their own folly. So a good rod fends off threats and dispenses correction.

Sheep also need to be guided on safe paths to green pastures and good waters, and reclaimed from ditches and mires. A shepherd's staff, maybe with a crook in it, rescues and keeps safe the sheep.

You may now be walking through darkness: a medical problem, loss of a job, or family tragedy. God does not promise you an absence of valleys, but to be with you in their midst of shadows. Trust the heart and path of the Good Shepherd who gave His life for you. His rod and staff will still shepherd your soul.

PRAYER: *Lord, thank You for being my Shepherd! As I walk through this world's dark valleys, help me to trust that You are with me and wield Your rod and staff for me.*

195

I have said these things to you, that in me you may have peace. In the world you will have tribulation. But take heart; I have overcome the world. (John 16:33)

A friend invited me to his home to watch a crucial game for his favorite basketball team. We both had to attend a meeting at the time of the game, so he recorded it for us to watch later.

As the game progressed, my friend's team was getting badly beat. But my normally expressive friend seemed unconcerned. Finally, I asked him why he was not acting like the fanatical fan I knew him to be.

He responded, "One of the guys in our meeting got a text about the game and told me that my team rebounds in the fourth quarter. I am not worried because I know we are going to win."

Jesus does not want us to be unprepared for the battles that we will face when we stand for Him in a world opposed to Him. He gives us a clear heads up, saying, "In this world, you will have tribulation."

Jesus warns us this way because He knows that we could easily turn away from Him if we had false expectations about a life with Him putting us on easy street. But He does not only warn of battles, He tells us the eventual outcome—His victory.

So, yes, we may face hard times and difficult people, but we need not be overwhelmed because we know who will overcome. The outcome is already determined: Jesus wins! And we are on His team!

PRAYER: *Heavenly Father, sometimes challenges of this world threaten to overwhelm my faith. Keep me faithful, relying on Jesus's assurance that He has overcome the world and His victory secures my eternity.*

196

We know that for those who love God all things
work together for good, for those who are called
according to His purpose. (Romans 8:28)

This astounding promise of God can sometimes become the worst of Christian two-by-four clubs. Those insensitive to others' pain can insist this verse should provide an instantaneous end to discouragement or grief:

"You have lost a job?" Don't worry. God will work it for good."
"You have lost a spouse? Don't grieve. He is in a better place."
"You are in a crisis? Don't fear. God's got it all under control."

As true as the statements may be, such blunt bashing with God's truth does not reflect the care of the apostle's words. He never says all things feel good—or seem fair or right. He says that God will work all things together for good. There is a *process* in God's plans that should allow us to work through grief, pain, and questions.

We work through such difficulties with the assurance that God will never leave or forsake us, nor allow our circumstances to overwhelm His eternal plans.

Such grace does not forbid our tears but gives us time to clear them from our eyes. In that space, we can look forward with faith in God's hand and look backward to the cross for reassurance of His heart.

Yes, everything in creation is being bent toward your eternal good by a sovereign God. That is a powerful truth—so powerful we should handle it with the care God intends.

PRAYER: *Jesus, thank You for assurance that pain and grief cannot undo Your purposes. Help me understand how to share the truth of Your sovereign hand with the tenderness of my Savior's heart.*

197

Blessed are those whose lawless deeds are forgiven,
and whose sins are covered. (Romans 4:7)

We have friends who adopted a child from another nation. When they went to the orphanage, they found the child wrapped in red, which in that culture was a sign of favor and love.

The red cloth signified that although she had been given up by an unknown biological mother, the child was loved. Yet, as these new parents moved the cloth covering the child's face, they discovered a facial feature that was unacceptable in that culture. That red cloth represented love, but it had also been used to hide a flaw that would cause rejection.

You and I are children with an even more compassionate covering. God covered our sinful flaws with the blood of Jesus in order to adopt us as His own. Our guilt and shame are forever hidden by Jesus's love poured out on the cross for all who put their faith in His grace.

We do not have to project a flawless face to God to know His love; rather, we can trust Him to cover all our flaws with His perfect grace to make us His children forever.

PRAYER: Father, thank You for covering my sin with Christ's blood so that I might know the love and favor that secures me in Your family forever. May this grace keep me loving You.

You are a chosen race, a royal priesthood, a holy
nation, a people for his own possession, that you may proclaim
the excellencies of him who called you out
of darkness into his marvelous light. (1 Peter 2:9)

Our world—even the church—has become celebrity crazy. We follow the actions, antics, and failings of the famous, constantly measuring if their performance still makes them worthy of our attention.

The consequence is not only measuring *their* worth by their ability to please us—we tend to look at *our* family, friends, coworkers, and selves the same way. The question that plagues us all is, "So, what have you done lately?"

Even if we had wonderful beginnings and early accolades, the pressure to maintain appreciation and adulation becomes crushing. We compare our appearances, our achievements, and our families' Facebook posts, constantly feeling pressed to stay acceptable. What can release the pressure?

As Christians, we have the privilege of embracing a new, unchanging, and precious status that identifies us as God's beloved, based not on what we've done but on what Jesus Christ has done for us!

When we come to Christ by faith, we become children of God—adopted into His family forever. With this unchanging status, we're not always looking for somebody's spotlight on our performance. We have been called into the marvelous light of God's eternal love. And if the Creator of the universe loves us, we must really be something!

> PRAYER: *Father, help me to view myself through Your eyes, relishing the marvelous status You have given me in Christ. May I not be driven by what others think of me but by my love for the One who has made me eternally precious to You.*

199

I tell you, my friends, do not fear those who kill the body, and after that have nothing more that they can do.... Are not five sparrows sold for two pennies? And not one of them is forgotten before God. Why even the hairs of you hear are numbered. Fear not; you are of more value than many sparrows. (Luke 12:4, 6–7)

No matter what's happening in your life, God assures you that He knows and is in charge of every detail. That truth was dramatically proven to a woman named Ashley Smith one dark night.

Ashley's drug-damaged life was spiraling when Brian Nichols broke into her apartment. He had just killed four people and was running from the police.

As Brian hid, waiting for the inevitable shootout that would end his life, these two desperate people "chanced" into a conversation about why each was there. They miraculously concluded that God must have a purpose for them.

God's truth in the midst of the crisis led to Brian turning himself over to police and to Ashley turning away from drugs.

Ashley now believes that God caused her and Brian's paths to intersect. Their encounter not only turned her away from drugs but back to God. Then God used Ashley to turn Brian to Christ, enabling his reception of eternal forgiveness despite the extreme measure of his sin. Prison will not bar him from Heaven.

Ashley and Brian remind us that God can use anyone, anytime, anywhere to deliver the limitless measures of His grace! Our circumstances are never too small, or too bad, or too desperate for God.

PRAYER: Lord, please help me to believe that You have all the details of my care in Your loving control, so that I will trust You and turn to You no matter what.

It was not with perishable things such as silver or gold that you
were redeemed from the empty way of life handed down
to you from your ancestors, but with the precious blood of Christ,
a lamb without blemish or defect. (1 Peter 1:18–19 NIV)

Have you ever wanted a special big-ticket item? Maybe you saved and saved until you had the full amount needed to make the purchase.

That's a bit like what God has done for you. He long ago established a plan to redeem you from sinful humanity, building the means of salvation from ancient times until He would purchase your soul for Heaven by the precious blood of His own Son!

Your redemption was not settled with the exchange of precious resources of this earth. No one can buy a place in Heaven. Instead, God established a purchase plan that was secured by a binding covenant declared at the dawn of humanity. The covenant was made for us but fulfilled by Christ's perfect sacrifice.

Those who rely on His provision have their sins fully paid for. Any other claim on the blessings of God's covenant is an empty sham of religious ritual or personal conceit.

Only by trusting that Jesus purchased Heaven's blessings for us by His sacrifice can we claim redemption from a sinful past and a home in Heaven forever. When we trust this purchase plan, God declares our salvation fully paid.

PRAYER: *Lord, thank You for redeeming me from empty efforts to save myself by providing for Your covenant love to be secured by Christ's blood and to be claimed by faith alone!*

201

If while we were enemies we were reconciled to God
by the death of his Son, much more, now that we are
reconciled, shall we be saved by his life. (Romans 5:10)

My grandfather was a tough-talking, chain-smoking manager of a dime store who was hard to get to know. Once, when we were at his house, I found an old wooden top to play with—until my older brothers took it from me.

I don't remember how I objected, but it was loud, causing a disturbed grandfather to point at me and order, "You, come with me."

Scared and not knowing what was going to happen, I followed him into the basement. There he presented me with his own fishing-tackle box. It was one of the last interactions I would ever have with him. I did not know it then, but he was dying.

His dying gift I have kept to this day. The reason is not because the tackle box was particularly valuable, but because that dying gift closed the distance between me and my grandfather. Because he provided what the child pitching a fit could neither earn or deserve, I have treasured the gift of his love.

That's the nature and the consequence of God's grace. Jesus's dying gift closed the distance between us and God, reconciling us so that we would treasure His love and live for Him!

PRAYER: *Father, even though I deserved nothing, You reconciled me to Yourself through the death of Your Son. You closed the distance between us. May that reality motivate me to walk closely with You today.*

202

You then, my child, be strengthened by the grace that is
in Christ Jesus, and what you have heard from me in the
presence of many witnesses entrust to faithful men, who
will be able to teach others also. (2 Timothy 2:1–2)

Why make a big deal about grace? Don't Christians hear the message of grace enough?

The message of God's unconditional love is carefully and lovingly unpacked throughout Scripture. The word "grace" appears many times. And there are hundreds of examples of God providing for those who cannot provide for themselves. Does God overdo it by repeating the message of grace so much?

The answer is no, but why is that so? The reason becomes clear in the Apostle Paul's instructions. Paul is approaching the end of life and emphasizing what is most important for the strength to live for God.

What is most important? "Be strengthened by the grace that is in Christ Jesus." The message of grace is so counter to human instincts of how we secure affection that it is hard to overemphasize. Preachers know that even when we preach *grace*, people hear *law*, presuming God's love is based on measuring up to His standards.

People who believe that God's love is based on their performance inevitably fall into pride or despair. Doing good works just to keep God at bay furthers the gap between us and Him.

It takes regular doses of grace from mature Christians to help counter our instincts. Grace is not a license to sin; it is strengthening the heart for godly service out of love for a sacrificial Savior.

PRAYER: Lord, strengthen my love by the message of Your grace so that I will live for You and help future generations to do the same out of love for the One who gave Himself for them.

203

*One will scarcely die for a righteous person—
though perhaps for a good person one would dare
even to die—but God shows his love for us in that while
we were still sinners, Christ died for us. (Romans 5:7–8)*

Early in ministry the Lord blessed me through the powerful testimony of the believing parents of a young woman killed by a drunken driver. I tremble still to remember accompanying police officers to their home to tell them of the loss of their only child.

Their grief was profound. In many ways I felt useless for the task of helping them. Yet, because the Lord had filled them with His Word, they grieved as those who had the confident hope of their daughter's eternity and their family's reunion in Heaven.

Their faith was as profoundly displayed as their grief when they crossed paths in a drugstore with the young man who had killed their daughter as he was awaiting trial. Said the parents to the one who had done such damage to their family, "Trust in Jesus, and He will forgive all your sins."

The words were the work of the Spirit of God—the Spirit sent to testify of Jesus. These dear parents spoke as the Spirit's witnesses of the One who died for us while we were still sinners. Their testimony was His truth for all who trust Jesus.

Do not believe that your sin is greater than God's grace. Jesus died to reconcile His enemies to God. His grace is greater than the greatest sin of the greatest sinner. Trust this Jesus!

PRAYER: *Jesus, when I doubt that You could love someone like me, remind me that You died for sinners just like me. Help me trust that Your grace is greater than my sin.*

204

If anyone is in Christ, he is a new creation.
The old has passed away; behold, the new has come.
All this is from God, who through Christ
reconciled us to himself. (2 Corinthians 5:17–18)

The Apostle Paul says, "If anyone is in Christ, he is a new creation." That doesn't mean all believers suddenly have the body of a pro athlete or the mind of a prophet. The changes are in our *spiritual* nature.

Before we were united to Christ, we had no ability to live a righteous life for God. Even nice things we did that seemed good to others and to us were not done to please God. We were living for ourselves—for our pleasure—others' approval, or to compensate for something in us. That self-focused lifestyle was the core of our *old* nature!

But through Christ, our nature was changed. Our sins were forgiven, and we were also made able to live for Christ and those He loves. In fact, that became our heart's deepest desire. We don't always express that desire well; our sin nature still influences us. But, for the first time in our lives, we have the desire and ability to live for God—that's our *new* nature.

Because of Christ's mercy and the indwelling of the Holy Spirit, we have Christ's pardon from past sin and spiritual power to resist more sin! We are not perfect yet, but we are no longer controlled by sin.

Now that we are new creations, we realize that God's grace is not our license to sin but Christ's release from its guilt and power!

PRAYER: *Heavenly Father, today help my words and actions to demonstrate that I am a new creation. Cleanse me from the guilt of my sin, and may gratitude for Your mercy compel me to act on the power You have granted me to resist sin.*

For God so loved the world, that he gave his only Son,
that whoever believes in him should not perish
but have eternal life. For God did not send his Son into
the world to condemn the world, but in order that
the world might be saved through him. (John 3:16–17)

In a hospital room, I faced a father whose son's life hung in the balance due to a freak accident. Through his tears, this father confided, "I know what is going on. God is punishing my son for my sin."

I was shocked. Standing before me was a wonderful man of faith who, during a moment of hardship, could only think of God as an ogre in the sky, demanding a pound of flesh for some past error.

I had no idea how to answer, but somehow the Holy Spirit supplied words: "God is not putting the penalty of your sin on *your* son, because He has already put the penalty of your sin on *His* Son."

I still wonder how the Spirit planted those words in the panic of my thought, but they have since helped me in times of my own hardship. When I am tempted to think God is getting back at me for my sins, I remember that He completely poured out His wrath on His Son so that I would have His mercy.

God is good all the time because His Son took all the punishment we deserve. God has promised your salvation, not your condemnation.

PRAYER: Lord, thank You for allowing Your only Son to pay the penalty for my sin. When I'm tempted to doubt Your care, remind me You gave Jesus for me so that my sins will not ever condemn me or my loved ones.

206

The Lord's servant must not be quarrelsome but must be kind to everyone, able to teach, not resentful. (2 Timothy 2:24)

The world is filled with opinions, and social media has expanded the opportunities for many persons to express theirs without fears about facing those their words buffet.

A lot of anger and criticism is aimed at Christians for beliefs that are rooted in God's Word. But we, too, often join in the fray, justifying blunt and cutting words with the supposed sin or faithlessness of those on the receiving end of our critiques.

Some may argue that Christian obligations to act lovingly only apply to brothers and sisters in Christ. They may also point to inspired prophets who spoke to enemies of God with sharp-tongued zeal.

It is important for us to remember that speaking for God should humble us before we seek to humble others. An inspired apostle did not limit speaking Christianly to Christians. Paul commanded those who would serve the church to be kind *to everyone* and not to be quarrelsome or resentful with anyone.

We may quickly point out that's not the way others are treating us, but that is precisely the point. The Christian community should display the alternative society the world cannot know apart from Christ. If we only echo the world, the message of grace cannot be heard.

Jesus could certainly speak with boldness, but His goal was to make the Gospel plain. God's truth without His gracious intent is not His will.

PRAYER: Lord, teach me to consider Your love for people with whom I disagree so that I will show the love and respect that make Your grace known to all who need it.

207

At the end of the days I, Nebuchadnezzar, lifted my eyes to heaven,
and my reason returned to me, and I blessed the Most High,
and praised and honored him who lives forever. (Daniel 4:34)

We love to hear a dramatic testimony. We delight in stories of radical change in people like the Apostle Paul, who turned from persecuting Christians to building the early Church!

Such stories are woven throughout Scripture because we keep wondering if God can work so powerfully and personally. Sometimes the unlikeliest persons are chosen to make clear that God can work precisely this way for people without any other hope.

We would have trouble identifying anyone more wicked than Babylon's King Nebuchadnezzar. He was a ruthless idolator, enslaver, and murderer. Yet, he ended up praising the God of the people of Israel that he had so cruelly enslaved and persecuted.

This king may be unique in his wickedness but not in his path to God. There is no way that this wicked man could have compensated for his sins to claim God's love. So how did he come to God?

When he was absolutely incapable of helping himself, he did not point to his achievements, or look down on anyone else to compare his goodness. Instead, he looked up to Heaven for God's help.

God blessed the humility of a man who possessed no good in himself. *That's Gospel gold!* God made a pagan king a member of Heaven's family by grace alone. We, too, become members of God's family by faith in His grace alone.

Look up to the One who sent Jesus down to you.

PRAYER: *Heavenly Father, thank You for enabling me to be a member of your family—not because of anything I've done but solely by Your grace. May humility be my path to You.*

208

*The LORD passed by, and a great and strong wind tore
the mountains and broke in pieces the rocks before
the LORD, but the LORD was not in the wind.
And after the wind an earthquake, but the LORD was
not in the earthquake. And after the earthquake
a fire, but the LORD was not in the fire. And after
the fire the sound of a low whisper. (1 Kings 19:11–12)*

Well-known Christian author Elisabeth Elliott recounts the story of a young woman who lost her father during the Great Depression—four days before her seventeenth birthday.

Without her father to support the family, the girl knew her life was going to be a struggle. The silence of his absence seemed almost to crush her. Then she heard a gentle sound that gave her hope.

It was the *whisk, whisk* of the broom her mother had not used in three days. That simple whisper of the broom said more about faith than anything her mother could have voiced. It said, "Life goes on. We have trusted the Lord. He has always provided for our needs. We will press on. We will live again."

An act so gentle, a little whisper of the assurance of God's care, powerfully rekindled faith, hope, and the willingness to move forward into God's future.

When the Lord swept our sins as far away as the east is from the west, and promised an eternity in His presence, the whisk of His broom became our assurance of abiding care for every day in every trial.

PRAYER: *Father, I sometimes long for You to speak to me in loud and dramatic ways. Help me to learn to recognize Your strongest and clearest voice in Scripture so that I will hear its gentle whispers speak to all of my life.*

209

But for Adam there was not found a helper fit for him.
*So the L*ORD *God caused a deep sleep to fall upon the man,*
and ... took one of his ribs and closed up its place
with flesh. And the rib that the Lord God had
taken from the man he made into a woman
and brought her to the man. (Genesis 2:20–22)

When God made a "helper" for Adam, the wife was fulfilling a role that God identifies as His own. He, too, is our *very present* help (Psalm 46:1). The coidentification reminds us that a wife is to help her husband be what *God* intends, not what *she* intends.

A wife who will only devote herself to the vision of the husband she wants him to become does not understand God's plan. God's plan is for our present love to be transformative. We are helped to mature in grace by the love and support that is reflected in the specific personality and experiences of our spouses.

In God's great wisdom and love He chose our spouse, out of all the persons in the world, to be the one to help us become the person He intends.

If a wife withholds some part of her love until her husband reflects the perfection of her makeover, she is depriving them *both* of the present joys of unconditional love. She is also depriving herself of the spiritually mature husband God intended her to have through her loving help.

Too often couples waste years in tension and conflict by withholding the fullness of their love until the other meets some criteria of deserving. We are most blessed when we recognize the love we share unconditionally will form the greatest and most joyful bonds of our present and future marriage.

PRAYER: *Heavenly Father, in all the days of my marriage help me to love in all the ways that help my spouse become all You intend—not only what I want.*

Beloved, let us love one another, for love is from God,
and whoever loves has been born of God
and knows God. Anyone who does not love does
not know God, because God is love. (1 John 4:7–8)

The Jefferson Barracks Memorial Bridge, which crosses the Mississippi River, reflects an architectural design called a *tied arch*. It's a series of cables suspended from a massive arch that supports the bridge's roadbed.

For the bridge to support the intended load, the cables must have a specific tension. To test that, each cable is plucked like a huge harp string to see if it has the proper resonance. Whether the bridge will hold is revealed by the tone the cable emits.

In a similar way, God's hold on us is revealed by the tone of our hearts. When our hearts are tuned to God's heart they resonate with His love for others.

Sometimes those heart strings are plucked harshly or unkindly by the actions of others, but the Christian heart reverberating with humble gratitude for Christ's mercy still resonates with His grace.

A heart tied to God's heart reflects His love; a heart that does not cannot claim to know God. That may sound harsh, but God loves us enough to give the warning sounds of spiritual danger. If loveless tones have come from you recently, tether your heart again to the forgiving heart of Jesus.

PRAYER: *Father, I pray that my heart will resonate with love and gratitude for what You have done for me in Christ. Help me to love when it is difficult, confirming Christ in me.*

For our sake he made him to be sin who knew no sin,
so that in him we might become
the righteousness of God. (2 Corinthians 5:21)

If you were in deep in debt for ten million dollars and someone wrote you a check for the full amount, you would be thrilled but not out of the woods.

After all, even after your debt was relieved, with no other funds added, you would still have an empty balance in your bank account. That's the way lots of Christians feel, when they only consider half of the Gospel.

The first half of the Gospel promises that the debt of our sin was fully paid when Jesus died on the cross. He became sin for us, taking the penalty for our sins on Himself. That's great, but we can still feel guilty that our sin caused His suffering. And there is another problem: You and I continue to sin.

God's standard for yesterday, today, and tomorrow is "Be holy, for I am holy." That means every day that we are not perfect, we accumulate new debt. And even if Jesus cancels that, we still only have zeros to our name in our spiritual account.

That's why we need the second half of the Gospel. Jesus not only paid for our sin, He provides His righteousness for us. Paul writes that Jesus provided so that "in Him we might become the righteousness of God." Jesus gives what God requires, making us rich in His righteousness even as He forgives our debt.

Praise God that your debt is paid and your spiritual bank account is overflowing with grace.

PRAYER: Lord, thank You for both halves of the Gospel: for paying my debt in full and for providing Jesus's righteousness in abundance. I need both. I praise You for such rich grace.

212

*Faith is the assurance of things hoped for, the conviction
of things not seen. For by it the people of old received their
commendation.... Without faith it is impossible to please him,
for whoever would draw near to God must believe that he exists
and that he rewards those who seek him. (Hebrews 11:1–2, 6)*

Without confidence in our relationship with Christ, we become like my children, who at a young age feared standing up to cross a rope-suspension bridge.

The anchors and ropes that held the bridge were perfectly secure, but my young children approached it with dread! They were far more focused on the depth of the chasm beneath them than on the security of the bridge that held them. So in fear and anguish, they would only crawl across the bridge, even as other people confidently walked past them.

My children's actions are at times reflected in believers who doubt their security in Christ. They crawl forward in their pursuit of God's purposes, far more focused on personal weakness and spiritual danger than on the promises of God. Doubting the certainty of His care, they take baby steps for Jesus instead of confidently marching forward in His care.

The chasms of potential failure are real, and dangers from spiritual foes are immense, but the bridge to God's purpose is supported by cables of His love and power that no earthly power can overcome. So walk forward on the bridge of obedience to His Word with the faith that it is secured by the wisdom, strength, and love of your sovereign God.

Take each step of faith with the drumbeat of these oft-repeated words from Billy Graham: "The will of God will not lead you where the grace of God cannot keep you."

PRAYER: *Lord Jesus, help me to walk by faith in Your sure provision this day, so that I step forward in Your purposes with courage and confidence and not with childlike fears.*

No temptation has overtaken you that is not common to man. God is faithful, and he will not let you be tempted beyond your ability, but with the temptation, he will also provide the way of escape, that you may be able to endure it. (1 Corinthians 10:13)

The Apostle Paul writes to people like us who have been tempted by the world's traps and snares to think there is no way out! He assures us instead, "When you are tempted, God will provide an escape."

Not only does God promise this escape from temptation, but He also promises escape from debilitating shame. Our tendency is to think, *The reason that I am so tempted is that I am weak and weird. If I were a mature person—a real Christian—then I would not be tempted this way.*

Instead, the apostle assures each of us that we are not alone. There are hundreds of thousands of others across the ages and across the world who struggle with similar things. Don't let Satan weaken you with the shame of believing that you are so unique or weird or awful that God's grace cannot help you.

The assurance of a way of escape from temptation to multitudes of persons like us also keeps us from creating our own exclusion clause from seeking God's help and obeying His commands.

God says, "Others have struggled like you, and have found victory in My provision. So can you." That assurance enables us to overcome our weaknesses and turn away from our temptations.

Believe that these promises of God are real. Then you will have power to fight your temptations and flee to the escape He graciously provides.

PRAYER: Lord, when I am tempted, enable me to believe You will provide a way of escape, to believe You will give me strength to run to it, and to run to it!

214

Not that I have already obtained this
[righteousness God requires] or am already perfect,
but I press on to make it my own, because Christ
Jesus has made me his own. (Philippians 3:12)

As followers of Christ, we must continually fight against sin, but that doesn't mean we'll attain perfection on this side of Heaven. Even the Apostle Paul acknowledged that he was not "already perfect."

We won't be perfect in this life because there's only person who was: Jesus Christ, our Savior. But the fact that we are not already perfect does not keep us from pressing on to live as He lived. One reason is that we have already been granted a perfect record by the grace of God—He has erased the record of our faults by the blood of Jesus.

When we understand how incredible God's love for us really is, our heart's desire is to live for Him. The Apostle Paul said it simply and compactly, "I press on to make [a righteous life] my own, because Christ Jesus has made me His own."

We long to reflect Christ's heart because He claimed ours. His love for us makes us want to live for Him and to be like Him.

Friends of ours adopted a child from an African village where food, medical care, and education were almost nonexistent. The adoption was truly *lifesaving*.

Years later, we noted the silhouette of that child—now a young man—approaching us at twilight. His gait was unmistakably that of his adopted father; so was his voice; so was his faith.

So also we delight to mirror our Messiah. We seek to make our own the life of the One who made us His own.

PRAYER: *Lord, You know I am far from perfect, but don't let that discourage me from seeking to honor You. Fill me with desire to make my own the life of the One who made me His own by His saving grace.*

Who shall separate us from the love of Christ? Shall tribulation, or distress, or persecution, or famine, or nakedness, or danger, or sword?... No, in all these things we are more than conquerors through him who loved us. (Romans 8:35, 37)

Have you ever wondered if life's trials prove that God has stopped caring for you? Such natural questioning is why the Apostle Paul assures us that we are more than conquerors of life's trials *through Him who loved us!*

Paul was trying to make it clear that Jesus's love for us is infinitely greater than all our circumstances or sins. The challenges of past, present, and future do not indicate that God is gone, nor do our flawed responses to them indicate that His love is.

What assures us of God's inseparable love? First, it was established by His grace, not by how good we or our circumstances were.

Second, God is everywhere. He is always near. He remains *Immanuel* (God with us) even when the earth is shaking. No trial or failure can distance us from Him.

Third, even when trials expose our weakness, God sticks close to provide a remedy. Greater is He who is *in you* than any power in this world (1 John 4:4). As a result, we are more than conquerors of fear, doubt, and disobedience through Christ's power.

We believe we have Christ's pardon for us, Christ's presence with us, Christ's power in us, and Christ's promises forever.

Knowing that God has made us able to stand and will always stand with us, we are more than conquerors of this world's evils.

PRAYER: *Heavenly Father, thank You for being the power of my power and providing it through a love that will not let me go. Give me faith in the grace that is greater than my sins or fears so that I will stand against all that You will conquer.*

*I acknowledged my sin to you, and I did not cover my
iniquity; I said, "I will confess my transgressions to the LORD,"
and you forgave the iniquity of my sin. (Psalm 32:5)*

When I was growing up, instant pudding had just hit the market. A little milk, a little powder packet, and, *voilà*, creamy, silky pudding.

But my mother, an expert cook, was not having it. One night she pulled her homemade pudding from the fridge and there was a thumb-sized hole in the middle of it. "Who did that?" she asked. Like a junior choir, all six kids sang out, "Not me!"

My mother wasn't having any of that. She lined up all six kids and said, "Stick out your thumbs." Then she began to measure each thumb against the pudding dent. My brother, Gordon, was the guilty one! We knew because the hole demonstrated the dimensions of what would fill it.

Similarly, God wants us to confess our sin, not because He needs it to discover our sin, but because the holes in our holiness indicate the dimensions of grace that will be needed to fill them.

Honest confession reveals to us, more than to God, the transgression that requires His intercession. When we identify the magnitude of our sin, we discover the magnitude of His grace.

As a result, seeking God's forgiveness yields the fruit of true repentance: confession of how long and wide and high and deep is the love of God that we each need.

PRAYER: *Lord, I confess my sins to You, knowing that You forgive and, by forgiving, ignite the love that compels my heart to beat for You. Show me the true dimensions of my sin that I may confess how great are the dimensions of Your love that I require.*

217

[Jesus] said to them, "How foolish you are, and how slow to believe all that the prophets have spoken! Did not the Messiah have to suffer these things and then enter his glory?" And beginning with Moses and all the Prophets, he explained to them what was said in all the Scriptures concerning himself. (Luke 24:25–27 NIV)

Have you ever been startled by the jarring surprise that comes with the last crank of a jack-in-the-box? God's grace was never meant to surprise us that way.

Instead, Jesus's words assure us that God was preparing His people to receive the grace of Christ long before His appearance on Earth. God began revealing His plan in the opening chapters of the Bible. There He promised a Son who would crush the powers of Satan, and the rest of Scripture progressively unveils what that should mean for us.

The message of salvation doesn't get dumped on humanity all at once. We couldn't receive it that way. Instead, we are led by laws, examples, and prophecies to understand the pervasiveness of human failing and the necessity of a divine solution. That's the Gospel message unfolding from Genesis to Revelation.

Why should we care that the Bible unfolds that way? Because this reveals how patient and persistent is the grace of God for sinners and strugglers like us.

God did not turn away because His people did. He did not abandon His children because they stumbled. Instead, as the light of dawn grows brighter toward the day, the message of grace grew clearer until it revealed the Savior we need every day.

PRAYER: Lord, help me always to read Your Word with Gospel glasses that reveal divine provision for human need. Let me not settle for simple "do good" lessons that do not lead me to my Savior as Your Word always does.

218

We do not have a high priest who is unable to empathize with our weaknesses, but we have one who has been tempted in every way, just as we are—yet he did not sin. (Hebrews 4:15 NIV)

Secular storyteller and popular professor Brené Brown says, "Empathy is the great antidote to shame." When we experience human empathy, we begin to heal through another's understanding of our difficulty.

Divine empathy from One we instinctively think would only judge us, offers soul-deep grace to heal our deepest shame. That's why the writer of Hebrews tells us Jesus can empathize with our weaknesses because He was tempted in every way we are—yet He did not sin.

Jesus experienced all the pressures upon His soul that this world can exert. Although none of these external threats to His holiness penetrated His spiritual armor, He now knows how threatened we are by them and what it takes to resist them.

Because Jesus understands what we go through, He's able to empathize. He's been there. So when He hears our cries for help, He really understands prayers about loneliness, suffering, cruelty, and abandonment. Not only does He hear, He responds as He has learned firsthand to strengthen, support, heal, and forgive.

Jesus knows our worst nightmares because He walked through this dark world. So He knows how to guide us, intercede for us, and provide the light for our plight. We go to Jesus because we know that, when no one else really understands, our God does!

PRAYER: *Jesus, thank You for becoming one of us so that You know what it means to be tempted. Thank You for assuring me that when no one else understands, I can know that You do. Because You empathize, I can endure.*

Our God whom we serve is able to deliver us from
the burning fiery furnace, and he will deliver us out
of your hand, O king. But if not, be it known to you,
O king, that we will not serve your gods. (Daniel 3:17–18)

Daniel's companions teach us what faith means by their confidence in God's *ultimate* rescue. These faithful men announced that God was able to deliver them from a pagan king's fiery furnace, but they also confessed their allegiance if He did not.

Their famous *"But if not..."* statement is their clear declaration that God is worthy of our worship and faith regardless of our circumstances. The young men knew that God had provided an eternal rescue that extended beyond this life and beyond a fiery trial. Even if they could not predict His present actions, they had faith in the eternal security He provides.

Don't let anyone convince you that trusting God means telling Him what He must do. We must declare our trust in God by entrusting our lives and our eternities to Him. We trust Him to be good to us and through us. That may mean delivering us from an immediate trial or giving us the strength to bear it.

Early in ministry, I visited a widow to provide pastoral care. She did more for me. Through tears she said, "I prayed for God either to heal my husband, or to give me the strength to bear his loss." Then, like a sunbeam after rain, a smile burst through her tears and she said, "And He did. God gave me the strength."

Her trust strengthened and informed my own—and maybe yours too. Trust the God of eternity for the grace you need today.

PRAYER: *Father, I know that You always have the power to deliver me. Help me to trust You to provide what is best for my eternal care regardless of present outcomes.*

220

For the moment all discipline seems painful rather than pleasant, but later it yields the peaceful fruit of righteousness to those who have been trained by it. (Hebrews 12:11)

When you take a turn off a highway and see a sign that says, "No Through Traffic," you don't think to yourself, *What cruel, hard-hearted person put that road sign there?* You feel thankful that somebody cared enough to instruct you that this road is a dead end!

The same is true with God. He doesn't just tell us what is right and then send us on our way with no more care for our wellbeing! God provides signs through His correction and discipline that get our attention. That's often how we know we've gotten off the path and are in spiritual danger.

God corrects us because He loves us and because His directions (and redirection) provide the way for our safety and care! God's discipline is never from "the ogre in the sky" who desires our harm, but from a Heavenly Father who is leading us from danger to "the peaceful fruit of righteousness."

When you recognize God's discipline, trust it to be an expression of fatherly care that would be absent without His grace. No discipline seems pleasant for the moment, but there would be no power in God's continuing spiritual care without it. His discipline never harms, even if it hurts, but always turns us from spiritual danger into His loving arms!

PRAYER: Lord, help me to walk in the righteous path You have laid and to believe Your warning signs and correction are for my spiritual safekeeping. Help me to believe Your discipline is always from a heart of fatherly love.

221

*When the goodness and loving kindness of God our
Savior appeared, he saved us, not because of works
done by us in righteousness, but according to his own
mercy, by the washing of regeneration and renewal
of the Holy Spirit, whom he poured out on us richly
through Jesus Christ our Savior. (Titus 3:4–6)*

Imagine the thief who died next to Jesus standing at the gate of Heaven. Also imagine some guardian at the gate asking the thief, "Why should I let you in?"

The only response the thief can give: "I got nothing. I lived a sinful life and died before I could do anything to make up for it."

"Yet," adds the thief, "the One who died next to me said, 'Today, you will be with me in Paradise.' I'm with Him."

The two claims of the thief are the only claims that will qualify anyone for Heaven: "I got nothing," and "I'm with Him." There is nothing we can do that will save us from our sin. Yet, Heaven is ours when we are with Jesus, uniting our souls to Him by faith in His provision.

God "saved us, not because of works done by us in righteousness, but according to His own mercy." He washes us from past sin, generating new life for us by His Spirit—even when we can't make up for our wrongs. So, whoever confesses, "I got nothing but Jesus" gets Heaven.

PRAYER: *Father, Your mercy for my messes is astonishing! Help me to count on Your loving kindness rather than my goodness when I stand before You in Heaven—or this day.*

222

He said to me, "My grace is sufficient for you, for my
power is made perfect in weakness." Therefore I will
boast all the more gladly of my weaknesses, so that
the power of Christ may rest upon me. (2 Corinthians 12:9)

Author Roy Atwood writes, "My father's illusions of independence and self-sufficiency were shattered" when he fell off the roof of his home while repairing the gutters during a rainstorm. Landing on the corner of a concrete sidewalk, he broke his spine. The fall almost killed him and in a split second, "his pride and dreams" were gone forever.

Atwood goes on to describe how his father's state of almost complete dependency turned his heart to Christ's sufficiency. The change was dramatic: anger was replaced with joy; bitterness by tenderness; and lifelong hardness with a gentleness of spirit.

Atwood concludes that his father's last years of physical weakness were his best, and the legacy that he will leave to his children's children will be of the transforming work of Jesus.

That transforming work always occurs when we come to the end of ourselves and discover the God of grace is waiting to heal our heart today and to prepare our soul for eternity where there is no more suffering or shame.

If you have come to the end of yourself, it's time to pray "that the power of Christ may rest upon me." Confess your weakness and Christ's transforming power will come upon you.

PRAYER: Lord, help me to embrace the sufficiency of Your grace when my inability overwhelms my spirit. Remind me that when I come to the end of myself, Jesus is there waiting to pardon and prepare me for eternity.

223

*This is his commandment, that we believe in
the name of his Son Jesus Christ and love one another,
just as he has commanded us. (1 John 3:23)*

God's eternal acceptance of us does not hinge on our ability to meet legal standards—divine or human. Does such grace mean we no longer have to concern ourselves with God's rules? No way.

Christians are compelled by God's love to honor Him as He desires. How do we express our love for God?

We love those that Jesus loves. Since Christians bear the name of Christ, we honor Him by loving His people—even the difficult and desperate ones.

John says those who believe in the name of Jesus love one another "as he has commanded us." The Apostle Paul echoes, "The whole law is fulfilled in one word: 'You shall love your neighbor as yourself'" (Galatians 5:14). These apostles echo Jesus, who taught that the greatest commandment is to love God, which requires that we love our neighbors as ourselves (Matthew 22:37–39).

We don't love others because they deserve it, but because Christ deserves our obedience. We don't gain God's love by obeying His commands, but we show our love for Him by obeying the commands that guide and guard all who are dear to Him.

Honoring Him is not simply about being right in religious understanding or practice; it is about being right in relationships. If you're not, He provides grace to forgive you and to help you love those He loves.

PRAYER: *Father, as I encounter others today, help me to share the love You have extended to me through grace I do not deserve. May I honor You by loving all whom Jesus loves.*

224

As each has received a gift, use it to serve one another, as good stewards of God's varied grace: whoever speaks, as one who speaks oracles of God; whoever serves, as one who serves by the strength that God supplies—in order that in everything God may be glorified through Jesus Christ. (1 Peter 4:10–11)

An old car wax commercial depicts a young woman preparing to sell her car. Aged and dull, the old vehicle no longer holds the allure it once had. Yet when the woman uses the "miracle" wax to put back the shine, the new gloss revives her affection for the car. She drives away, tossing the FOR SALE sign.

The commercial speaks to a deeper truth. We love what we invest in. When we labor with God's gifts to improve the security, maturity, and understanding of other people, we spread Christ's glory to them *and* they become more precious to us.

Bringing out the glory of Christ in others by the various gifts and graces He provides, helps them, and at the same time, seals our relationships with them. The result is greater glory to Jesus reflected in the love we share for those who needed our help.

Our churches, our families, our neighborhoods, fellowships, and the people in all of them become more precious to us as we invest in them, and Jesus shines brighter because we do.

PRAYER: *Lord, help me today to use the gifts You have given me to serve and bless others You love. May my investment not be begrudging but a way of making Your glory so evident in them that I delight to serve them to see more of Your glory.*

225

Therefore confess your sins to each other and pray for each other so that you may be healed. The prayer of a righteous person is powerful and effective. (James 5:16 NIV)

During America's Great Awakening, Pastor Jonathan Edwards gathered eight hundred men together to pray. During this meeting, a woman sent a message to the men, asking them to pray for her husband. The note described a man whose spiritual pride had made him unloving, prideful, and difficult to live with.

Edwards read the message aloud, hoping that the unidentified man would raise his hand to acknowledge his need and accept the prayers of the assembly. But when Edwards asked for the man whose spiritual pride had made him so unloving to raise his hand, three hundred men raised their hands.

When the Holy Spirit is active among us, He not only convicts our hearts of sin, but makes us willing to confess our sin to God and to one another. Such mutual confession encourages believers that they are not alone in their sin and not alone in fighting it.

God powerfully works among His people to heal and to accomplish His purposes when we are transparent about our need of Him and about our gratitude for His grace. In church communities where people find safety and acceptance for the confession of their sin to one another, pride withers, humility grows, and the Gospel spreads.

PRAYER: Lord, I confess that I sin against You daily in thought, word, and deed. If I believed I were alone in this, I would hide my faults from others, perhaps from myself, and even from You. Thank You for fellow Christians who help me grow in Your grace by confessing they need it, too.

Whoever would be great among you must be your servant,
and whoever would be first among you must be your slave,
even as the Son of Man came not to be served but to serve, and
to give his life as a ransom for many. (Matthew 20:26–28)

Many people unconsciously expect their church to serve them. The expectation shows with the checklist we bring to worship. We ask, "Did the pastor preach a sermon to my liking? Did the music suit my taste? Does the building have the right décor?"

Of course, we are right to be concerned that our church does what is right. The Bible tells us to be vigilant about God's priorities. But sometimes God's priorities get confused with our preferences. Whether we are expressing greater concerns about the latter than the former may take serious heart examination.

That examination, if it is biblical, often begins with asking whether we really are willing to follow Jesus by denying ourselves (Matthew 16:24). Are we more seeking to serve or to be served?

Of course, we are all ready to testify that we are willing to be a servant—until someone treats us like one. Then, we must ask if Jesus only calls us to an occasional act of service, or to a life of selflessness for the sake of others knowing Him.

The charge to put God's priorities above our own often can reduce our checklist to one item: Does this church help me serve Jesus better?

PRAYER: *Jesus, thank You for coming to serve rather than to be served. Help me to follow Your example by being willing to give my life in the service of helping others know You better.*

227

Let all bitterness and wrath and anger and clamor
and slander be put away from you, along with all malice.
Be kind to one another, tenderhearted, forgiving one another,
as God in Christ forgave you. (Ephesians 4:31–32)

The story made headlines in Christian media. In post-apartheid South Africa, a frail black woman stood in a courtroom in front of the man who had murdered her husband and son. The judge asked her, "What do you want?" Her answer stunned everyone.

She replied, "I want three things: To know where my husband's body is, so I can bury him properly. Then, I want the accused to become my son, so that he can visit me, and I can show him the love I have. Finally, I want him to come forward now so that I can I forgive him, as Jesus forgives."

That story could not be confirmed. Many suspected a hoax. Perhaps it was. But why did so many Christians embrace it so readily? Because we know the account, however suspect its details, accurately reflects Jesus's calling to love as He loves—to forgive as we have been forgiven.

Maybe the story serves best because we cannot pick its particulars apart. Instead, we must let the principles enter our heart, as from a modern parable, and consider how Christ's mercy should motivate us.

Who needs your forgiveness this day? I know that you and I will want to pick apart the particulars of why we need, or need not, show mercy. Still, our Lord has already declared what He wants: "Forgive as God in Christ forgave you."

> **PRAYER:** Lord, as I have received Your grace, please help me to extend mercy toward those who have hurt me. Help me to forgive as I have been loved by You. Nothing that You require is harder or clearer in Scripture—or more blessed in life.

228

*Now a Jew named Apollos, a native of Alexandria,
came to Ephesus. He was an eloquent man, competent
in the Scriptures.... He began to speak boldly
in the synagogue, but when Priscilla and Aquila heard
him, they took him aside and explained to him
the way of God more accurately. (Acts 18:24, 26)*

Soon after a young man professed faith in Jesus, he began preaching in a small church. He didn't know much about the Bible, people, or preaching, but he knew God wanted others to know Jesus. So, the young man prayed that God would do a "mighty work" in that little church.

Unfortunately, the church did not flourish. In fact, it closed. Grief over not reaching people in that community deepened the man's desire to minister effectively. So, freed of the daily obligations of running a church, the man pursued further training that taught him deeper truths of Scripture, how God's people grow in faith, and how to preach.

He is now one of the finest preachers in the country. God truly did a "mighty work" in that little church, humbling and preparing a man for God's work.

God answered prayer as He knew was best, placing a talented servant on a path to greater service. In God's graceful timing, He always answers faithful prayers as He knows is best.

PRAYER: Father, help me to remain faithful in my prayers with the confidence that You will answer in Your graceful timing as You know is best.

229

Jesus, looking at him, loved him, and said to him, "You lack one thing: go, sell all that you have and give to the poor, and you will have treasure in heaven; and come, follow me." Disheartened by the saying, he went away sorrowful, for he had great possessions. (Mark 10:21–22)

To love God with all our hearts we need to understand the barriers to such love in our hearts. We see one displayed in the story of the man who chose earthly wealth over a relationship with Jesus.

The young man's preoccupation with himself is revealed early in this account. He asks Jesus, "*Good* teacher, what must *I do* to inherit eternal life?" Jesus hears the assumption that one can *do* enough to qualify for Heaven and points down a different path.

"Only God is *good*," says Jesus. Sadly, the young man misses the point, and seconds later claims that he is as good as God, deserving an eternal inheritance.

All along, the goal of the man's devotion was the expansion of his own affluence—wealth on Earth *and* in Heaven. That's why he cannot engage in devotion that would threaten his bank account. His sin is not his wealth, but his assumption that God would owe him for his own extraordinary goodness.

The heart humbled by grace does not send God a bill for our goodness but devotes itself to the One who paid it all.

PRAYER: *Heavenly Father, help me to see the treasure of grace for which my merits could never pay so that I will live in gratitude for the salvation my Savior fully purchased. Make my devotion a response to grace, not a demand for it.*

The thief comes only to steal and kill and destroy.
I came that they may have life and have it abundantly.
I am the good shepherd. The good shepherd lays
down his life for the sheep. (John 10:10–11)

I had my head down, trudging along a jogging path while worrying about a church problem. Then, as I topped a hill, I suddenly found my head directly in the path of a low-flying and rapidly approaching goose.

I instinctively dodged right, but the goose ducked to his left, keeping our noggins on a collision course. Then, as people describe car-crash experiences, I felt everything go into slow motion. I watched the approaching goose tweak his tail, lift his leg, and twist his body so that he veered over my shoulder with outstretched wings grazing the top of my head.

Once I got over the shock of the near crash, I was amused by what had almost happened. "Man," I thought, "wouldn't that have been a way to leave this world. I can see the headlines now, 'Preacher Taken to Heaven by a Goose.'" I began to laugh out loud.

Then I realized what my Good Shepherd had done. Knowing that I had been near despair with worry, God had sent a migrating goose from hundreds of miles north to fly low over that hill at the very moment I would reach the top. Then, contemplation of God's amazing power and timing would so reassure me of His love that I could laugh in the midst of worry—and carry on with renewed faith.

We entrust our eternities and everyday lives to our Good Shepherd because Jesus came with perfect timing and love, laying down His life to prove He will protect our paths.

PRAYER: Jesus, because You are the Good Shepherd who cares for His sheep, help me to trust You for the eternal protection that You know is best to keep me walking (or jogging) Your paths.

*Do not worry about your life, what you will eat or drink;
or about your body, what you will wear.... Look at the
birds of the air; they do not sow or reap or store away in
barns, and yet your heavenly Father feeds them. Are you not
much more valuable than they? (Matthew 6:25–26 NIV)*

Don't worry, be happy. If a Caribbean singer with a big smile and a melodic voice sings the words, we smile.

But if the Creator who examines our hearts says, "Don't worry," then we worry. How can we not? We wonder what's around the corner to test our obedience to such a command. It's almost as if we're hardwired to do the very thing we're told not to do.

So how do we keep from anxious worry? One way is to imagine ourselves in the scene as Jesus teaches. He points to the flying birds that have God's provision despite how vulnerable they are.

Our eyes follow His gesture to look at the birds in the skies and we want to believe He has such care for us. But does He?

The answer comes as our eyes return to the One speaking. What is the greatest evidence of God's care for vulnerable creatures like us? He is!

The One sent from Heaven to tell us, "Do not worry about your life, what you will eat or drink..." is the One who assures us of God's care. If He came from beyond the skies to save us for eternity, we can trust Him for today.

So today—really—*don't worry!* Yes, make your plans and be responsible, but trust that the One who sent Jesus for your eternity will provide what is best for today.

PRAYER: Lord, help me to trust that You not only care for the birds of the air but also for me. Let the reality of Jesus on Earth bolster my heart for the realities of today so that worry does not lead me to despair in trial or doubt in You.

When Daniel knew that the document had been signed,
he went to his house where he had windows in his upper
chamber open toward Jerusalem. He got down on his
knees three times a day and prayed and gave thanks before
his God, as he had done previously. (Daniel 6:10)

The "document" was a death sentence for anyone praying to anyone other than Daniel's pagan king. Its signing was the bottom falling out of Daniel's life.

What do you do when the bottom falls out? Well, if it's a sack of groceries, the remedy is simple enough: you clean up the mess. But what happens when the bottom falls out of your life—your marriage, your finances, or your health? What do you do when you can't clean up the mess?

Believers are not insulated from life's crises, and the bottom can fall out for us too. Like everyone else, we can face crippling disappointments and disasters. We aren't in Heaven yet.

Daniel wasn't in Heaven yet, either. So, when the bottom fell out of his life, he fell to his knees in prayer. Daniel offered prayer and thanksgiving to God, seeking Him for needed help.

Perhaps that sounds too simple but, during crises, it can be easy to forget God. Don't forget. Before you send the text, write the email, or formulate the plans of your wisdom, pray to God for His. Depend on Him and He will delight to answer as He knows is best.

PRAYER: Father, I know that life in a fallen world is full of disappointments and disasters. But in difficult times, help me to remember You and to follow Daniel's example, coming to You in devoted and dependent prayer.

*Do you not know that the unrighteous shall not inherit
the kingdom of God? ... And such were some of you,
but you were washed, but you were sanctified, but you
were justified in the name of the Lord Jesus Christ and
in the Spirit of our God. (1 Corinthians 6:9, 11)*

At the Great Sand Dunes National Park in Colorado, the mountains of sand rise to more than seven hundred feet. The sight of the dunes is spectacular, and wonder surrounds their formation.

The sand forming the dunes is first blown through mountain passes, coating the lower dunes with what would seem only to be dirt. Then the Medano River running through the dunes washes tons of that dirt into lower mountain valleys. From there, mountain winds from a different direction pick up the sand and lift it even higher onto the dunes from which it came.

You would expect that water and wind would erode the dunes and whittle them down. But God uses the processes of washing and wind to build the dunes higher and higher! They become more and more glorious as God works through natural processes to make His handiwork spectacular.

We also are God's handiwork. God washes and whittles away our sins, cleansing our souls and sanctifying our lives. But the process does not lessen our significance; it builds us up into the glory He intends for our lives!

PRAYER: Father, thank You for washing away my guilt and whittling away the sins that beset me. As You lift me higher and higher toward Yourself, help me reflect Your glory by making Your handiwork apparent and appealing to others.

234

God raised us up with Christ and seated us with him in the heavenly realms in Christ Jesus, in order that in the coming ages he might show the incomparable riches of his grace, expressed in his kindness to us in Christ Jesus. (Ephesians 2:6–7 NIV)

At times, God uses language intended to shake believers by the shoulders so we face our new reality.

Here the Apostle Paul tells us that God has already raised us and seated us with Christ in Heaven. That hardly seems possible. My GPS indicates that I am still alive on this earth, seated at my desk in a building in a big city in the United States. How can I already be resurrected and seated in Heaven?

Paul speaks in such startling terms so we understand the certainties of God's grace. Our tendency is to base our identity on temporal realities—our locale, our sin, our shame. But present spatial dimensions or spiritual dynamics will not do.

Living on Earth now does not deny that I am a spiritual being with heavenly citizenship already assured by Christ. I am no more a citizen of Earth than I am a citizen of China when I temporarily visit there.

My permanent home provides my identity. So also my eternal citizenship is determined by my permanent residence in Heaven. There I already have a seat with Christ, a home with God, and a destiny of eternity.

Why does all that matter? Because neither present sin nor circumstances can undo my heavenly identity. My eternal residence marks my truest citizenship that this earthly sojourn cannot mar or remove. Jesus is mine and I am His forever!

PRAYER: Father, I'm grateful You have already seated me with Christ. Help me not to despair over temporal sin or circumstances but to be strengthened by eternal realities!

235

*I will instruct you and teach you in the way you should go;
I will counsel you with my eye upon you. Be not like a horse or
a mule, without understanding, which must be curbed with
bit and bridle, or it will not stay near you. (Psalm 32:8–9)*

The Bible encourages us to set goals, but if we attempt to better ourselves without seeking God's instruction, we forfeit the peace He intends and the accomplishments He enables.

When I was about to graduate college, I had my eye on goals whose sole purpose was my wealth and others' approval—my glory. I was a believer and knew these could not be God's only goals, but I wasn't sure of my alternatives.

Only when a spiritual father counseled me to deepen my study of Scripture did I rediscover the beauty and fulfillment of seeking God's glory above my own. The path was long, but in its steps I found the career, the family, and the purpose God had in view long before I saw the blessings.

God's eye of blessing and protection is on us whenever we seek His counsel rather than stubbornly holding to wayward paths of worldly priorities. The path of a gracious God is always best. When we are questioning our course, it's always better to be God-led rather than mule-headed.

PRAYER: Lord, keep me trusting Your path to goals that You have graciously prepared. On Your path are blessings long apparent to Your eye. When Your eye is on me and I am on Your path, then Your best for me is ahead of me.

236

It is God who arms me with strength and keeps my way secure.
He makes my feet like the feet of a deer;
he causes me to stand on the heights. (Psalm 18:32–33 NIV)

My family loves vacationing in the mountains of Colorado. There we have often visited a unique stone castle that has a winding staircase leading to a breathtaking but precarious mountaintop view.

When my sons were little, they would climb the stairs with me even though there were no banisters. At the lower levels, I would have to remind them to hold my hand, but as we ascended the stairs, the less reminding they needed. By the time we reached the top, I felt as though my hands were being crushed by two tiny vises! My sons realized that the greater the height, the greater the danger.

God wants to take you to the heights of His purposes, but not for you to be afraid. He assures that you are held firmly in the grasp of the One whose infinite strength rules the heights, even if you can't hold onto Him.

He will not let you go. So you can go wherever He leads, willingly and unafraid. No height He calls you to climb is too high for the King of Heaven to hold you safely!

PRAYER: *Father, as You lead me to greater heights in Christ, help me to go willingly and unafraid, knowing that You hold me—and will not let me go.*

237

One will scarcely die for a righteous person—
though perhaps for a good person one would dare
even to die—but God shows his love for us in that while
we were still sinners, Christ died for us. (Romans 5:7–8)

Messages that are *entirely* "be good," or "be like someone in the Bible," or "be more disciplined" sound biblical but torpedo the Gospel.

While there's nothing wrong with these messages *in* themselves, *by* themselves they're insufficient. They imply, "You just have to be good enough for God, or be better than other people, or be more disciplined than you were, and *then* God will love you."

Jesus says quite the opposite: "When you've done all you can do, you're still an unworthy servant" (Luke 17:10 Paraphrase). So how can we possibly have a relationship with God if we cannot earn it?

The Bible verse above explains the alternative to faith in our performance: "But God shows His love for us in that while we were still sinners, Christ died for us!" That's the good news of the Gospel. God doesn't base His love on what we do but on the grace provided by the sacrifice of His Son, Jesus Christ!

We are not commanded to *be good*, or *be like so-and-so*, or *be more disciplined* to gain God's love, but to respond to His grace by trusting Him and loving as He commands. Our deeds do not earn His love but show ours. Our faith is not in our goodness but in His grace.

PRAYER: Heavenly Father, thank You for loving me even when I was Your enemy. Help me to respond to Your grace with loving gratitude displayed in faithful obedience.

238

Open my eyes that I may see wonderful things in
your law. I am a stranger on earth; do not hide your
commands from me. My soul is consumed with longing
for your laws at all times. (Psalm 119:18–20 NIV)

I left for a long trip early one morning, driving east into a bright sun. I did not know the danger until I heard a truck but never saw it pass me. I had literally been blinded by the light. Overexposure to the sun had temporarily taken my vision.

Unfortunately, this can parallel the experience of some Christians as they read Scripture, attend worship services, and practice daily Christian disciplines. We get so much exposure to God's truth that we stop seeing or appreciating it.

What's the solution to being blinded by the light? The answer is *not* to start avoiding God's truth—it's imperative that we know God's good and safe path.

The answer lies in keeping our hearts sensitive to the wonders of God's heart evident among the truths to which we are being exposed.

If all we see are glaring commands, then we will ultimately look away from words that condemn us. But if we learn to see those commands as God's provision of a path of safety and blessing being extended to all who long for His help, then we begin to sense again the grace of God that first warmed our hearts to seek Him.

So when you consider Scripture today, allow God to show you if you are starting to go blind to the light of His Word. If you are, then pause to put on your Gospel glasses to read again with the eyes of your heart open to seeing the Light of the World all Scripture reveals.

That light is Jesus, and in His light we see the grace that keeps our hearts committed to Him on the journey He designs for us.

PRAYER: *Father, I ask You to open my eyes so that I may always see Your heart in Your Word and live in light of the truth Your care makes bright.*

239

*I want you to know, brothers, that what has happened to me
has really served to advance the Gospel, so that it has become
known throughout the whole imperial guard and to all
the rest that my imprisonment is for Christ. (Philippians 1:12–13)*

Kenneth Bae experienced God's faithfulness while imprisoned in North
Korea. Kenneth was traveling in that country when authorities uncovered an email message on his computer that spoke of praying with others for
more North Koreans to know Jesus.

Such prayer was against the law, and Kenneth was sentenced to a hard
labor camp. He became North Korea's longest-held American prisoner. His
health was not good and his deprivations were great. But he maintained his
testimony, which became a curiosity to his guards.

One asked, "If your God is so good, why are you here?"

Drawing encouragement from the Apostle Paul's testimony to Roman
guards, Kenneth replied, "If my God were not good, I would not be here to
tell you about Him."

Through the many hardships, Kenneth never lost sight of God's grace
and faithfulness. His imprisonment and his eventual release put his faith and
prayers before the world. As a result of his trials, Kenneth's original prayers for
more people to know Jesus were more powerfully and expansively answered
than he could ever have personally arranged or imagined.

> **PRAYER:** Lord, help me to trust that my trials can be used to
> advance the Gospel for my neighbors, loved ones, and per-
> secutors. You will never waste my trials. Help me to trust You
> through them for Jesus's sake.

240

When the fullness of time had come, God sent forth his Son
...to redeem those who were under the law,
so that we might receive adoption as sons. And because
you are sons, God has sent the Spirit of his Son into our
hearts, crying, "Abba! Father!" (Galatians 4:4–6)

Friends recently sent us a video of their daughter barreling down a hall and shouting as her father came through the door, "Daddy, you're home!" The inexpressible joy of this child was evident, but the family's back story was not. Feeling called to adopt a child, the parents found themselves in a nation where girls were not wanted, particularly those with physical disfigurements.

When the little girl's orphanage allowed an outing so these prospective parents could get to know her, glares and snide comments came from many passersby. The cruelties made the couple even more conscious of the child's needs and more convinced they wanted her.

Such love for the unloved expressed by these sweet parents came from the Gospel of grace written on their hearts. God has so loved us. When our souls were disfigured by sin that would seem to disqualify us from God's affection, He came to save us and to make us part of His family. Such grace should make us run to our Heavenly Father and delight in pleasing Him.

> **PRAYER:** *Father, You adopted me as Your child even though there was nothing beautiful in me. May your love for the unlovely cause me to delight in You and make evident to all the beauty of Your grace by how I also love others.*

Wives, submit to your own husbands, as to the Lord.
For the husband is the head of the wife even as Christ is the
head of the church, his body, and is himself its Savior.
Now as the church submits to Christ, so also wives should
submit in everything to their husbands. (Ephesians 5:22–24)

The Apostle Paul tells us that wives should submit to their husbands in "everything." But does that mean a wife should do whatever a husband wants regardless of whether it is moral, kind, or good?

The biblical answer is *no*! Each wife should submit to her own husband *as to the Lord.* The Lord never commands evil and never approves submitting to it. That means a wife is never obligated to do anything contrary to God's Word.

A wife submits to her husband *as the church submits to Christ.* That means wives remain spiritually responsible to order their lives for Christ's witness and worship. Being married does not negate a wife's primary obligation to honor God in *everything*.

Honoring God may actually require resisting a husband's desire to do what is evil, doing damage to a family, or being harmful to himself. That's because submitting one's desires and talents to the good of another does not require abandoning gifts but applying them selflessly for God's purposes.

So we don't use God's gifts to bless others because *they* deserve it but because God does!

> **PRAYER:** Lord, I know that submission to the spiritual needs of others is ultimately an act of worship. Even when it's hard, help me to honor You by conscientiously and selflessly using the gifts You have given to bless another for Jesus's sake.

242

You, therefore, have no excuse, you who pass judgment
on someone else, for at whatever point you judge another,
you are condemning yourself, because you who pass
judgment do the same things. (Romans 2:1 NIV)

A Christian businessman tells of a personal experience that transformed his understanding of the Gospel. He had an employee who was stealing from the company. Though the boss gave the employee opportunity to change, the man just kept on stealing.

At his wit's end, the businessman sought out his pastor for guidance. But the more the boss described the man who kept sinning despite the grace offered him, the more the boss recognized he was describing his own habitual sin.

Through the experience, the businessman experienced the Gospel at a level beyond Sunday school courtesies. He realized how much he desperately needed God's grace, and how generous was the heart that offered it.

Of course, stealing has to stop, but we are best equipped to deal with such sin when we understand how God has dealt with our sin. He disciplines when He must, but never without the goal of reaching the heart and redeeming the person.

PRAYER: *Lord, I know that I am more ready to judge others than to face my own sin. Help me not to forget the grace that is Your goal as I deal properly with the sin of others by remembering how You have dealt with mine.*

243

*I saw in the night visions, and behold, with the clouds
of heaven there came one like a son of man,
and he came to the Ancient of Days and was
presented before him. And to him was given dominion
and glory and a kingdom. (Daniel 7:13–14)*

In the book of Daniel, the precision of the ancient prophet's predictions about the temporary triumphs of evil across the world are astounding and, at times, hard. Daniel's visions twist in wild gyrations, describing the realities of a broken world.

He predicts that, for centuries, the enemies of God will have their day, the honor of God will go away, the people of God will suffer, and all of it without apparent purpose. So how do we deal with such hard realities of our sinful world?

We respond in faith by recognizing that nothing surprises God. God saw it all coming, and He did not give up on our world or on us.

Evil may have its day, but God will have the final say. He knows the measure of evil, but He also knows its end. Christ will have "dominion and glory and a kingdom" over all. That is what He ultimately revealed to Daniel and what Daniel revealed to us.

God has the final authority, and there is none greater than He. Because of God's powerful and resolute grace, restoration is possible, renewal is promised, and redemption is our certain future!

> **PRAYER:** Lord, I am as troubled as Daniel that life in a broken world sometimes doesn't make sense. Help me to trust that the troubles are temporary, and evil will not triumph. As You ruled the past, so also You determine the future that I may live in the present with confidence of Your final grace.

244

*Consider the lilies of the field, how they grow: they
neither toil nor spin, yet I tell you, even Solomon in all
his glory was not arrayed like one of these. But if God
so clothes the grass of the field, which today is alive and
tomorrow is thrown into the oven, will he not much more
clothe you, O you of little faith? (Matthew 6:28–30)*

In His Sermon on the Mount, Jesus directs us to faith by observing God's
care of the natural world.

On another mountain a botanist introduced my family to a vast array
of wildflowers. Then he took out a jeweler's glass to show us the details of
individual flowers. Under magnification, we could observe the intricate engineering and amazing design of each flower down to the cellular level.

Each flower marvelously represented the hand of the Creator. We had
admired the beauty that we could naturally see; now we marveled even more
at the engineering and art the jeweler's glass revealed.

Then the botanist directed our gaze to the surrounding mountains and
said, "The hand that designed each flower's cells also made these great mountains and every molecule of every rock."

It was hard to take it all in, but we got the message: To take even a small
glimpse into God's amazing care for His creation is to marvel at the hand that
created us and carries us through His intricate design for our lives. Such a
hand can be treasured and trusted, especially since it sent Jesus to tell us about
the heart behind the hand.

> **PRAYER:** Lord, thank You that the wisdom that engineers the
> lilies and mountains guides the hand that provides for me. And
> thank You that the hand that received the nails for me reveals
> the heart that can be trusted to design what is best for me.

God chose what is weak in the world to shame the strong; God
chose what is low and despised in the world, even things that are
not, to bring to nothing things that are, so that no human being
might boast in the presence of God. (1 Corinthians 1:27–29)

We marvel at world-class musicians, actors, and athletes. These superstar achievers receive constant media attention and high-paying salaries that are not available to ordinary humans of lesser talent and ability.

We understand the acclaim and reward such high achievers receive, but the reverberations of our society's performance worship can deeply affect our own hearts.

If we begin to estimate our worth based on how well we (or others) think we perform in our jobs, classrooms, or relationships, then we will begin to believe that we are loved well only if we *do* well. This is simply not the message of the Gospel.

Yes, God honors and treasures our obedience, but it's not the *reason* He cares for us. God cares for us because of what Jesus did for us and Jesus's claim upon us.

We are precious to Him regardless of our performance. That's why we desire to serve Him with devotion that is deaf to any other evaluation.

So serve God with peace of mind and strength of heart, knowing that Jesus's performance, not yours, has already determined the treasure you are to God!

> **PRAYER:** *Father, I know that You do not accept me because of my performance but rather because of what Jesus has done on the cross to claim me. Help me always to treasure His provision as He always treasures me!*

246

Stand firm in the one Spirit, striving together as one
for the faith of the Gospel without being frightened
in any way by those who oppose you. This is a sign to
them that they will be destroyed, but that you will be
saved—and that by God. (Philippians 1:27–28 NIV)

In the book of Philippians, the Apostle Paul shares his deep affection for the believers in Philippi. They must wonder what good is his love for them, or theirs for him, as he languishes in prison.

Paul answers by assuring them that they further his witness as they stand firm against opposition without fear of those who oppose them. The absence of fear does not remove the dangers but testifies to faith in a greater God. In this way, the far-distant Philippians join Paul in his witness of God's care.

How comforting to know that the Spirit uses our unity as believers to transcend time, geography, and circumstances, releasing us from the physical limitations of life for spiritual testimony.

In God's plan, Paul ministers across nations and ages from an ancient prison cell, and we join in his ministry when we do not fear opposition to our witness.

Our fearlessness shows confidence in God's eternal care to people across town and across generations. In this way the solidarity of believers in Christ makes Jesus known to the world!

PRAYER: *Heavenly Father, help me to live beyond fear so that I may join with fellow believers in sharing Christ's message by my evident confidence in Your eternal care.*

247

Whoever would be great among you must be your servant,
and whoever would be first among you must be your slave,
even as the Son of Man came not to be served but to serve, and
to give His life as a ransom for many. (Matthew 20:26–28)

When Columbia Bible College President Robertson McQuilkin told people of his decision to resign so he could care for his Alzheimers-stricken wife, he was startled by the responses he received.

It was a mystery to him why people reacted with overwhelming appreciation. His own oncologist explained: "It is not rare for women to give themselves for suffering husbands; but few men do the same for their wives."

The reason McQuilkin's decision made him a spiritual leader for people across the world is that his actions reflected the very heart of the Gospel. His goal was to serve, rather than be served.

McQuilkin willingly made himself a "slave" to the needs of a loved one, and in doing so freed himself from the grip of self-interests to promote the wellbeing of another and the witness of his Savior.

We lead for Christ most clearly and most effectively when we follow Christ in the selflessness He modeled for us.

PRAYER: *Lord, help me to follow Your example each day by a willingness to serve others for their wellbeing, for Your witness, and for my own growth in understanding Your grace.*

248

For from his fullness we have all received, grace upon grace. For the law was given through Moses; grace and truth came through Jesus Christ. (John 1:16–17)

Where are you on the grace-and-truth spectrum? Some people are all about God's grace and ignore the truth of the Bible. Others major on the truth of God's expectations and have little patience for strugglers. Yet the Scriptures tell us that grace and truth can't be separated.

The Apostle John writes that grace and truth came through Jesus Christ. And Jesus said, "If you love me, you will obey what I command" (John 14:15).

So, being under the Gospel of grace does not make obedience to God's truth optional. When God removes good works as a condition for His acceptance, He does not remove righteousness as a requirement for living. That's because the truth of Scripture reveals laws for life that glorify God while guarding His people from harm.

God warns us not to use His unconditional love as an excuse for selfish indulgence. That's not because He is an eternal killjoy who doesn't want us to have any fun. To the contrary, He wants us to have the delights of life His grace designed.

Grace revealed the law designed by His love to guide us, and grace releases us from the guilt of failing its standards. But grace would not be grace if it freed us from sin's guilt and sent us into sin's harm.

By Moses's law we learn the guidance of God and the guilt of our sin. By Christ's grace we are loved beyond our sin, but never allowed to deny the truth of God's law or sin's consequence.

PRAYER: *Heavenly Father, may both the grace and truth of Jesus Christ be seen in my life as I seek to serve You today.*

249

*We are God's masterpiece. He has created us anew
in Christ Jesus, so we can do the good things he
planned for us long ago. (Ephesians 2:10 NLT)*

While at a local fair, I received a call from my son. He told me he had gone to share the Gospel in Ferguson, Missouri, where racial injustice had just resulted in a man's death.

My first impulse was to say, "What are you thinking? Get out of there." But my son spoke before I could voice my objection, saying, "I will not let hatred stop me from showing Christ to my neighbor."

My son knows he's a product of our family's genetics, nurture, and environment, but he also believes that he has been created by God for Christ's purposes. My child is God's workmanship, a product of divine intention and craft, designed in eternity for God's eternal purposes.

Such a perspective makes me gasp to consider the responsibility I have in raising God's child, and it makes me bow to God's purposes for him. Of course, I am not the first parent to question whether it's good for me if my child serves Christ on the mission filed, in charitable endeavors, or on the streets of Ferguson—or Bangladesh or Afghanistan. Still, I need to remember Christ has dibs on his life.

I'm not talking about being cavalier or irresponsible about life choices; I am affirming that God loves my children more than I do. He fulfills their hearts' desires by engaging them in His designs. I want my children to be happy. So does Jesus. That's why He calls them to fulfill their creation purpose.

PRAYER: *Heavenly Father, help me to remember that I and my loved ones are Your workmanship, created in Christ Jesus to do good works that You prepared long in advance for us.*

250

*Now I, Nebuchadnezzar, praise and extol and honor the King
of heaven, for all his works are right and his ways are just;
and those who walk in pride he is able to humble. (Daniel 4:37)*

As a pastor, I wrestle with trying to convince people of how sure is God's promise of grace to those who ask for forgiveness. Some have been helped by simply considering the life of Nebuchadnezzar. He was the murderous, arrogant, and idolatrous king of Babylon who enslaved God's people. Yet God claimed his heart.

As long as the king paraded his greatness, looking down on everyone else, he was a pathetic mess before God. But once he looked up to God, confessing his lowliness of heart and mind, the Lord restored him.

You may wonder if God could or should forgive someone like you. But if God would restore a person as awful as Nebuchadnezzar, then He can restore you.

Nothing can stand between us and the grace of God. Once we confess our utter need of Him, His ultimate love for us is sure. His gracious provision for the lowly is deep and wide. When we confess that our sin has brought us low, God's lifts our hearts and restores our purpose!

PRAYER: *Father, I confess that I am weak, sinful, and lowly. Thank You for Your merciful pardon of the messes I have made, and for lifting the load of sin from me as I look to You.*

251

*Now the Lord is the Spirit, and where the Spirit of the Lord
is, there is freedom. And we all, with unveiled face, beholding
the glory of the Lord, are being transformed into the same
image from one degree of glory to another. For this comes
from the Lord who is the Spirit. (2 Corinthians3:17–18)*

We live in a spiritually deceptive world that constantly seeks to trap us in
paths and patterns that keep us away from the blessings God intends.
So God in His grace came to set us free from dead ends and awaken us to a
better life and a truer reality, where lasting love and significance are assured.

Already we have the glorious blessing of our sin being covered by God's
grace, which grants us His holiness. But that is not our final glory. As the
Holy Spirit indwells our hearts, He uses God's Word to transform us more
and more into Christ's likeness.

The affections, priorities, and ambitions of Jesus, our Savior, increasingly
become ours. We live more for the Father, delighting more in His love. Our
hearts beat in rhythm with His, and His joys become ours.

There is wondrous glory in the life of every newborn child, but there is
greater glory when that life is lived selflessly, heroically, and in full expression
of God's gifts. So also the glory of our new birth is transformed into even
greater glory as the Spirit matures us into Christ's likeness.

We are never loved more by God than when we are born again, but His
love becomes even more glorious as we mature by yielding to His Spirit.

PRAYER: Heavenly Father, thank You for the glory of my new
birth. Now groom me for greater glory by making my heart
sensitive and submissive to the Word of the Holy Spirit.

252

My mouth will tell of your righteous acts, of your deeds
of salvation all the day, for their number is past my
knowledge. With the mighty deeds of the Lord GOD I will
come; I will remind them of your righteousness, yours
alone. O God, from my youth you have taught me,
and I still proclaim your wondrous deeds. (Psalm 71:15–17)

Some time ago, Jim Orders, a senior board member of our school for pastors, was diagnosed with a deadly cancer. When I visited him, he smiled and spoke with a trust in God's plan that had matured over a lifetime of faith. He said, "I always wondered how the Father would take me home. Now I know."

In his last days, Jim had a final task he strove to complete. He wrote the history of his family and business as a way of celebrating the grace he had experienced. He longed to leave a legacy of faith for those he loved so they might also have deep confidence in Jesus, no matter what life brought.

This is always the desire of faithful parents, pastors, friends, and neighbors. Our joy increases as we see others share it. Our confidence in God grows as we witness others growing in faith. Our sense of purpose deepens as we see God deepen our faith in new generations of believers.

Your joy also will increase as your witness spreads. You don't need to wait until you are dying to experience such joy. The One who rose from the dead will walk with you and work through you as you tell loved ones His wondrous deeds. So, tell!

> **PRAYER:** Lord, help me to remember all the wonderful things You have done in my life. Then please give me opportunities and a loving heart to share my joy with those who need You.

253

*Whatever was written in former days was written
for our instruction, that through endurance
and through the encouragement of the Scriptures
we might have hope. (Romans 15:4)*

As Christians, we lean on God's promise that He will work all things together for our ultimate good (Romans 8:28). But how do we know that promise is real, and how does it reach deep into our hearts, banishing all fear and doubt?

The Apostle Paul reminds us that everything in the Bible is painting a picture of God's purpose through time, trials, and triumphs that culminates in the saving work of Jesus.

When we see how comprehensive is God's plan, how resolute His love, and how eternal His purpose, then we are encouraged despite present trials and enabled to endure them. God is working all for good; He's proven it over and over—especially at the cross.

Scripture's grand design helps rescue us from debilitating worry and anxiety as we face the troubles of a fallen world. Since nothing on Earth can separate us from His eternal love, we persevere in God's grace until His purposes for us and our world are fulfilled!

PRAYER: *Heavenly Father, I am so thankful that my life both now and forever is in Your hands. Help that wonderful truth to banish my fears and doubts, and to build the encouragement and endurance needed for every trial!*

Since we are surrounded by so great a cloud of witnesses,
let us also lay aside every weight, and sin which
clings so closely, and let us run with endurance the
race that is set before us, looking to Jesus, the founder
and perfecter of our faith. (Hebrews 12:1–2)

When I saw my son's energy wane during his cross-country meets, I'd shout encouragement from the crowd to revive his resolve and keep his focus on the goal. I could have voiced threats or showed my frustration, but I knew such things would eventually sap his strength—even if they might momentarily spur him on.

God, who is a better father than I am, ensures that His grace-filled encouragement rings powerfully, lovingly, and *continually* through the witnesses that testify to His grace throughout Scripture. There the heroes are spurred on by His faithfulness and supported by His mercy, even when they falter.

As we press toward the goal that God has laid out for us, the Bible's cloud of witnesses surrounds us and supports us so that we constantly gain confidence of God's grace for our race.

The course may be steep and long, but His witnesses keep us strong with encouragement: He is with you, as He has been with us. He will never leave or forsake you. So run hard and run strong.

> **PRAYER:** My Father, thank You giving me a cloud of witnesses as I run the race of the Christian life. May their assurance of Your abiding care give me strength and endurance to finish the course You have set for me.

255

*So, being affectionately desirous of you, we were ready to share
with you not only the Gospel of God but also our own selves,
because you had become very dear to us. (1 Thessalonians 2:8)*

What does it mean to "do life" with God's people? The Apostle Paul
explained when he wrote to the church in Thessalonica. He reminded
them that he was ready to share not only the Gospel but himself.

When we "do life" with people, we seek to know them in deeper ways, to
pray for needs, to forgive flaws, to share understanding of God's Word, and to
support in times of pain and joy. We weep with those who weep and rejoice
with those who rejoice.

By sharing our lives as well as our words, we help others sense the difference the Gospel has made in our hearts, and we grow in grace by seeing the
same in them—especially in the sensitive situations. When we become dear
to one another, we recognize and honor how precious each is to God.

We put our youngest daughter to bed every night with the words, "You
are precious to us." As she got older, she thought she didn't need to be treated
as a child so she waved off the phrase one night—until we left her room. Then,
she called us back in tears. "You didn't say it," she cried.

So we said it again, and say it to this day, knowing that it is as important
to share our hearts as to share our words in order to show God's heart to all
His loved ones.

> PRAYER: Lord, help me to share the Gospel not only in the
> words I say, but also in the life I share with those around me.

256

In my Father's house are many rooms. If it were not so, would I have told you that I go to prepare a place for you? And if I go and prepare a place for you, I will come again and will take you to myself, that where I am you may be also. (John 14:2–3)

When my youngest daughter went off to college, she was determined to be brave. So she did nothing but smile and chatter as we took her clothes and boxes to her dorm. Even as we were getting into the car to drive away, her face showed only sunshine.

When I went to give her a final hug, I first held her at arm's length and looked her in the eye. I told her what my father had told me many years ago, "No matter what happens here, you are my precious child, and nothing will change that. Our home is always your home."

That did it. The smile vanished, her face flushed, and she hugged me hard, crying and saying, "Oh, Daddy, that's not fair!" To which I replied, "Of course, it's not *fair*. It's grace!"

PRAYER: *Heavenly Father, thank You for making me Your child by the work of Christ, and for the promise that my performance will never lessen Your love. I will always have a place in Your heart and in Heaven prepared by Christ for me.*

257

Let your adorning be the hidden person of the heart with the imperishable beauty of a gentle and quiet spirit, which in God's sight is very precious. For this is how the holy women who hoped in God used to adorn themselves. (1 Peter 3:4–5)

How strange—and significant—that the impulsive, quick-tempered, and pushy Apostle Peter would advise seeking to win a spouse to faith in Christ by "a gentle and quiet spirit."

The apostle's words remind us that God bestowed great dignity, value, and spiritual power on women who reflect the heart of their Savior. The world teaches that those who exert the most pressure from the highest position have the most influence; the Gospel teaches that hearts are most influenced by us when Christ's character is most evident in us.

Peter addresses women whose husbands are not believers. Such wives may think that verbal pressuring, emotional manipulation, or reasoned demands are best to convince a man to change—for his own good. The apostle, who had been such a hothead, instead urges holiness with trust in God.

Peter knew that showing Christ to others is far more effective than shoving Jesus on them. The more we try to leverage change, the less our spouses feel loved. The more we treat a spouse with respect—providing a gentle word, a non-combative spirit, and a beauty of heart—the more the Jesus in us is attractive.

A woman who would win her husband to Jesus is wiser in seeking to display her Savior than to control her husband. Show Jesus and let the Spirit sway the man.

PRAYER: Lord, help me to show my Savior and be willing to have Your Spirit sway my loved one. Work through my humility and holiness to reach my spouse.

*I prayed to the LORD my God and made confession,
saying, "O Lord, the great and awesome God, who keeps
covenant and steadfast love with those who love him
and keep his commandments, we have sinned and done
wrong and acted wickedly and rebelled, turning aside
from your commandments and rules." (Daniel 9:4–5)*

Flipping through a family photo album, a rebellious son called his mother to him and pointed in sadness to a picture of himself as a small child. "Mom, in this picture I can see such hope in your eyes as you look at me. But I have dashed all your hopes. I know that's why you can no longer love me."

The wayward son had so often protested his innocence or minimized his guilt that his mother doubted her son could ever turn from his destructive paths. And it was true, his selfish rebellion had hardened her heart. But when he confessed his guilt, her hardness towards her child broke. She embraced him with the hope and the heart that was depicted in the photo taken so long ago.

Once again, she offered her love and help to her difficult child. She had not been moved by a denial of wrongdoing, but by a confession of desperation.

The Bible tells us this is also what moves God's heart on our behalf. His embrace is most evident not when we trumpet our goodness or deny our sin, but when we call out in desperation for His forgiveness. Our Heavenly Father's love and help are always available when we confess our need of His grace!

> PRAYER: *Father, I know that I have sinned against You in my words and actions. I ask You now for forgiveness and help not because I deserve them but out of my desperation. Nothing I can do will make up for my sin. I trust Jesus will.*

259

I cried out to him with my mouth; his praise was on
my tongue. If I had cherished sin in my heart, the Lord
would not have listened; but God has surely listened
and has heard my prayer. (Psalm 66:17–19 NIV)

If we want our prayers to be answered, we must be concerned to do God's will, because God will never contradict His purposes. The psalmist writes, "If I had cherished sin in my heart, the Lord would not have listened."

God does not answer prayers that undermine what's best for our souls. If we ask God to make our lives pleasant while pursuing sin, His granting our request would only damage our souls.

God does not turn a deaf ear to sinners' prayers, rather He listens with sovereign sensitivity to the priorities and affections behind our requests. He is not punishing our sin by His silence but guiding our hearts to His by depriving us of our own selfishness.

Out of His fatherly care, God's Word and Spirit convict our hearts of sin, reveal self-deception, and renew our appreciation for fellowship with Him.

If we are paying attention to the way God responds to our prayers, we will understand the misery of selfishness, the goodness of God, and the privilege of praying to One who only listens to prayers that will shower His grace upon us.

PRAYER: *Father, make the desires of my heart Your own.*
Help me not to ask You to bless or ignore my sin, but to lead
my heart in Your paths by how You respond to my prayers.

260

*Wives, be subject to your own husbands, so that even if
some do not obey the word, they may be won without
a word by the conduct of their wives, when they see
your respectful and pure conduct. (1 Peter 3:1–2)*

After becoming a Christian, Heather had faithfully committed to living for her Lord despite the indifference of her husband, James.

As a hardened police captain, he wanted nothing to do with her faith and often mocked it. Still, she honored and loved him for more than thirty years.

I once asked her what kept her living sacrificially for her husband when his gruffness and mockery were so painful. She simply said when she became a Christian, she fell in love with Jesus. That love made her *want* what Jesus wanted for her husband.

Being subject to a spouse as the Bible requires is never mousy meekness that demeans a woman. The Bible intends courageous, faithful, wise, and persistent living for Heaven's purposes. Such living refuses to cling to bitterness or selfishness, but yields and wields every gift and resource that God provides for the sake of another's soul.

Such yielding and wielding are living the Gospel message with respectful and pure conduct, even when human reasoning and rewards seem far off.

When thirty years of acting like a gruff billy goat did not drive his wife away from her faith or from him, James turned to her God. He had seen the worst of the world in his profession and wanted the realities of another world he had seen in his faithful wife.

PRAYER: *Father, please enable me to live a respectful and pure life in front of my spouse and others, so that they can see the changes Jesus has made in me and be drawn to Him.*

261

God shows his love for us in that while we were
still sinners, Christ died for us. (Romans 5:8)

Our human instinct is to believe we have to become a better person for God to accept us—that we have to achieve a certain level of holiness before we can have a relationship with God.

Common experience teaches, "Measure up! You have to hit the mark before you get my heart. Achievement before acceptance!" The Gospel of Jesus Christ is gloriously and graciously different!

God shows His love for us in that Jesus sacrificed Himself for us before we measured up, hit the mark, or achieved anything—while we were still sinners! Jesus invites us to come to Him even though He knows everything about us—the good and the bad. He knows our sin, and loves us still.

To come to Him as He desires, we resist the instinct that says, "He won't accept me until I get good enough." That would deny how good He is and would keep us from ever coming to Him.

Instead, we believe that Jesus really wants us to come to Him acknowledging our sin rather than trumpeting our achievements—in meekness, confessing we have missed the mark.

We don't need to wait until some future day of better resolve. We can run to the rescue that is ours today as we trust the Savior of sinners to love us before we become saints—to embrace the messed-up before we have cleaned up.

> **PRAYER:** *God, I can hardly believe that You love and accept me despite my sins. So help me to believe. I come to You now, confessing that I don't deserve to come but that Jesus gave Himself for me while I was still a sinner. Forgive me and help me live and love as You desire to honor Jesus's grace for me.*

262

*In your hearts honor Christ the Lord as holy, always being
prepared to make a defense to anyone who asks you for a
reason for the hope that is in you; yet do it with gentleness
and respect, having a good conscience, so that, when
you are slandered, those who revile your good behavior
in Christ may be put to shame. (1 Peter 3:15–16)*

For about three years, Betty had been witnessing to a neighbor, giving as gentle and respectful a defense as she could muster for her hope in Jesus. Though the neighbor belonged to a cult, the two women remained on friendly terms as each tried to tell the other about the *true* meaning of faith.

Then, for reasons Betty could not discern, the relationship took a bad turn. The neighbor got angry about the placement of some flowers along Betty's fence, then refused to continue their conversations and complained to other neighbors about Betty.

The two didn't speak for six months. Then one day, the neighbor showed up at Betty's door without warning. She told Betty, "I wasn't really upset about flowers, but about what I was beginning to see about God's grace in the way you explained the Bible!"

Later Betty told us through grateful tears, "I have always understood the work of the Father and of the Son, but now I understand how the Holy Spirit works through His Word."

Praise God that we are not dependent on our wisdom to share God's love but have the blessing of the Holy Spirit working by and with the Word He gives us to reach the hearts of loved ones.

> **PRAYER:** Lord, help me to share the Gospel with those around
> me with gentleness and respect, trusting that Your Holy Spirit
> is at work with the power and truth of Your Word.

263

Let us not grow weary of doing good, for in due season
we will reap, if we do not give up. So then, as we have
opportunity, let us do good to everyone, and especially
to those who are of the household of faith. (Galatians 6:9–10)

Christians can be so fickle. Sometimes we reason that because others do not love the Lord, we don't have to be kind to them. We become like those cult members who think it's okay to take advantage of us in airports because we aren't honoring their god.

Other times we use social media or simple gossip to rage at believers we think are not living up to our God's standards of thought or behavior. We rationalize our rage with excuses about others being undeserving of our kindness or respect.

The Apostle Paul declaws all arguments for acting with thoughtless disregard for anyone's soul. He, who makes the strongest arguments for correct doctrine, nonetheless urges doing good toward all—especially those in the household of faith.

Never would Paul argue that we should be unconcerned about thoughts or deeds that dishonor God. Yet, because he wants others to love God, the apostle reminds us that the Gospel is powerfully made known by expressions of goodness foreign to our character apart from the work of grace in us.

Always the Spirit urges us to act on behalf of others, to show the love of Jesus Christ to every person—in ways small and great. As we do good to all, we honor our Savior and show the priorities of His Kingdom to our world. That's our mission!

PRAYER: *Father, as I have the opportunity today to show the realities of Christ's grace, enable me to do good to all, especially those in the household of faith.*

264

*He said to me, "My grace is sufficient for you, for my
power is made perfect in weakness." Therefore I will boast
all the more gladly of my weaknesses, so that the power
of Christ may rest upon me. (2 Corinthians 12:9)*

Years ago, at my graduation from seminary, God revealed His grace in a way
that initially frightened me. As I looked down the line of friends graduating into ministry, I had a shocking realization. Every one of my friends had been through a major life challenge while in seminary. I, too, had suffered deep heartache.

In that moment, I thought to myself, "Someone has tried to stop us from ministering for Christ."

I have continued to witness the opposition of Satan against my friends and me in every life stage and every place of ministry. His relentless attacks have revealed our weaknesses time and again.

But they have revealed something else: the strength of God in and beyond our weakness. Those that have humbly sought God's aid, honor, and forgiveness have been powerfully used to accomplish what no one could have done in his own strength.

God has poured His goodness through our weaknesses to show that the surpassing greatness of His power is all of grace. Through Christ's mercy rather than our merits, marriages have been healed, churches built, leaders restored, and souls saved for Heaven forever.

None of us can take credit for these spiritual transformations. All we can say is, "Praise God." Our weaknesses have made His power evident to us, if to no one else. The grace we have received makes our confidence in the Gospel all the more sure. Our weaknesses prove His strength.

PRAYER: *Lord, pour mercy through humility, making the power of Your grace more evident by the confession of my weakness that You have overcome—and blessed!*

265

*For his sake I have suffered the loss of all things and
count them as rubbish, in order that I may gain Christ
and be found in him, not having a righteousness of my
own that comes from the law, but that which comes
through faith in Christ. (Philippians 3:8–9)*

When God looks at us, he does not value us based on our talents and accomplishments. Since our best works are tainted by our human imperfections and pride, any thought that God's love would be based on our deserving it will always be countered by God's infinite holiness.

For this reason, the Apostle Paul counts as rubbish whatever good works he had once counted to his credit for God's acceptance. Paul now has faith that God looks at him through the lens of what Jesus perfectly accomplished on the cross—not through the lens of human performance.

An old example reminds us that when you look at something white through a red lens, it looks red. But when you look at something red through a red lens, it looks white.

Similarly, when we try to hold up our works as pure to God, He observes them through the lens of the cross as bloodstained. But when we confess that our sins required the blood of Jesus, God looks at our scarlet stains through the lens of the blood of Christ, and they look as white as the wool of a lamb.

The example is ancient, but we need the truth every day and eternally. When we trust that Jesus's blood covers our sins, then we need not count on our rubbish to provide for our redemption. Trust that, though your sins be as scarlet, Christ's blood will make them white as snow. His grace will cover you.

PRAYER: Lord, thank You for covering my sin with Christ's blood. May Your lens of grace be the source of my hope and the lens through which I learn to see others' need, too!

266

Now to the one who works, his wages are not counted
as a gift but as his due. And to the one who does not
work but believes in him who justifies the ungodly,
his faith is counted as righteousness. (Romans 4:4–5)

I heard an old tale about a man who died and faced the Angel Gabriel at Heaven's gates. Gabriel told him, "In order to get inside you need one hundred points, so tell me all the good things you've done."

Assured of his qualifications, the man excitedly recounted his accomplishments: He never cheated on his wife, he attended church, he supported missionaries, and he helped the needy. "Fantastic," Gabriel responded. "You have five points!"

Upon hearing this, the man cried aloud in desperation, "What? At this rate, the only way I'll get into Heaven is by the grace of God!"

Then Gabriel welcomed him inside.

The man had discovered that we can't stand before God because of anything but belief in the One who justifies the ungodly!

Our faith in the grace provided through Christ is our great and sure hope. To all who confess their need of Him, the King of Heaven says, "Come in."

> **PRAYER:** Lord, I look forward to the day I'll be with You in the joys of Heaven. Thank You that my qualification is not by anything I have done, but solely through faith in the grace You have provided! I have no hope of Heaven but Jesus. Please help me live the thanksgiving He deserves.

*Resist the devil, and he will flee from you. Draw near
to God, and he will draw near to you. (James 4:7–8)*

I have seen the wall where the ink left its stain. A spattered shadow still appears where Martin Luther is said to have thrown his inkwell at the devil's appearance. The story is famous for its dramatic features and important because of its representation of spiritual warfare.

Luther wasn't running from God or pursuing an evil path when he felt most assaulted by Satan. The spiritual attack came while Luther was translating the New Testament into the language of his people.

After enduring great personal sacrifice and engaging in efforts that would change the face of the Western world, Luther's faith was severely tested. His experience should teach us we are never immune to spiritual assault—not even when we are immersed in noble spiritual endeavors.

Thus, we must resist the devil, not only by doing important things for God, but by drawing near to Him. Great men and women of God often receive their greatest spiritual challenge when engaged in their most important spiritual work. The key to our spiritual safety is not the greatness of our endeavor but the nearness of our God.

Our temptation is to be fulfilled by doing a great work for God, but He first desires a great heart for God. We want the achievements; God wants our hearts.

PRAYER: *Father, help me to recognize and resist the attacks of the evil one. Let me not substitute the importance of doing work for You with the necessity of drawing near to You.*

268

He said to me, "My grace is sufficient for you, for my power is made perfect in weakness." Therefore I will boast all the more gladly of my weaknesses, so that the power of Christ may rest upon me.... For when I am weak, then I am strong. (2 Corinthians 12:9–10)

Perhaps the first children's song we learned was "Jesus Loves Me." The song teaches us about Jesus *and* about ourselves: "Little ones to Him belong; they are weak but He is strong." We may get too old for the song's tune, but should not mature beyond its truth.

Even the Apostle Paul did not outgrow the confession of his weaknesses. If that seems humiliating, then we have not fully grasped the blessings of Jesus's love.

Our Savior delights to show Himself strong in behalf of those who confess their need of Him. When we acknowledge that our sins and our trials are beyond our resources, then we are signaling for our Savior to rescue us with His.

Our grownup tendency is to trust our abilities. Childlike faith that trusts Jesus's love and power, confesses, "Jesus, I need Your help." Then, the same Jesus that loves the little children responds, "My grace is sufficient for you, for my power is made perfect in weakness."

PRAYER: *Father, thank You for promising sufficient grace. Help me rely on my Savior's strength more than mine by a willingness to boast of my weaknesses that require His rescue.*

269

Depart from me, all you workers of evil, for the LORD has heard the sound of my weeping. The LORD has heard my plea; the LORD accepts my prayer. (Psalm 6:8–9)

When I was pursuing graduate studies at a secular college, I discovered how dangerous Christian commitments can be. Before the approval of my final project, a professor on my examining committee said that he would block my graduation because I had written that the Bible had dependable truth for today.

I was devastated. I had sacrificed thousands of dollars, thousands of hours, and tons of family focus for this degree. So I doubled down on all my efforts to counter the professor's opposition. I made calls, wrote memos, tried to get the man off my committee, and pleaded for understanding from university officials. None of the frenetic activity was working.

Only when I came to the end of my solutions did I recognize that I had not really, humbly prayed.

Convicted of my willingness to depend on my resources rather than my God, I did finally ask His help. He mercifully answered by having a senior professor that no one would challenge decide to support me.

We are such silly creatures at times. We depend on human slingshots to fight for ourselves when Heaven's artillery is locked and loaded to accomplish Christ's victories for us.

A battle may still be necessary, and the victory may not be in our ability or timing, but prayer is the signal for God's artillery to bless as He knows is best.

PRAYER: *Lord, help me to turn to You more than my resources for the help I need. Remind me that prayer is Your distant artillery for every Christian in a battle for You.*

The LORD answered Moses, "Go out in front of the people. Take with you some of the elders of Israel and take in your hand the staff with which you struck the Nile, and go. I will stand there before you by the rock at Horeb. Strike the rock, and water will come out of it for the people to drink." (Exodus 17:5–6)

Many of us remember Bible stories as they were presented in Sunday School. I recall the picture in my children's Bible depicting what happened after Moses struck the rock to bring forth water in the wilderness. The illustration showed a little stream flowing gently into a pool for few surrounding children and sheep.

But when we realize that this water had to supply more than a million people and millions of animals, we know that children's Bible picture was far from adequate. The stream was a torrent of water needed for the masses of people and herds God blessed.

The torrent understanding is needed not just for explaining God's greatness, but also His grace. God provided the river of blessing for people who were fearful, complaining, and rebelling. God had every right to turn off the spigot of His blessing; instead, He opened the floodgate—and He would do it again, when the people and Moses sinned worse.

If you think God will only provide streams of mercy from thimbles of grace for a few worthy creatures, come to Him with millions of other sinners and bring a big bucket to get all the mercy you need!

> **PRAYER:** *Father, thank You for sending Jesus to provide a river of mercy for millions of sinners like me—and me! Help me to believe and rejoice that You have enough grace to fill my bucket of need.*

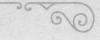

My son, do not despise the LORD's discipline or be weary of his reproof, for the LORD reproves him whom he loves, as a father the son in whom he delights. (Proverbs 3:11–12)

A father who delighted in his son was genuinely surprised at an act of foolish rebellion. As was the habit of that family in that era, the disobedience resulted in a trip to the bathroom for a few whacks of mom's hairbrush to "the seat of education."

The son's reaction to the punishment also surprised the father. The child shook with spasms of tears, expressing far more pain than the controlled discipline could have inflicted.

The father said, "Son, why are you so upset? You have never reacted this way before. Did I hurt you more than I intended?"

"No, Dad," the child replied. "But always before, you left the bathroom door open. This time you shut it and in the mirror on the door I could see the pain in your face as you disciplined me. I did not know how much I hurt you until I saw your face."

So also our God takes no delight in our discipline, but because He delights in us, He will act to protect us from the harm of unchecked sin. How much our sin hurts Him was revealed at the cross.

PRAYER: *Father, no child enjoys discipline—including me! Help me to realize and receive Your discipline as an act of love intended to turn me from harm and to help me grow to maturity in Christ's blessings.*

*As far as the east is from the west, so far does he
remove our transgressions from us. As a father shows
compassion to his children, so the LORD shows compassion
to those who fear him. For he knows our frame;
he remembers that we are dust. (Psalm 103:12–14 NIV)*

Driving through the flat fields of our area, we often have an unobstructed view from one horizon to its opposite.

When our children were small, we would encourage them to look one direction out our car windows, and then scan the horizon all the way to other side of the car. Then we would say, "That's how far God has removed our sins from us."

The perspective that keeps us adults from fully appreciating that wideness of God's mercy is one obstructed by our own sin. We imagine the heavenly expanse blocked by a God looking down on us with arms crossed and frowning face.

That's why the Bible not only tells us about how distant God makes our sin, but how open are His arms to draw us near.

Our Maker remembers we are creatures of dust, needing His compassion, and He shares it as readily as a compassionate father embracing a child in need!

PRAYER: Lord, help me remember Your love removes my sins as far as the east is from the west, and You have fatherly compassion for all who confess they need such grace.

273

Do not conform to the pattern of this world, but be transformed by the renewing of your mind. Then you will be able to test and approve what God's will is—his good, pleasing and perfect will. (Romans 12:2 NIV)

Maybe you're like me. I was raised in a Christian home, but in my teens, my parents' marriage was in crisis, and I retreated to my room most nights to escape the tensions and stress.

So when I went off to college, and even when I began ministry, I didn't have good perspectives on marriage or relationships of any kind. I lived in a protective shell, cool and aloof. I limited any expression of love or emotion, protecting myself from pain while actually wanting love and connection.

When the Lord first brought, Kathy, my future wife, into my life, I was sure that I could help her grow in spiritual understanding. I now praise God that He used her to teach me far more of His grace for battered souls like mine.

Kathy loved me past my aloofness, forgave my pride, and allowed me to grow in tenderness. Had she not expressed grace better than I can explain it, I shudder to think of the father, pastor, or man that I would have become.

God's transformation occurs when our minds are renewed by understanding how good, pleasing, and perfect is His will. His Word reveals that will; our relationships also have the power to make it real. Teaching and showing grace to one another breaks the patterns of the world and renews hearts for Jesus.

PRAYER: *Heavenly Father, continue to transform my heart and mind by the Word and work of Your Holy Spirit, so that I can know Your good, pleasing, and perfect will.*

274

The Sovereign Lord *is my strength; he makes my feet like the feet of a deer, he enables me to tread on the heights. (Habakkuk 3:19* NIV*)*

Driving through Colorado mountains on a vacation, my family discovered how easy it is to mistake an *up* for a *down*.

Winding through an extremely difficult mountain pass where stony peaks arced away from the car at steep angles, it seemed as though the towering rock enveloping us was forcing us downward.

Yet, despite our visual sensations, the struggling noise of the car engine indicated we were in fact on an incline. Only by looking in the rearview mirror could we compensate for the optical illusion and see that we were really climbing higher.

In a similar way, when faced with God's discipline or the world's difficulties, we may feel as though we're being brought down, but as we look back over the path the Lord has enabled us to tread, we'll see He was actually taking us to spiritual heights.

The journey may be steep and hard, but God only works to lead us higher and closer to His heart.

PRAYER: *Sovereign Lord, You are my strength. Enable me today to walk through the valleys of this life and to the spiritual heights that are closest to Your heart.*

These words that I command you today shall be on your heart. You shall teach them diligently to your children, and shall talk of them when you sit in your house, and when you walk by the way, and when you lie down, and when you rise. (Deuteronomy 6:6–7)

As parents, we all make mistakes. My wife, Kathy, and I have made our fair share. We can recall times of improper discipline, impatience, and poor judgment that we hope God will erase from our kids' memories. But even if they remember, we won't despair.

As Scripture describes the day-in, day-out patterns of biblical parenting, we are blessed by the realization that our patterns are more critical than a particular mistake. Momentary errors will not wreck our children's souls. Otherwise, conscientious parents could become paralyzed, fearing to do *anything* with the concern that *something* might ruin our children.

God's grace not only pardons our sin, it provides the instruction that fallible parents need to establish home and life patterns that are more influential than any particular error resulting from temporary fatigue or an overwhelming day!

Our gracious Heavenly Father gives us second chances *and* long patterns to enable us to steer children in His ways! We may take an occasional wrong turn, but the road is long and forgiving. Praise God, and don't give up on yourself or His map for the long journey of parenting.

PRAYER: *Father, I know that I make mistakes, but I thank You for always forgiving me in Christ. Please help me to trust Your unconditional love and follow Your patient plan as I raise children to know You.*

276

This light momentary affliction is preparing for us an eternal weight of glory beyond all comparison. (2 Corinthians 4:17)

When a child is born, the precious new life is cause for rejoicing that we all sense and share.

But imagine that someone tried to dampen our joy by saying, "I'm sorry. This child has a very fair complexion and is likely to be burned by the sun or chapped by the wind in days to come."

The parents would respond, "The wonder of this new life and the joys our child will experience in years to come far outweigh such temporary afflictions. We will not let our joy be lessened by what will soon pass."

In this same way, Christians rejoice in the wonder of our new life in Christ and the glory that we will experience in the life to come. The eternal joys that are ours (pardon of sin, restoration of bodies, reunion with loved ones, life with Jesus) far outweigh our very real, but still temporary, afflictions.

No matter how difficult your present reality is, don't let it blind you to the eternal realities whose glory far outweighs your temporary afflictions.

PRAYER: Father, I rejoice that You saved me from sin and also made me Your child to receive eternal blessings. While I live on Earth, help me to focus more on the eternal glories that await me than the temporary afflictions that weigh on me.

277

*Are not two sparrows sold for a penny? And not one them will
fall to the ground apart from your Father. But even the hairs
of your head are all numbered. Fear not, therefore; you are
of more value than many sparrows. (Matthew 10:29–31)*

Church forefathers captured the essence of Christ's assurance with this
question and answer:

Question: What is your only comfort in life and death?

Answer: "That I am not my own but belong with body and soul, both
in life and in death, to my faithful Savior Jesus Christ. He has fully paid for
all my sins with His precious blood and has set me free from all the power
of the devil. He also preserves me in such a way that, without the will of my
Heavenly Father, not a hair can fall from my head; indeed, all this must work
together for my salvation. Therefore, by His Holy Spirit, He also assures me
of eternal life, and makes me heartily willing and ready to live for Him."

The One who cares for the sparrows gave His life for you. You are worth
more than many sparrows and can count on His eternal care. When it's hard
to believe that, still believe. This truth will be your abiding comfort in life and
in death—and forever! Believe it and rest easy.

PRAYER: Lord, help me to live for my Savior, not with a spirit
of fear, but with the certainty that not even a hair can fall
from my head without the will of my Heavenly Father.

In him we have redemption through his blood, the forgiveness of our trespasses, according to the riches of his grace, which he lavished upon us. (Ephesians 1:7–8)

What does it take for a marathon runner to power through the final miles? Grit ... determination ... willpower ... *oxygen*!

To take in adequate oxygen in those final miles, even the fittest runners open their mouths. Of course, they don't think that by opening their mouths they're going to manufacture oxygen. No amount of human effort could do that! Instead, the runners open their mouths to take in what is *already* surrounding them.

In the same way, we shouldn't read our Bible or pray or worship God with the expectation that we're going to manufacture God's grace for us. His free, unconditional, unlimited grace has already been fully provided by the work of Jesus.

When we read God's Word, pray, and worship, we are relishing the grace that's already been provided for us so that the joy of the Lord would be our strength (Nehemiah 8:10).

We are not manufacturing grace by our performance of these Christian disciplines. We are practicing these disciplines because we rejoice in the grace they reveal and are strengthened by the joy they promote.

So, use every means of grace to breathe in deeply the beauty of God's grace that every verse and every prayer and every true act of worship celebrates!

Ready, set, breathe! Breathe in the goodness of God by using His Word, worship, and prayer to fill up your heart with celebration of the grace that is His free gift for your forever joy.

PRAYER: *Heavenly Father, thank You for the grace that You lavishly supply through Jesus Christ. Help me this day to use every means of grace You provide to breathe in the goodness of Your care so that Your joy would be my strength.*

And Jesus answered them, "Have faith in God. Truly, I say to you, whoever says to this mountain, 'Be taken up and thrown into the sea,' and does not doubt in his heart but believes that what he says will come to pass, it will be done for him ... whatever you ask in prayer, believe that you have received it, and it will be yours." (Mark 11:22–24)

D o you know how to win baseball's World Series? Decades ago, when the New York Mets were the surprise champions, the team's young pitchers told the secret: *You gotta believe!*

In almost every championship series since, people take up that same slogan for their favorite team.

Belief, it seems, is the magic potion to get what you want. Unfortunately, this superstitious notion of "believing" gets transferred to spiritual matters without spiritual priorities. For example, we can begin to think of prayer as a way of persuading God to give us the trinkets and treasures we desire as long as we "believe" enough that we will get them.

This genie-in-the-bottle approach to prayer misses the words that began Jesus's teaching: "Have faith in God." Our belief is in God, not in the urgency of our desires or the degree of our belief. Our faith is in His wisdom, not ours; His plans, not ours; His fatherly care, not our childish understanding.

Biblical prayer surrenders control to God, believing that He is already ahead of us, sovereignly responding to our prayers better than we can imagine. We offer meager desires to God, believing the One who made the mountains will move Heaven and Earth to bless those who have faith in His greater grace.

PRAYER: *Heavenly Father, help me to trust that the One who made the mountains will move Heaven and Earth to bless me, so that I will pour out my heart's desires to You in faith.*

*Your word is a lamp to my feet and a light to my
path. I have sworn an oath and confirmed it,
to keep your righteous rules. (Psalm 119:105–106)*

With an ascent that approaches fourteen thousand feet, Horn Peak is one of my favorite hikes in the Colorado Rockies. But on one sunny day, as our group reached the tree line, clouds rolled over the mountain. The peak was still visible and I had hiked the trail before, so I wasn't concerned. But I should have been.

As we climbed back down from the peak, dense fog enveloped us, hiding the trees and rocks we used to navigate our course. Without a familiar path to follow, we lost our way, came to a sheer drop off, retraced our steps up the mountain, and had to descend through increasing fog, then rain, then snow, then darkness.

As daylight waned and we prepared to spend a desperately cold night on the mountain without shelter, we wandered across a well-worn trail. God had graciously provided a path in the remaining light for our rescue!

Similarly, when we have been endangered by wandering from God in spiritual darkness, He provides for our rescue. Not only does His grace alone keep us from a fall into Hell, but it also marks for us a path of safety and blessing by the law that shines His love on our path through this life.

PRAYER: Lord, may Your Word be a lamp unto my feet and a light for my path as I seek to follow You in the ways You have graciously designed and revealed for my life's blessing.

281

*All the paths of the LORD are steadfast love
and faithfulness, for those who keep his covenant
and his testimonies. (Psalm 25:10)*

In our national parks and forests, trails are designed to maintain the safety of the hikers, bikers, and campers. Similarly, the principles of God's law establish the safe path for God's people through all of life.

So, taking such a path should not be something we dread but something we desire in order to experience God's guidance and safekeeping.

Still, our spiritual safety requires that we remember staying on the path never earns us God's grace. If God were not already gracious to us, the path would never have been laid.

The path of God's law is an expression of God's constant care. That's why the psalmist could sing to God, "Oh how I love your law! It is my meditation all the day" (Psalm 119:97).

Rejecting God's good and safe path is not a walk into a carefree life, but foolish wandering from His steadfast love and abiding care.

Today, walk in the safe and good path God graciously provides, and you'll discover more and more of the character and care of God!

> **PRAYER:** Heavenly Father, Your Word lights the path that enables me to discover the greatest blessings You intend for my life. Please provide the grace I need today to walk this path with confidence in the love and care of the One who laid it.

282

Be imitators of God, as beloved children. (Ephesians 5:1)

Before my wife and I really understood the Gospel of grace, we would discipline our children the way we heard others discipline their kids. I would say to my son, "Colin, you're a bad boy because you disobeyed."

Such words were so common in our upbringing that we didn't grasp their flaw. We were teaching our children that *who* they were was based on *what* they did—that because they did a bad thing, they were bad. We based their *who* on their *do*. That's not the Gospel!

The good news Jesus came to share is that our identity is not determined by our behaviors but by the relationship His grace alone secures. We don't imitate God to become beloved; we imitate Him as *already* beloved children.

To reflect this Gospel in parenting, I had to learn to say, "Colin, don't disobey, because *you are my son*, and I love you!" I wanted him to know in every way possible that our deeds do not determine our identity; our identity motivates our deeds!

We do not obey God to gain His love, but to offer thanks for the grace that granted it. Grace prompts the gratitude of joyous devotion.

Today honor the One who loves you, not because of what you do, but because you are His. Love Him with the devotion of the child that you are by His grace alone. Such devotion will be your joy, not because it earns anything for you, but because Jesus gave everything for you.

> **PRAYER:** *Heavenly Father, thank You for making me Your child through the grace of Jesus Christ alone. Help me so to treasure this identity that my life reverberates with works of thanksgiving that honor You and demonstrate the depth of my affection for You.*

Wives, submit to your husbands, as is fitting in the Lord. Husbands, love your wives, and do not be harsh with them. Children, obey your parents in everything, for this pleases the Lord. Fathers, do not provoke your children, lest they become discouraged. (Colossians 3:18–21)

The Bible has a lot to say about how husbands and wives are to love each other *before* it speaks to how we should parent. The implicit message is: a healthy marriage is the foundation of biblical parenting.

A healthy marriage supplies the spiritual support that each parent needs to provide the nurture and discipline a child needs. A wife doesn't fail to discipline because she's needing a child to supply the love her husband won't. A husband doesn't over overdiscipline to prove he is the man his wife will not acknowledge.

If the marriage is as God intended, neither parent feels solely responsible or to blame for difficult decisions. If the two are really one before God, then there is a united front in dealing with a child's rebellion, depression, or faith struggle.

Biblical marriages are the sacred soil in which God matures healthy children. We cultivate such marriages to honor the Lord, knowing He intends to use godly unions to bless us and our children.

This doesn't mean that a less-than-ideal marriage cannot produce godly children. No marriage is perfect, and God provides grace for all kinds of homes. But if you are wondering what is the best gift that you can give your children for their long-term health of mind and heart, the biblical answer is: love your spouse as God loves you.

PRAYER: *Heavenly Father, help me to love my spouse as You have loved me, and use our support of one another to be a firm foundation for the spiritual nurture of our children.*

284

*The Spirit helps us in our weakness. For we do not know
what to pray for as we ought, but the Spirit himself intercedes
for us with groanings too deep for words. (Romans 8:26)*

In the classic play *Cyrano de Bergerac*, a young man named Christian tries to court a beauty named Roxane. Christian doesn't have the words to profess his love, but Cyrano does.

Standing in the shadows beneath Roxane's window, Cyrano prompts the young suitor with lavish prose that softens Roxane's heart for the young man. The words are powerful and ring true, not only because they are beautifully formed but because they come from Cyrano's own deep love for Roxane.

Cyrano speaks not only with greater eloquence than Christian can muster, but with greater fervor than the younger suitor's heart can actually feel.

While the parallels are not exact, Cyrano's story relates the dynamics of divine intercession. Though we may not know all the right words to say to God, another speaks for us—the Holy Spirit. And He does not merely correct the content for our prayers, but the fervor. With groanings deeper than we can feel, He makes heartfelt petitions to God for us.

So even when you don't know what or how to pray—pray, trusting the Holy Spirit to intercede with the petitions and the heart you need.

PRAYER: *Lord, even though I don't always know what or how to pray, keep me coming to the God I love by trusting the Holy Spirit to intercede for me!*

285

*You yourselves like living stones are being built up as a
spiritual house, to be a holy priesthood, to offer spiritual
sacrifices acceptable to God through Jesus Christ. (1 Peter 2:5)*

When construction began on a new development in our community, the builder placed a large fence around the property. He wouldn't allow anything inside the gate *except* what would advance the building of those new homes.

In a similar way, God puts a construction fence around our lives and allows nothing to enter except what will develop us more into the likeness of Jesus.

This fence of God's care is one of the Christian's greatest comforts. It assures us that nothing enters our lives except that which is for our ultimate good. The fence of God's care doesn't signal that everything will be easy or finished all at once, but it does mean that whatever we encounter inside the fence will have a purpose in the plan of the Architect.

So, remember, Christians are not perfect, but under construction. We have been fenced about with God's love so that we can be built up according to His perfect plan, and nothing enters our lives except what will be used to make us more like Christ in holiness and service to God!

PRAYER: *Lord, whatever I face today, help me to remember that it would not have come if it did not have a purpose in Your design for my life. Help me to respond with the faith that nothing can enter my life that does not help me better to understand and reflect my Savior.*

> *You felt a godly grief, so that you suffered no loss through us. For godly grief produces a repentance that leads to salvation without regret. (2 Corinthians 7:9–10)*

When we grieve for our wrongdoing, we are experiencing the conviction that our sins have hurt the heart of God. No one should want to feel such pain, but God uses it to assure us of the Holy Spirit's presence in our lives.

If the Holy Spirit were not in our hearts, then we would not grieve that our sin grieves our God (Ephesians 4:30). The heart not indwelt by the Holy Spirit is hostile to God and cannot feel true conviction for sin (Romans 8:7).

It is certainly possible to feel the guilt of having been caught or the shame of failing loved ones without being a true Christian. However, it is impossible to experience sorrow for grieving our Heavenly Father without believing that our sins have betrayed the One who loves us. Such conviction is entirely and only by the work of the Holy Spirit.

So, strange as it may sound, godly grief is confirmation of God's Spirit in our hearts. We need not despair that our sin has forever separated us from God when our godly sorrow is the absolute proof of His continuing presence.

The conviction that confirms God is still with us gives us fresh incentive to love and serve Him. In fact, the Spirit uses your godly sorrow to grant confidence that He has not rejected you in order to encourage your prayers of repentance.

Conviction of sin is the assurance of the Holy Spirit's indwelling that makes us willing to confess sin and want to please Him again!

PRAYER: Father, thank You for the confirming work of the Holy Spirit! May He convict my conscience to assure me that I am Yours and to lead me to the blessings of repentance.

You were dead in the trespasses and sins in which you once walked.... But God, being rich in mercy, because of the great love with which he loved us, even when we were dead in our trespasses, made us alive together with Christ. (Ephesians 2:1–2, 4–5)

Long ago, there lived a king who looked out from his palace window to see his young child gathering flowers for a royal bouquet. But the child did not only gather flowers. Because he was a child, he collected weeds as well.

To help his laboring child, the king tasked his eldest son with a mission: to go and remove the weeds from his younger sibling's bouquet and replace them with flowers gathered from his own garden.

The older son did just as his father instructed. Soon the beaming younger child approached his father's throne to present the beautiful bouquet to the king. "Here, my father," he said, "are the flowers I have prepared for you."

Only later would the younger child understand that his bouquet had been made acceptable by the gracious provision of his father, who had sent the older brother to make it right.

In a similar way, our Heavenly Father provided Christ (our elder brother) to turn our works into acceptable gifts for God. Christ's righteousness has been substituted for our flawed and weedy works by the gracious provision of our Heavenly Father!

That's not simply a truth to claim at the end of life as we approach God's throne room, but rather is a grace to claim every day as we celebrate Christ's provision that makes us acceptable to God.

> **PRAYER:** *Father, thank You for making the bouquets of my works acceptable to You by the work of Jesus—not just at the end of my life, but every day of my life. May His gracious provision for my flawed flowers make me all the more desirous of bringing more to glorify You this day and every day.*

Elisha prayed and said, "O LORD, please open his eyes that he may see." So the LORD opened the eyes of the young man, and he saw, and behold, the mountain was full of horses and chariots of fire all around Elisha. (2 Kings 6:17)

When our children were small, we sometimes worried about their safety on the stairs of our home. The long staircase offered no landing to ease the danger of its steep slope. But the more we worried, the more the kids seemed attracted to the stairs—our youngest daughter especially.

Normally, we would scold the toddler for heading up the stairs alone, but one time, she was trying so hard that I didn't have the heart to stop her. Instead, I followed close behind with my hands ready to catch her.

When she reached the top, she was so proud of her accomplishment that she raised her hands in triumph. If she had been a rooster, she would have crowed.

She did not realize that her success and safety were secured by hands other than her own. Likewise, as much as we may think our accomplishments are all our doing, God is actually holding us in His hands, and directing the hosts of Heaven to keep us secure for His purposes.

PRAYER: Father, when my trials or my pride threaten to overwhelm my spirit, help me to remember the heavenly hosts that guard my soul and also Your hands that secure me more than I ever fully realize on Earth.

*In this is love, not that we have loved God but that he loved us
and sent his Son to be the propitiation for our sins. Beloved, if God
so loved us, we also ought to love one another. (1 John 4:10–11)*

I think it's fair to say that many people honor God out of mere duty—or because they dread His anger. How many times have you heard someone say they did something wrong, and now they're waiting for the proverbial bolt of lightning to strike?

Yet God wants the prime motivation of His children to be very different! That's why His greatest commandment is for you to love the Lord, your God, with all your heart, soul, and mind (Matthew 22:37–8).

That love relationship changes everything in our Christian walk. God's love assures us that His rules are for our benefit, not the arbitrary commands of an eternal killjoy.

When we truly understand God's heart of grace through the revelation of Jesus Christ's sacrifice that turned God's wrath from our sin (as a propitiation), then we never fear His condemnation. Instead, we're drawn into a relationship that's filled with love.

That love causes us to obey God not out of fearful dread or slavish fear, but out of a childlike love and willing heart. Our greatest delight is delighting Him. A heart of gratitude (rather than desire to gain material rewards or to avoid an ogre in the sky) becomes the supreme motivation and power of those who grasp how great is God's love for us.

What communicates that love? Jesus. As we gaze upon His cross and marvel at His provision for sinners like us, we live to love Him. That was the plan from the beginning. So live to love Him, and love living for Him!

PRAYER: Father, thank You for loving me so much that You sent Your Son as a propitiation to pay the penalty for my sins. May I respond to Your love by loving to live for You.

Now that you have been set free from sin and have become
slaves of God, the benefit you reap leads to holiness, and the
result is eternal life. For the wages of sin is death, but the gift
of God is eternal life in Christ Jesus our Lord. (Romans 6:22–23)

A mother of teens was arranging the evening's snacks in the church youth room when she glanced at the white board. There a lesson on "grace" was outlined. Then, with a firmness that betrayed a hint of anger, she turned to the youth pastor and said, "My children don't need more grace. They need more rules."

Now, the mother's words might sound unkind, but the pastor understood her concern. He knew she was a godly woman who was truly worried for her kids—and other kids in the church. We are right to be concerned about a faith without boundaries.

Whenever we broadcast that God's unconditional love has provided an escape from sin, fears arise that teens and adults alike will abuse God's kindness. But grace frees us from the enslavement of sin, not the guidance of God.

Hearts captured by grace are enslaved to God's heart with a loving compulsion to honor Him (2 Corinthians 5:14–15). Grace frees us *from* sin not *to* sin.

Faith without standards is folly, not grace. We cannot please the One we love if we don't know what pleases Him. There is no grace to experience if there is no way to respond in love to the One who gave Himself for us.

PRAYER: Lord, thank You for the gift of eternal life! Help me to use my freedom from the guilt and power of sin to demonstrate love for my Savior that gives my life its most profound joy.

291

The prayer of a righteous person has great power as it is working.
Elijah was a man with a nature like ours, and he prayed fervently
that it might not rain, and for three years and six months it did
not rain on the earth. Then he prayed again, and heaven gave rain,
and the earth bore its fruit. (James 5:16–18)

God doesn't need our prayers to fulfill His purposes. But for reasons that aren't entirely clear to us, He promotes His glory and our significance by using our prayers to advance His Kingdom. The Bible says, "The prayer of a righteous person has great power."

That promise is not just for spiritual giants like the prophet Elijah. The Bible says, "He was a man with a nature like ours," assuring us that we can pray with as much authority and effect as he did.

Much as an old-fashioned steam engine uses coal to power a train, God uses our prayers to empower the engine of divine transformation. Of course He could transform our world without our prayers, just as He could make trains run without natural resources. But He has not chosen to operate that way.

So that we would treasure our role in God's plan, He reveals that He uses our prayers to work all things together for good—even when we don't know how to pray (Romans 8:26–28).

How it all works I cannot fully understand, but if our meager petitions fuel God's divine engine, then let's keep "shoveling coal" by praying. The destination and timetable are always subject to God's wisdom, but His power is in our prayers. So get on board and pray!

> **PRAYER:** Lord, help me to follow Elijah's example by praying fervently that Your will would be done, so that my prayers would be an instrument of Your blessings for many.

I will make them and the places all around my hill a
blessing, and I will send down the showers in their season;
they shall be showers of blessing. (Ezekiel 34:26)

Have you ever considered how strange it is that you can keep your balance in the shower when shampooing your hair?

Think about it. There you are with eyes closed, standing without support, your hands flailing through your hair while you shake your head like a rock star. Yet despite the frenzied gyrations, you keep your balance. What keeps you from falling? The water from the shower nozzle tapping you on the shoulder keeps you oriented.

Similarly, the blessings of God gently shower over our lives to keep us spiritually oriented and in balance for His calling.

When we are experiencing trials, there is never total absence of blessings. So we praise God for the good we can see, as well as the grace we cannot yet see.

It may be good to remember the example of Bible commentator Matthew Henry. A man once stole his wallet. Henry's response: "I am thankful he never robbed me before; that he took my wallet and not my life; although he took all I had, it was not much; and, I am glad that it was I who was robbed and not I who did the robbing."

Awareness of the constant stream of grace that flows over us keeps us steady for God's service.

> **PRAYER:** Heavenly Father, You have poured down showers of blessing in my life. May the good I can see prepare me for the grace I cannot yet see as You orient me toward Your purposes.

*Love is patient and kind.... It does not insist on
its own way.... It does not rejoice at wrongdoing,
but rejoices with the truth. (1 Corinthians 13:4–6)*

Early in our marriage, my wife, Kathy, and I agreed not to belittle one another in public, even though it was a common way our friends joked.

Our agreement came after noticing how often these friends would use the protection of a public gathering to make embarrassing comments about a spouse's habits, flaws, or foibles.

Now don't get me wrong, Kathy and I enjoy teasing one another, but we have learned that trying to correct or manipulate one another through public embarrassment, even in jest, isn't helpful. Demeaning another for the sake of getting a laugh or gaining control is not a path to marital health.

Scripture is clear that we're to exercise love and mutual respect toward our spouses. Our marriages should be places of mutual support—where we are secure enough to enjoy a tease and loving enough not to use it to mask manipulation.

Mutual respect builds marriages. Teasing can make them fun. But public embarrassment, where the one teased cannot respond or defend without further embarrassment, is unfair.

God's grace flows through marriages where love does not seek its own way, does not rejoice in another's discomfort, and teases for mutual fun, not to embarrass anyone.

PRAYER: Father, help me to express love and honor in the way I speak to and about my spouse. Help me to build up another in love as You knit us together by Your grace.

I am sure that neither death nor life, nor angels nor rulers, nor things present nor things to come, nor powers, nor height nor depth, nor anything else in all creation, will be able to separate us from the love of God in Christ Jesus our Lord. (Romans 8:38–39)

God knows our assurance of His love *can* be shaken. So in one of the most sophisticated New Testament books, God has the Apostle Paul pause and return to simple themes at the heart of the Gospel; Jesus's love will not let us go.

The assurance comes in such a way that you can almost hear God whisper to Paul, "Now Paul, a lot of these doctrinal truths can be rather difficult for my people to grasp. So, lest they get discouraged, remind them Jesus loves them, and nothing can change that."

So Paul writes in Romans that *nothing* can separate us from the love of God in Christ Jesus—not sin, not circumstances, not spiritual opposition. If you have trusted Jesus to be your Savior, then you are His on this day and every day to come!

Such assurance of His strong hold on us is meant to make our witness strong for Him. If He will not let us go, then why would we ever let Him down? Neither fear nor doubt nor guilt should drive us away from following Him. We come to Him, hold to Him, and return to Him because He will not let us go.

PRAYER: Lord, it is difficult for me to realize that nothing can separate me from Your love. Today, renew my assurance of Your hold on me so that I will cling to You and will return to Your arms no matter how great the distance I have created.

*Stand therefore, having fastened on the belt of truth, and
having put on the breastplate of righteousness, and, as
shoes for your feet, having put on the readiness given
by the Gospel of peace. (Ephesians 6:14–15)*

My father-in-law's unit was assigned to face down a line of tanks barreling toward Allied troops at the Battle of the Bulge during World War II. The weapons in his unit were totally inadequate for the task. He later said, "Those tanks cut through us like we were paper."

I cannot imagine the experience of those men, trying to stand against such an onslaught as the ground beneath them shook and death for many approached.

The Apostle Paul's imagery puts us into a setting of similar spiritual warfare. We are forced to picture ourselves standing before powerful evil. We are up against the powers of overwhelming wickedness that cause our world and our hearts to shake. But then God speaks: "Stand firm!"

Our doubts and fears, driven by honest assessment of our inability cause us to cry out, "How can I possibly stand against this?" Then our God replies, "You have My armor. Evil will not prevail over you. Stand firm."

The Bible never promises an immediate end to all your trials, but God promises to equip you with all that is necessary for your spiritual victory. Believe Him. In Christ you *can* stand against the onslaughts of evil. So stand firm!

> **PRAYER:** Lord, enable me to stand firm in the realities of spiritual warfare, putting on Your armor and trusting Your grace to provide all that is necessary for Christ's victory.

*Now for a little while, if necessary, you have been grieved
by various trials, so that the tested genuineness of your
faith—more precious than gold that perishes though it is
tested by fire—may be found to result in praise and glory
and honor at the revelation of Jesus Christ. (1 Peter 1:6–7)*

Often, we experience Jesus more intimately during times of trial. Though no one should desire such seasons of difficulty, Scripture describes the beauty that comes of emerging from them by faith.

The Apostle Peter's words remind me of the Japanese art of mending broken pottery with melted gold. Kintsugi pottery is renowned as "more beautiful for having been broken."

As much as I don't want to be broken, I am thankful for the example of how something damaged can be made more beautiful than the original. A wise preacher once said, "It is unlikely that God can use anyone for great purposes until that person has been broken by trials."

When I've been bruised, battered, or broken, I am reminded that Jesus helped me through those difficulties, and He can do the same for others. If I never had to turn to Him or ask His healing, then how would I or others know His grace?

When we reflect the beauty of Christ that comes from our mended brokenness, the world sees more of God's grace and so do we.

PRAYER: *Heavenly Father, when I'm tested by fiery trials, may You refine me like gold, so that I can glorify You and shine the beauty of the Savior who mends me. May my witness for You be more beautiful because Your grace has mended my brokenness.*

297

*We know that our old self was crucified with him
[Christ] in order that the body of sin might be brought
to nothing, so that we would no longer be enslaved to
sin.... Let not sin therefore reign in your mortal body,
to make you obey its passions. (Romans 6:6, 12)*

The question can be fairly asked, "If as Christians, we are no longer slaves to sin, then why do we still sin?"

The answer, while not pretty, is pretty simple: We sin because we love it. Consider this: If a sin did not attract us, then it would have absolutely no power over us. The object of our lust, bitterness, ambition, or greed ultimately controls us—not because we are helpless before it, but because we are desirous of it.

Sin gains power over us not by its indomitable force, but by our divided heart—torn between love for Jesus and love for the sin.

So, if our love for sin is what grants it power over us, how do we drive such love out of our heart? The scriptural answer is plain: with a greater love. When our love for Christ is supreme, it drives out the passion for sin that is its power source.

What will make love for Christ supreme in our hearts? Remembering—really being gripped by—how great is His love for us (1 John 4:19). When the dimensions of Christ's sacrificial love and eternal care fill our hearts, sinful affections lose their grip on us. When Christ is our first love, walking with Him is our first priority and greatest passion!

PRAYER: Lord Jesus, help my heart to be gripped by how great is Your love for me so that I love You more than my sin. May my passion for You become preeminent, so that walking with You becomes my first priority.

We were gentle among you, like a nursing mother taking care of her own children. So, being affectionately desirous of you, we were ready to share with you not only the Gospel of God but also our own selves, because you had become very dear to us. (1 Thessalonians 2:7–8)

The Apostle Paul describes his ministry not only as sharing God's Word, but also sharing his life in affection for others. Our purpose in the body of Christ should not be seen as merely mouthing God's love but mimicking it.

Others will hear His Word from us only as they see His heart in us. Church is not only a place to declare God's Word but a place where selfless care demonstrates it.

The power of selfless care was demonstrated powerfully in our church by a childless woman named Marlene. She desperately wanted children but married too late in life. She didn't let that stop her spiritual mothering.

The neighborhood children of all races, economic backgrounds, and educational differences became Marlene's spiritual children. Though their backgrounds were often rough, she was as gentle (and firm when needed) among them as a mother taking care of her own children. She embraced all, often filling in the gaps for absent biological parents.

This godly woman provides us a glimpse of our gracious God, whose grace and mercy embraces all of us with His unmerited and unlimited grace.

PRAYER: Heavenly Father, in response to Your unlimited grace, help me share and show Your love, selflessly caring for the members of Your family—just as You care for me.

299

Christ himself gave some to be the apostles, some prophets,
some evangelists, some pastors and teachers,
to equip his people for works of service, so that the body
of Christ may be built up. (Ephesians 4:11–12 NIV)

My sons are best buddies, even though they are very different personalities. One is a deliberate thinker; the other a spontaneous adventurer.

Their distinctive personalities came out when we built a backyard swing set with a tall slide. One of my sons went to the slide, stood aside to measure its height, and then climbed carefully up the steps to get the best angle of descent to the adjoining sandpile.

The other son donned his roller skates and leaped to the top of the slide to achieve maximum velocity!

Without one of our sons, life would have been a lot more dangerous; without the other life would have been a lot less exciting. Without one, there would be fewer doctoral degrees in our house; without the other, there would be fewer mountaintops in our lives.

These two men remain best friends, and when they are working together, our family experiences are the absolute best!

That's what our Lord intends for the family of God, also. He provides unique personalities, using our diversity for experiencing and sharing the Gospel in ways we could not as individuals.

The Apostle Paul writes, "To each one of us grace has been given as Christ apportioned it" (Ephesians 4:7). Embracing this wisdom makes the body of Christ the amazing instrument of grace God intends.

PRAYER: *Jesus, help me to discover the gifts You have given me and to appreciate those You have given others as You build up the body of Christ for the full reach of the Gospel.*

300

*Do not lay up for yourselves treasures on earth, where
moth and rust destroy and where thieves break in and
steal, but lay up for yourselves treasures in heaven, where
neither moth nor rust destroys and where thieves do
not break in and steal. For where your treasure is, there
your heart will be also. (Matthew 6:19–21)*

It's almost a human reflex to think that greater obedience to God guarantees that we will have a problem-free family, material comforts, and a successful career. But that's clearly not the case for many persecuted or impoverished believers throughout history or across our present world.

Our reflex mistake is trying to assess God's faithfulness by earthly measures rather than eternal blessings. Not all Christians will have what the world most treasures, because worldly things are not what God most treasures.

The blessings of living for Christ will always include being able to look in the mirror without shame, having spiritual peace in a troubled world, and absolute confidence that God is working all things for the eternal good of those who love Him.

Righteousness, peace, and eternal joy are the blessings God grants His people that the world cannot grant nor take away. Be encouraged today—even if it's a tough day—knowing that you can always trust in the perfect plan and gracious provision of your eternal God!

PRAYER: Lord, please help me not to assess Your faithfulness by earthly measures. Rather teach me the certainty, beauty, and eternity of Your spiritual blessings that the world can neither give nor take away.

301

*I pray that out of his glorious riches he may
strengthen you with power through his Spirit in
your inner being, so that Christ may dwell in your
hearts through faith. (Ephesians 3:16–17 NIV)*

The Apostle Paul's example encourages us to pray for the Holy Spirit to strengthen others. When others are strengthened by the Spirit through our prayers, our own hearts are encouraged and we become more aware of the power of prayer to build the community of faith that supports us.

I have stood in pulpits with hopeful and supportive faces waiting to be fed with the Word of God. I have also stood facing suspicious and angry faces unwilling to hear anything I would say.

I know that God's Word can work in both, but I treasure the sense of soaring power that comes from evidence of supportive prayer for me from the congregation; and I know the sense of power being sapped from me by lack of support.

These differences remind me of Jesus's lack of miracles due to the lack of faith from His hometown (Mark 6:5–6). Advancing God's work is not just about praying for personal effectiveness, but praying for those around us—that God's Spirit would strengthen them for His work and that His Son would indwell their hearts.

Such a shared spirit fuels the power of the church to shine God's heart and to do His will. So today, take a moment to pray that God's Spirit would supply the strength of faith for those around you!

PRAYER: *Father, today graciously supply me with the desire to pray that others would be strengthened by the Spirit and indwelt by Christ so that we all might be united in and equipped for Your service.*

We have had earthly fathers who disciplined us and
we respected them. Shall we not much more be subject
to the Father of spirits and live? (Hebrews 12:9)

If hardships are not punitive, then why does God allow them? The writer of Hebrews provides the answer: "He disciplines us for our good, that we may share in his holiness" (Hebrews 12:10).

God has no desire to harm His children, but like an earthly father, He wants to train us in character and conduct that will guard us from danger and lead to future blessings.

When a mother took her fevered child to the doctor, she promised the needed shot "would not hurt." The doctor knew that was not true, and he spoke honestly to the child: "I may hurt you, but I will not harm you."

God's discipline operates similarly. It may hurt (all discipline does), but its design is never for our harm. Instead, God produces a harvest of righteousness and peace for those trained by His discipline.

Our God is a good, good Father who loves us with the tenderness, wisdom, and power that are best for our spiritual health and eternal blessing!

> **PRAYER:** Father, I must admit that I don't enjoy Your discipline. But help me to accept correction and training from Your gracious hand, realizing that Your goal is to make me mature and complete in Christ.

Though you have not seen him, you love him. Though you do not now see him, you believe in him and rejoice with joy that is inexpressible and filled with glory, obtaining the outcome of your faith, the salvation of your souls. (1 Peter 1:8–9)

Pro basketball star Jeremy Lin was having a bad year. In the midst of a terrible slump, he posted on the internet, "I am in the fight of my life for joy.... Only when I focus on who God is ... and how much He loves me, am I able to live with joy and freedom."[3]

How could he say this? Because he put on his Gospel glasses. Then he read sports headlines of criticism through the lenses of God's approval and affection that would remain long after critics were gone. He used the absence of the world's acclaim to focus on the eternity of God's love.

The same can be true for us! No matter what we're presently facing, when we focus on the grace of God that has no limit in amount or duration, then we're able to live with continuing joy. Such joy is true freedom from voices of criticism in the world or from within.

PRAYER: Father, when the outcomes of my life seems joyless, please help me to focus on the outcome of my faith, the salvation of my soul and eternity with You.

304

Our God whom we serve is able to deliver us from the burning fiery furnace, and he will deliver us out of your hand, O king. But if not, be it known to you, O king, that we will not serve your gods or worship the golden image that you have set up. (Daniel 3:17–18)

All kinds of false faiths are promoted in the world. "If you give enough money ... " or "If you pray enough ... " or "If you summon up enough confidence, then God will give you what you want." Such promises cannot be found in Scripture, but prey on the poor, the desperate, and the needy.

True faith is not deciding what we want and demanding that God make it happen. True faith is doing what God commands and trusting Him to provide what is best for eternity.

The book of Daniel provides a perfect example. When the prophet's friends were tested with threats of a fiery furnace, their faith did not waver. They said, "Our God is *able* to deliver us." Then they added, "*But* even if He does not, we will still serve Him."

Whether they lived or died, they had faith that God would deliver them from evil in the way that He knew was best for their eternal good.

The God who sent His Son for you can be trusted. Do as He desires. He will supply the rescue that is right.

PRAYER: Lord, help me to do as You desire by trusting You more than my desires. Focus my faith on Your unwavering faithfulness so that I may fulfill Your eternal purposes.

*For I have the desire to do what is right, but not the ability
to carry it out. For I do not do the good I want, but the evil
I do not want is what I keep on doing. (Romans 7:18–19)*

Imagine a Little League coach instructing some young pitchers as they watch game films of historic major leaguers. "Now watch how these pitchers work. I want you to focus on the catcher's mitt, as they do. And square your shoulders to the plate, as they do. And follow through after the pitch, as they do."

But then the film displays a pitching great whose course of life became tragic. When the young players see this pitcher, the coach says, "See how he tries to make every pitch perfect and gets frustrated with every flaw. Don't do that! If you expect yourself to be perfect, that will destroy you from the inside."

Could the Apostle Paul be coaching Christians similarly? He uses himself as an example of one who strove to do everything perfectly for God and confesses, "I ... have not the ability to carry it out."

If even a spiritual major leaguer can't always do what he or God wants where does that leave the rest of us? Depending upon the grace of God! Just as Paul did, when he concluded, "Wretched man that I am! Who will deliver me from this body of death? Thanks be to God through Jesus Christ our Lord."

A holy God could destroy us were it not for His gracious provision. By faith in Jesus we have the holiness we could not achieve and the encouragement to live more devotedly for the One who has loved us despite our imperfections.

> **PRAYER:** Father, thank You for freeing me from the pressure to be perfect to know or keep Your love. You knew all my faults when You provided Jesus to save me. Help me to grow in that grace as I keep living in thanksgiving for Jesus.

306

Let each one of you love his wife as himself, and let the
wife see that she respects her husband. (Ephesians 5:33)

Proverbs 31 describes a godly woman as one who brings honor and blessing to her husband. But is a husband the only one who benefits from the respect of a godly wife? *She* benefits as well!

No woman wants to be married to a man she does not respect. So the respect a wife offers her husband does not only benefit him. It provides the deep levels of marital fulfillment that *her* heart yearns for. The more a wife treasures her husband, the more satisfying and precious she will find their union.

Of course, this instruction seems unfair when a husband seems unworthy of respect—and one apostle even tell wives to "reverence" their husbands. *None* are worthy of that. So how can we accept these instructions?

The answer lies in understanding that respect for others depends as much on what is in our hearts as what is in their lives. Everyone has flaws that we cannot respect, and everyone has features we can choose to respect. From Scripture we learn that the more we respect the features we can, the less we see the flaws we cannot.

Yes, it's hard. But the grace God extends to you is the grace available to you to love another as you have been loved. Fulfilling marriages are built on mutual respect from mutual sinners. You have to respect the spouse you married to be married to a spouse you respect.

> **PRAYER:** Lord, thank You for my spouse! Help me to learn from Your grace toward me so that I will love my spouse as You have loved me, and will respect as I wish to be respected.

Truly, truly, I say to you, everyone who practices sin is a slave to sin. The slave does not remain in the house forever; the son remains forever. So, if the Son sets you free, you will be free indeed. (John 8:34–36)

I have lived in the Land of Lincoln, a region in Illinois where legends and facts about the sixteenth president are so intertwined that it's sometimes difficult to determine all that's true. But the tales of his life consistently reflect the principles he held.

One account is that he collected all the savings of his meager income as a young lawyer to cast the highest bid at a slave auction. After purchasing the slave, he immediately set her free and told her she could go wherever she wished. She replied to him, "I wish to go with you!"

Such loyalty naturally results from gratitude for being freed from slavery. Similarly, when we have been supernaturally released from slavery to sin by the Son of God, our hearts are freed for loyalty to Him.

Biblical gratitude does not attempt to repay the debt for grace our meager efforts could never offset, but responds in grateful loyalty, going with Jesus wherever He desires to do whatever He requires!

> PRAYER: Lord, thank You for removing my chains and setting me free in Christ. Now that I am no longer a slave, fill me with such gratitude for my freedom that my heart is bound to You in loyalty and love!

308

Count it all joy, my brothers, when you meet trials of various kinds, for you know that the testing of your faith produces steadfastness. And let steadfastness have its full effect, that you may be perfect and complete, lacking in nothing. (James 1:2–4)

Understanding that God's primary goal for allowing the trials we face is our spiritual transformation helps to explain why He delays His response to some requests. Though we may be interested in a change of *circumstances,* God is more interested in changing *us!*

When we want a quick solution, God may be wanting us to grow in patience! When we want a troublesome coworker removed, God may desire a greater understanding of His heart for them—and us. We want closure for all our problems, but God wants us to learn to trust Him in everything!

God never hesitates because He is incapable or unwilling to bless. As Richard Trench once wrote, "Prayer is not overcoming God's reluctance; it is laying hold of His highest willingness." What is He most willing to do? Make us reflect ever more the heart, the hope, and the eternal joy of Jesus.

As an anonymous person wrote long ago: "God is perfect love and perfect wisdom. We do not pray in order to change His will, but in order to bring our will in harmony with His."

PRAYER: Lord, help me to pray for Your will more than mine, so that whether You change my circumstances or me, I will know and reflect more of my Savior. May confidence in Your perfect grace for me grant Your perfect peace to me.

309

Our struggle is not against flesh and blood, but against the rulers,
against the authorities, against the powers of this dark world
and against the spiritual forces of evil in the heavenly realms.
Therefore put on the full armor of God. (Ephesians 6:12–13 NIV)

Many attempts have been made to classify the demonic forces of darkness the Apostle Paul identifies in Ephesians 6. Most of the classifications are speculative, but there is no doubt that the Apostle Paul wants us to know that Satan works through evil forces that are present in this world —though not apparent to natural eyes.

Our natural inclination when facing enemies we do not see is to assume that they are not present and pose no threat. Yet when we put on the spiritual glasses that Scripture provides, we see that Satan's forces constantly threaten our spiritual wellbeing.

Wicked leaders, lustful pursuits, unchallenged injustice, and blinding materialism are but a few examples of the weapons wielded by those who intend our undoing.

Forget the sham impressions of Halloween costumes and horror movie spooks. The evil one appears as an angel of light, blinding us to the devastations of "acceptable" sins, distracting us from his destruction with promises of painless pleasures.

The Bible reminds us that we are to be on guard, equipping ourselves with the armor God graciously provides for those who otherwise would be no match for demonic powers and pervasive deceits. Apart from Christ, we are helpless against evil; with Christ, the demons flee.

PRAYER: *Father, help me not to be distracted or deluded by evil. May Your spiritual armor protect me from spiritual foes as I depend upon Christ's strength rather than my own! Open my eyes to real spiritual dangers and a stronger Savior.*

*Let us consider how to stir up one another
to love and good works. (Hebrews 10:24)*

W hen our youngest daughter was in high school, her life became an incredibly busy whirlwind of activities. With my own hectic schedule, connecting with her was sometimes a challenge.

But I wanted to connect with her, so my wife suggested I get up early to fix my daughter breakfast the mornings I was home. Nothing special—just a bowl of cereal.

On those mornings as I joined my daughter, I would often consider what was my most important responsibility as the father of this young Christian woman. As I filled her cereal bowl, I realized what it was: my most important task was so to fill her heart with love for Christ.

Why? Because all responsible parents know there are trials and temptations ahead for each child. But if my child's heart is full of love for Christ, she cannot be more spiritually safe or strong.

That is not only true of my child but of every child of God. When our hearts are full of love for Christ, then we are never more spiritually safe or strong.

We stir up one another to love and good deeds by filling up hearts with love for the One who loved us and gave Himself for us. Such encouragement is spiritual power!

> PRAYER: *Father, help me to stir up loved ones to honor You by filling them up with love for Jesus. May a supreme love for Him keep us all spiritually safe and strong by diminishing all other desires that would lead us from Him.*

My little children, I am writing these things to you so that you may not sin. But if anyone does sin, we have an advocate with the Father, Jesus Christ the righteous. He is the propitiation for our sins, and not for ours only but also for the sins of the whole world. (1 John 2:1–2)

We all know that two wrongs don't make a right, but do two rights make a wrong? Maybe.

If we think that doing more good will compensate for the wrong in our lives, then we are trusting a mistaken math to make us right with God.

The Bible says our best works are only filthy rags to a holy God, and Jesus said when we have done all the good that we should, we are still unworthy of Heaven. There is too much of our sinful self in our best works for them to make us right with God.

Does that math make our situation hopeless? Not at all. We simply must turn from our math to our Advocate. True repentance is not simply about shifting from doing bad things to doing good things. True repentance is humbly acknowledging that we could never make things right with God by our math, so we trust His grace alone for our pardon.

We turn entirely from our solutions and turn entirely toward God's provision. That means we ask for God's forgiveness and trust Jesus to be our Advocate. We accept that His sacrifice on the cross paid the penalty for our sin (that's what a *propitiation* does) and we rely on His work alone to compensate for all our wrongs.

He rights our wrongs in ways we never could. That's the math of grace that makes living for the Savior add up right.

PRAYER: Lord, thank you for making Jesus the Advocate that I need to do the spiritual math I could not complete. Give me confidence that His righteousness will cancel my worst wrongs, since it's sufficient for the whole world.

I will instruct you and teach you in the way you should go;
I will counsel you with my eye upon you. (Psalm 32:8)

A new computer, a new car, or a new phone with no instruction manual —that's a recipe for frustration! That's why a new life in Christ comes with God's Word as our instruction manual.

Following the instructions doesn't make us new, but it sure makes the life God intends for our eternal blessing much easier to figure out and to live.

The world is still complicated enough that we can feel like we're on our own, but we're not. God's instructions are an expression of His continuing care, a key way that He keeps His eye on us.

The care provided by the instructions is matched by the grace of a watchful God whose Holy Spirit provides the wisdom to understand Him, the care to protect us, and the pardon to bless us.

The grace that provides God's instructions simultaneously protects and forgives to stimulate love and trust of His Word. Then the more we follow that counsel, the more we sense His care. He keeps His caring eye on us by keeping His Word before us.

> **PRAYER:** Lord, thank You for Your Word that instructs me in the way I should go, and for Your watchful eye that protects me as I do. Please help me to treasure all the aspects of Your grace that keep me following You and returning to Your care.

313

The Spirit helps us in our weakness. For we do not know what to pray for as we ought, but the Spirit himself intercedes for us with groanings too deep for words. (Romans 8:26)

Have you ever wondered what the Apostle Paul meant when he wrote that the Spirit is interceding for believers with groans beyond words? Paul had a specific meaning in mind. Earlier in Romans, he said that creation *groans* for the fulfillment of God's purposes with the cries of a mother giving birth.

The reference reminds us that the Holy Spirit is advocating for our concerns with greater fervor than we can muster. We may be nodding off in our own bedtime prayers, but the Spirit is appealing to God with the fervor of a mother in the final stages of bringing new life into the world.

Not only does the Spirit intercede with such fervor but with such intent. We can be praying with cold or selfish hearts, but the Holy Spirit is interceding for the sake of new life on Earth and in us.

While our prayers may be reflecting desires that are immature, ill-informed, or self-seeking, the Spirit is transforming our prayers into petitions for God's purposes and priorities to be born in us.

We pray and the Spirit brings the fervor and power to petition God for new life in and through us.

> PRAYER: Lord, thank You for the Spirit who makes my prayers into godly petitions that have the power to bring new power and priorities into my life that are birthed by You.

314

Put on the whole armor of God, that you may be able to stand against the schemes of the devil. For we do not wrestle against flesh and blood, but against the rulers, against the authorities, against the cosmic powers over this present darkness, against the spiritual forces of evil in the heavenly places. (Ephesians 6:11–12)

We all know, "It's not the size of the dog in the fight that counts, but the size of the fight in the dog." But as believers, what is our fight?

In Ephesians 6:12, the Apostle Paul makes it clear that our fight is spiritual in nature, not physical. He tells us that our struggle is not against flesh and blood but against the powers of this dark world.

So how do we prevail in spiritual warfare? First, admit *it's real*! Then, remember what the Apostle Paul teaches—your strength is not in *your* armor. Your strength, stamina, and smarts are not Satan's equal.

Instead, remember that God provides *His* armor for you: His truth, His righteousness, His peace, His faith, His salvation, His Word, and His prayer. Rely on these!

An old hymn reminds us the Lord is "power of my power, and sword for my fight" ("Be Thou My Vision," attributed to Dallan Forgaill). So stand firm in His protection and provision. The battle may be fierce, but evil will not ultimately prevail. Our Gospel armor is secure, and our victory is already won in Christ.

> **PRAYER:** Lord, thank You for giving me all the spiritual armor I need in Christ. Help me to stand firm as I wrestle with evil, trusting in Your provision and protection.

315

*He said to them, "O foolish ones, and slow of heart to believe
all that the prophets have spoken! ... And beginning with
Moses and all the Prophets, he interpreted to them in all the
Scriptures the things concerning himself. (Luke 24:25, 27)*

Every page of Scripture contributes to our understanding of the grand
theme of God's intention to rescue people who cannot rescue themselves
from a world of sin.

Unlike every other religion that details what humans must do or think
to escape the pains and pressures of this world, the Bible teaches that God
Himself provides our rescue.

We don't climb to Him; He reaches to us. That message is so counterintuitive even disciples of Jesus were "slow of heart" to receive it. So like a
legendary coach at a pro training camp saying, "Gentlemen, this is a football,"
Jesus goes back to the basics.

Beginning with Moses and all the prophets, He explained how all the
Scriptures related to Him. He had said it all before, telling the religious leaders
of that day, "You search the Scriptures because you think that in them you will
have eternal life; and it is they that bear witness to me."

Jesus was not saying that every verse of Scripture mentioned Him, but that
all passages coordinate to reveal our spiritual inadequacy and God's gracious
provision. Thus, the message of the whole Bible culminates in the revelation
of our Redeemer.

When we see through the many centuries of biblical revelation how resolute, unrelenting, and undeterred our God's grace toward us has been, then
our hearts' greatest priority is to glorify and enjoy Him.

PRAYER: *Jesus, open my eyes to see how Your Word has
revealed Your grace—from Genesis to Revelation—so that
I will love and live to serve You above all and for all my days.*

316

Do nothing from selfish ambition or conceit,
but in humility count others more significant than yourselves.
Let each of you look not only to his own interests,
but also to the interests of others. (Philippians 2:3–4)

A selfie taken by a police officer with a Houston-area teen went viral. The picture got such attention because it was such a contrast to recent events.

A week earlier, in the same city torn by racial tensions, a policeman had been gunned down while pumping gas. So when this teenager offered to stand behind a police officer in the rain as she pumped gas—"to make sure you are safe"—that was a contrast and a picture the world was longing to see.

The officer later said, "I'm the one with the gun on my hip ... but he for sure 'had my six' while my back was turned."

The message of "I've got your back" is exactly what we should be saying and showing to each other in our churches and in our communities. Biblical faith is not selfish but considers the needs of others more significant than our own.

Jesus exposed His back and body to cruelty to secure our eternity. The world should see in us this grace that Jesus selflessly provided to make His message plain—even viral!

> PRAYER: Lord, help me to consider the needs of others more significant than my own, praying for them and offering needed support to demonstrate the grace of my Savior.

317

Submit to one another out of reverence
for Christ. (Ephesians 5:21 NIV)

Each one of us possesses a unique personality, a unique set of talents, and a background that God desires to use to make our churches, homes, and each other *better*.

But if you're dealing with a difficult person, their foibles and faults can make it difficult to assess why the Lord allows such people in our lives. Why would God do such things?

Difficult people require Christlike patience. The loveless require Christ's love. We require God's character to express His care to those without His character.

God expects us to confront error in ways that are boldly faithful and humbly submissive to His will. In this way, He builds aspects of our faith that we may not even want.

That's why biblical submission to one another's needs is not the suppression of gifts but full expression for mutual benefit. The one receiving the care—and the one giving it—grow in Christlikeness.

When we submit to one another, we are not backing away from challenges, we are using the heart and gifts of God to reflect His goodness and character into the life of someone He loves—including us!

PRAYER: *Lord, thank You for saving me despite my flaws. As I reflect this grace boldly for Your sake and humbly for others' sake, help me to remember that difficult people are meant to bring out the grace that You poured into me.*

For if you keep silent at this time, relief and deliverance will rise for the Jews from another place, but you and your father's house will perish. And who knows whether you have not come to the kingdom for such a time as this? (Esther 4:14)

Her uncle's strong words to Queen Esther ring through the ages to remind us not to doubt God's purposes for our lives.

You may think you are serving your Savior in insignificant places or against insurmountable odds, but an infinitely wise God has put you on this earth and with specific people "for such a time as this!"

Forty years before making their escape from an Islamic government that had forbidden Christianity, the Ooduck people had learned of Jesus's grace from two young, single missionary women serving with Sudan Interior Mission.

The women could not have imagined the full impact of their mission. So deeply did their witness reach into others' hearts that many fled to a refugee camp in Ethiopia rather than abandon their faith.

Many years later, when the mission organization learned of the Ooducks' perseverance, it organized a return visit of the two now-elderly missionaries. In the refugee camp the women discovered thirteen thousand Ooducks who were living for Jesus. They would be safe in eternity despite their earthly deprivations.

We will not fully know the impact of our lives for our Savior until we are with Him. But we are assured that "for such a time as this" He put us on this earth for the people He puts in our lives!

> **PRAYER:** Lord, help me remain faithful in the face of discouragement, hardship, or apparent insignificance to others, knowing that You prepared me for such a time as this.

What then is Apollos? What is Paul? Servants through
whom you believed, as the Lord assigned to each.
I planted, Apollos watered, but God gave the growth.
So neither he who plants nor he who waters is anything, but
only God who gives the growth. (1 Corinthians 3:5–7)

Here the Apostle Paul reminds us never to depend on human heroes alone to fulfill divine plans. Why?

Is it entirely honest to talk about David's victory over Goliath but never mention his sin with Bathsheba? Is it fair to recite David's psalms and disregard his murder of Bathsheba's husband? If we only talk about David when he was good, are we really teaching the *whole* truth of Scripture?

The truth is, there's only one untainted hero of the Bible—Jesus. Everyone else needs Him.

To focus on the Bible's human heroes without mentioning the grace of God that enabled their heroism or overcame their flaws warps the biblical message. Every flawed figure served God's process of planting and watering the seeds of the Gospel in Scripture until the time was ripe for Jesus.

Grace is written on every page of the Bible, as God gives victories to the weak, pardon to the flawed, and purpose to the failures. He's the hero of the helpless and the heroes!

So next time you read about a "hero," look for how God is planting seeds of grace to blossom for times and trials when the "hero" label is not part of our identy.

PRAYER: *Lord, help me to see the real hero to which every story in the Bible points. May I see Christ's grace sprouting on every page so that I turn to Him on my non-heroic days.*

How then will they call on him in whom they have not believed? And how are they to believe in him of whom they have never heard? And how are they to hear without someone preaching? (Romans 10:14)

The Navigators is an international ministry founded in 1933 by Dawson Trotman. It all started at a Texaco service station in Lomita, California. Trotman offered a baked-bean dinner to two young sailors in order to share his testimony and the belief that God would use them if they trusted in Him.

A few months later, the sailors persuaded Trotman to become a missionary to the fleet. None knew the assignment ahead—Pearl Harbor.

By the time of the attack, 120 to 130 men were regularly meeting in Bible studies aboard ship. And when their ship was destroyed, the surviving Bible study sailors were distributed on ships across the Pacific Fleet. By the end of the war, there were eight hundred ships with Bible studies being led by the Navigators.

Trotman's story is a great reminder that others will call upon Jesus when they hear what to believe. And they hear what to believe when someone loving and bold enough speaks of Him.

Jesus works when we speak!

PRAYER: *Lord, help me to share Your good news with my family, friends, and neighbors. How can they believe in You if they do not hear of You? Help me to speak for You.*

321

Let each one of you love his wife as himself,
and let the wife see that she respects her husband. (Ephesians 5:33)

The Apostle Paul's description of the biblical role of a wife in marriage culminates in a single word: *respect*. That's a word that seems to make half of humanity applaud, while the other half cringes.

The cringe factor only increases when we realize that the apostle uses the same word to describe the reverential awe that all Christians should have toward our Lord. No human and certainly no husband would seem to deserve that kind of regard.

The impossible requirement embedded in the word *respect* actually signals its purpose. A wife's respect cannot be rooted in her husband's deserving, but in God's purposes. We revere a divine design.

A wife's obligations of attitude and action have to come from her respect for God's purposes more than her husband's perfections. A husband will never deserve the reverential regard that he needs to fulfill God's calling on his life. It is only granted by a gracious wife.

As the spiritual head of the home, the husband will stand before God and give account for his family's spiritual nurture. The wife who reveres that calling will support her husband with the respect that helps him to honor God for the whole family's sake.

> **PRAYER:** Lord, help me to honor my spouse more for divine purposes than for human perfections. Your perfect love did not await my deserving. Nurture such grace in my family as I love and honor an imperfect person for Christ's sake.

322

For this is the love of God, that we keep his commandments.
And his commandments are not burdensome. (1 John 5:3)

If grace doesn't erase God's commands, how does it affect the way we teach them? Can we teach His commands without becoming legalistic?

The answer is a resounding, "Yes!" But only when we understand the purpose of God's commands for our life. If we think they are given so that we might earn or retain His love, that can't work because our best works are like polluted garments to Him (Isaiah 64:6). Manufacturing divine affection will always be beyond our abilities!

God has given us His law so that we will experience, not earn, the good He intends for our lives. When we teach that God's law is an expression of His gracious care for those He redeemed through the sacrifice of His Son alone, then we will teach the law to bless, not to burden.

The commandments of God demonstrate His love for us; they are not how we extract love from Him. Teaching the standards God outlines for us to experience the best this life can offer is not the teaching of legalism, but of love.

When we teach the grace that gave the law and the grace that secures our hearts despite our transgressions of it, then destructive legalism gives way to compulsive love.

PRAYER: *Heavenly Father, I know that Your commands are given for my good and are an expression of Your grace. Help me today to show my love for You by obeying Your Word, repenting of my sin, and growing in Your grace.*

If you then, who are evil, know how to give good gifts to your children, how much more will your Father in heaven give good gifts to those who ask him. (Matthew 7:11 NIV)

My first car was an import that an American car company sold for only one year. The maintenance record made the compact car a giant nightmare for all its owners. Not until my income allowed me to purchase another did I realize that cars aren't supposed to break down every few weeks.

One of those breakdowns occurred as I was heading home from college for the holidays. I was still a hundred miles from home, but I didn't panic. I called my father.

Even though I knew my late-night rescue would take my father's time and energy, I knew I could call on him. All my life he had proven his commitment to my care.

That is why Jesus reminds us that we are calling to our Heavenly *Father* when He teaches, "Ask, and it will be given to you. Seek, and you will find; knock, and it will be opened to you. For everyone who asks receives, and the one who seeks finds, and to the one who knocks it will be opened" (Matthew 7:7–8).

When our lives have become a nightmare of our own mistakes and miscalculations, we still can call out to our Heavenly Father who has proven His eternal care through the grace of Jesus. He will answer your call and provide what is best to help you.

PRAYER: *Father, thank You for always hearing my prayers and for always responding with the best care that divine wisdom and a gracious heart know to provide!*

324

*Do not be anxious about anything, but in everything
by prayer and supplication with thanksgiving let your
requests be made known to God. (Philippians 4:6)*

Sometimes we fear to approach God, thinking it's not appropriate to bother Him with the little things. But He wants us to connect with Him *in everything*.

As a Christian teen, I grew impatient with an experienced carpenter who paused on our mission project to find a fallen nail. "Just grab another nail," I said. "Well, Bryan," he replied, "I just prayed that God would help me find it. So I think I ought to look."

I scowled. "Maybe we shouldn't bother God about nails."

"Oh no, Bryan," the carpenter replied, "God says to pray to him about 'everything.'"

The carpenter was right. When the Apostle Paul says to take everything to God in prayer, he really means *everything*. We can pray about finding nails or keys—or about finding our way through stormy nights or relationships. We can pray about minor worries and major catastrophes, about our discomforts and others' tragedies.

If my children only came to me when the issues were serious, I'd rarely hear from them and we'd grow distant. It's our regular conversations about the small things that knit our hearts together.

The gracious Heavenly Father who knows this truth and desires to knit our hearts to His urges us to seek Him in *everything*. So we should thank Him for His meticulous care and come to Him in frequent prayer.

PRAYER: *Lord, I can be anxious about many things. Assure me by Your fatherly heart that I can bring everything before You in prayer, and that You want me to!*

325

One of them, when he saw he was healed, came back, praising God
in a loud voice. He threw himself at Jesus's feet and thanked him—
and he was a Samaritan. Jesus asked, "Were not all ten cleansed?
Where are the other nine? Has no one returned to give praise to
God except this foreigner?" (Luke 17:15–18 NIV)

Several years ago, a young mother found her son in his sister's room, eating a chocolate teddy bear she'd received as a gift.

Backing against the wall like a cornered criminal, the boy knew he could not hide the guilt on his chocolate-smeared face! He sobbed his sorrow, but his mother insisted he confess to his sister.

The sister was still in school; the hours until she came home magnified the boy's dread of facing her. When she finally arrived at home, the boy's pent-up anxiety exploded. He ran to his sister's arms and blurted out in tears, "Oh, Sally, I am so sorry I ate your chocolate teddy bear."

The sister could have been upset, but she used the opportunity to love up her little brother. She took him in her arms, kissed him, and told him she would always love him. At that point, the boy's anxious crying turned to joyous laughter. He thanked his sister, hugging her with all his strength.

Likewise, when we confess our sins with genuine sorrow, yet receive the wonder of God's gracious pardon with thanksgiving, then the joy of the Lord becomes our strength.

> **PRAYER:** Lord, I confess that I am guilty of sin, both in what I do and what I fail to do. Thank You for gracious love that relieves my anxious spirit and gives me renewed strength through the joy of Your embrace!

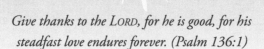

*Give thanks to the LORD, for he is good, for his
steadfast love endures forever. (Psalm 136:1)*

The psalmist encourages us to give thanks to the Lord because of His goodness to us. He demonstrates His glory by caring for us, making His enduring love our constant cause for worship.

We damage that worship when our relationships—which are intended to display His glory—do not reflect His enduring care. In relationships that reflect God's nature, our priorities are geared toward doing what's best for others. But that's easier to say than do.

For example, in the early years of our marriage, when my wife, Kathy, did something that frustrated me, my tendency was to freeze her out through angry silence. I thought that was to my credit for not losing control of my temper, but in reality I was trying to control my wife by denying the grace I preached.

Every marriage has its rough patches with things we have to work through, but God calls us to work in harmony with the grace we have received. We prioritize the good of each other—whether we are correcting or caressing. Our advantage is not our priority, but rather the enduring good of our spouse.

Without thanks for God's goodness filling our hearts, our natural reflexes are selfish, relating to people based on their actions toward us rather than on our enduring love for them.

Grace that claims us changes us so that selfless love permeates our lives, making every relationship an opportunity for displaying our Savior's nature and care. We honor Him by reflecting Him, making gracious love true worship.

PRAYER: Lord, as I encounter people today, may I seek to reflect Your grace toward me so that my relationships are an offering of worship to You.

The Father himself loves you, because you have loved me
[Jesus] and have believed that I came from God. (John 16:27)

No matter how much we feel the need to display our good works before God in order to merit His acceptance, our accomplishments are never the reason God loves us.

This realization that our good works will not move Him to love us runs counter to our natural reasoning. Most people readily admit "nobody's perfect," and yet many still think that their standing with God depends on their good works outweighing their bad.

Such persons are shocked to discover the Bible teaches our best works are filthy rags to a holy God (Isaiah 64:6), and that Jesus said when we have done all we should do, we are still unworthy (Luke 17:10).

Countering all of that terrible news is the good news of the Gospel: our gracious God loves all who trust in Christ, despite their unworthiness. Jesus came from God to provide the holiness we cannot attain.

We don't have to balance the scales of divine justice with our good works (that aren't good enough) because Jesus balanced the scales for us with His righteous life and perfect sacrifice. We live for Him not to balance God's scales, but to demonstrate love and thanksgiving for the One who did.

Trying to make trophies of your good deeds won't carry much weight with a holy God. Trust instead that Jesus came from God to balance the scales of divine justice for you.

PRAYER: *Heavenly Father, thank You sending Jesus because of Your mercy rather than my merit. Help me to show my love and thanksgiving by living for the Holy One who balanced the scales of divine justice by paying the penalty for all my sins.*

328

*I do not cease to give thanks for you, remembering you
in my prayers, that the God of our Lord Jesus Christ, the
Father of glory, may give you the Spirit of wisdom and of
revelation in the knowledge of him, having the eyes of your
hearts enlightened, that you may know ... the immeasurable
greatness of his power toward us who believe, according to
the working of his great might. (Ephesians 1:16–19)*

Along the Mississippi River near my hometown, I have a favorite viewing spot. It's just beyond the power plant where the river is diverted into a channel to turn giant turbines that supply the city's power.

As the water roars through the river channel, frothing, tumbling, and swallowing everything in its path, I'm awed by its power. I am also reminded of when the Spirit of God moved upon the face of the waters to create the world as we know it.

The immense power I can observe in the boiling waters of this one river's channel is but a drop in the bucket compared to the immeasurably great power of the Holy Spirit at creation. And it is that same Spirit who now lives in me—and you!

He makes His power visible to the eyes of the heart so we can see by faith that He is transforming creation again, working all things together for the good of those who love Him.

PRAYER: *Father, thank You for the gift of Your Holy Spirit.
Please open the eyes of my heart to see the immense power
at work in my behalf, so that I live with unceasing thanksgiving
for You and with unyielding confidence in Your plans for me.*

329

For God so loved the world, that he gave his only Son, that whoever believes in him should not perish but have eternal life. For God did not send his Son into the world to condemn the world, but in order that the world might be saved through him. (John 3:16–17)

What is the difference between love and grace? Love is affection. Grace is provision. Grace is a gift from a loving heart. Grace shows the love of the one who gives it and prompts love in the one who receives it.

God's love is different from ours in that it is not prompted by our love. His love originates solely from His heart because none of us loved Him before He loved us, and none of us could do anything to deserve His love.

Our thoughts, words, and actions gave God just cause to condemn us. So the love He has for us is unconditional. He loved us while we were yet sinners.

When God expressed unconditional love by giving Jesus to save us from the condemnation our sins deserved, that was grace—amazing grace! Such favor cannot be earned; it can only be received by trusting that Jesus's sacrificial provision was for you.

So grace and love are vitally connected, but grace is the gift of God's love that prompts our love. God's love causes us to love Him. His grace causes our gratitude. Then our love and gratitude make us desire to live for Him, since His love and grace provide for us to live eternally with Him.

We live every day in thanksgiving when we remember, "For God so loved the world that he gave his only Son, that whoever believes in him should not perish but have eternal life!"

> **PRAYER:** Father, thank You for the gift of Your Son. Help me every day to believe the grace Your love provided to save me from the guilt and penalty of my sins so that I might live and love in eternal gratitude.

330

To you, O God of my fathers, I give thanks and praise,
for you have given me wisdom and might, and have now
made known to me what we asked of you. (Daniel 2:23)

As the prophet Daniel's life demonstrates, we can bear almost anything when we see God working on our behalf. Daniel was given special insights into the nature and working of God, but that did not make his life easy. In fact, acting on the revelations—such as the portion quoted above—often put Daniel's life at risk.

To make the Lord's Word known, Daniel had to speak to those who did not want to hear it or would consider it offensive, even a threat. So what kept Daniel faithful?

He knew that God had already acted with extraordinary grace to claim His soul, so Daniel trusted the Lord for whatever was still to come. He kept that trust strong by praising God for what He had done, despite not knowing what He would do.

Daniel's situation was not so different from ours. We also must learn to trust God for what will come by focusing on what He has done—including saving our soul for eternity.

Our thanksgiving and praise keep our trust honed and engaged for the challenges that we still must face. Proclaiming God's glory takes our focus off the magnitude of our challenge and fastens our trust on the greatness of our Lord.

A heart that overflows with gratitude and praise for our eternal salvation is guarded from being overwhelmed by the circumstances of this life.

PRAYER: Lord, help me praise You for grace You have already provided in order to enable me to trust You for the grace I need for present or future trials.

*As he who called you is holy, you also be holy in
all your conduct, since it is written, "You shall
be holy, for I am holy." (1 Peter 1:15–16)*

Even if there were no tangible benefits in this life for holy living, we would still be called to holiness. The reason is that our calling is not rooted in earthly rewards but in the holy character of God.

Because He created us in His image, united us to Himself by the sacrifice of Jesus Christ, and transforms us to be more like Himself by the work of the Holy Spirit, our lives should reflect our God. Our salvation is really just the start of a process of becoming more and more like Him.

It's possible, of course, that we may be called to live for God in situations where there is no apparent gain for us as we represent the character of the One who made and saves us. In those situations, we demonstrate that living for Him is still better than bowing to any other pressure or priority of the world.

This is the high calling of every believer. We honor what is honorable in Him because nothing gives us more pleasure than living for the One who gave His life for us. Out of love for Him, every day we exchange old desires for new affections and every day His love transforms these affections into priorities and personalities that are more and more like His!

So even when we face ongoing challenges and temptations, the calling to holiness is not onerous or sad, but is the privilege of walking more closely with the Savior we love in a way that pleases Him and increasingly pleases us.

PRAYER: Lord, thank You giving me a holy calling that enables me to live for You and to show my love for You. Today, help me to be holy because You are holy and because it brings me joy so to live for the God who sent His Son to die for me.

332

*I call upon you, for you will answer me, O God; incline
your ear to me; hear my words. Wondrously show
your steadfast love, O Savior. (Psalm 17:6–7)*

I have had the incredible opportunity to raft down the Colorado River through the length of the Grand Canyon. The magnificent sights and scary rapids wondrously showed the power of God's hand. But I also learned more of His grace from a flaw of mine.

One evening a terrible rainstorm hit camp. As the clouds rolled in, I was able to get my rain gear on faster than most. As the rain pounded us, I smiled smugly at the discomfort of others and rejoiced to be snug as a bug in a rug— until the rain started running down my back, the consequence of a leaky seam that made me as miserable as everyone else.

The necessity of God's grace for everyone should remind us that we've all got leaky seams. If you don't confess that, then you won't seek the shelter that God alone can provide.

When you do admit you have some sinful leaks and call out to God for His help, then you have the promise of the One who controls the storms that He will hear above the tempest and will provide His care.

He promises that no matter what mess you've gotten yourself into, when you call Him, He will answer as is absolutely best to seal your soul in His grace.

PRAYER: *Dear Savior, I have many "leaks" in my life. As I call out to You for help, please send Your grace to seal my soul from sin with Your love and for Your purposes.*

333

*You shall love the Lord your God with all your heart
and with all your soul and with all your mind
and with all your strength. (Mark 12:30)*

When we love Christ above all, then all loves find their proper order and proportion in our lives. Jesus explained that our first priority should be to love the Lord God with all our heart, soul, mind, and strength.

When our love for God becomes our highest priority, then that love helps us to love what and whom He loves. Since He loves our neighbor, we do. Since He loves us, there is a proper love for self, too.

Does that sound strange? It won't when we are trying to help a young person caught in an addictive or self-destructive life pattern. Then we naturally say, "Jesus loves you," knowing that, when the person values themselves as Jesus does, new life is possible.

Self-love is destructive if it's our first priority. But if Jesus is our first priority, then protecting and promoting the health of one He loves is a priority that He uses to bring beauty and health to broken lives.

We honor the God who made us when we treat our bodies, souls, and consciences with His care. Neglecting or beating up on ourselves never honors the One who made us a temple for His Holy Spirit.

> PRAYER: Lord, help me to find the beauty and health that come from loving You as my first priority, and then discovering that loving what and whom You love instills proper love for the unlovely, the broken, and me!

God is our refuge and strength, a very present help in trouble.
Therefore we will not fear though the earth gives way, though the
mountains be moved into the heart of the sea. (Psalm 46:1–2)

At a large conference, I struggled with how to worship when a young woman whom I have known all her life walked onstage to lead us in song.

She was raised in a home with an unbelieving father, nurtured in a church torn by controversy, and still she learned to love Jesus and achieved fame.

Then she married a musician who, despite his claims of faith, betrayed her, making headlines of public shame and pain. As the betrayed wife now led us in worship, I could not help but notice her loss of weight, the sorrow lines around her eyes, and the ache beneath her praise.

I wondered if it were fair to her or to us to have her lead us in God's praise. She addressed my wondering in the first song she chose for us:

> Though Satan should buffet,
>   though trials should come,
> Let this blest assurance take control:
> That Christ has regarded my helpless estate,
> And has shed His own blood for my soul.
> It is well with my soul.[4]

This world's trials had surely buffeted her life, but her God was still her refuge. She was as qualified as anyone could be to sing of the God who knew her helpless estate and still provided the assurance to sing, "It is well with my soul."

God had provided her strength for every trial. She was safe with Him forever. Her strength changed the attitude of my worship!

PRAYER: *Lord, You are my refuge and strength. Help me to proclaim the certain truth: "It is well with my soul."*

Friend, I am doing you no wrong. Did you not agree with me for a denarius? Take what belongs to you and go. I choose to give to this last worker as I give to you. Am I not allowed to do what I choose with what belongs to me? Or do you begrudge my generosity? So the last will be first, and the first last. (Matthew 20:13–16)

Coming to faith in Jesus happens on God's timetable, confirming the purpose and value of each person.

Those saved early in life are God's lifeboats, gathering others by a lifelong witness to the blessings of grace. Those saved late in life are God's lighthouses, rescuing those who are still sailing amid rocky shoals with beacons of grace. These beacons signal, "It's not too late to turn from danger to your salvation."

God's lifeboats and lighthouses are both products of His gracious heart. If all whom God saves were children, there would be no hope for the mature without Christ. If only the mature could receive the Savior, then children would be neglected.

No guilt can seem greater than that of parents converted in their mature years who raised their children without Jesus. Relief from such guilt comes by trusting God's timing, wisdom, and heart.

An adult convert can be the lighthouse God always intended for others (including one's adult children) to receive the message: By contrast, Jesus's love for a child can be God's most powerful sign of grace for those who could never earn it.

The wonder of God's grace includes His working individually in each of our lives. He knows the best timing for each human heart and how best to use each personal story.

PRAYER: Lord, help me to be a beacon of grace to those around me, proclaiming that it's never too late to come to Christ, or too early to be used to bring others.

336

Husbands, in the same way be considerate as you live with
your wives, and treat them with respect as the weaker
partner and as heirs with you of the gracious gift of life,
so that nothing will hinder your prayers. (1 Peter 3:7 NIV)

Depending on the ages of our children, our financial needs, and the demands of my job, my wife, Kathy, has varied her time and energy spent in occupations outside our home.

In doing this, she has never wavered in submitting her own interests to the needs of the family God has entrusted to her care. In this confusing age, many have questioned or criticized her choices, but I respect them—and *her*. And that is not just my personal choice or any husband's option.

The Apostle Peter *commands*, "Husbands ... be considerate as you live with your wives, and treat them with *respect*." He uses the same root word in the previous chapter to instruct believers how they should regard an emperor.

The apostle's words require me to respect my wife for her sacrifices, her heart, and her faith, and to believe that she, though physically not as strong as I, is as much an heir of God's gracious gifts as I. Neither I nor our family would have known the all the treasures of God's blessings without her staunch commitment and care.

Spouses are not to gauge one another's value by arm-wrestling matches. And no spouse should take individual credit for the family blessings God prepared by wedding two as He knew was best. Selfish pride will always hinder our prayers and damage our families.

God has a better plan: husband, honor your wife.

PRAYER: *Heavenly Father, help me to show my spouse respect in how I honor her for the commitments and sacrifices made for the good of our family and the testimony of Jesus.*

At the right time Christ died for the ungodly.
For one will scarcely die for a righteous person—
though perhaps for a good person one would dare
even to die—but God shows his love for us in that while
we were still sinners, Christ died for us. (Romans 5:6–8)

Cathedrals, churches, and museums are filled with iconic images of Jesus. Many seek to draw comfort from these artistic representations of our Savior's holiness and perfection. But for Christian artist Don Tiemier, the images brought a crisis of faith.

As Tiemier contrasted the depictions of Jesus's perfections with his own flawed humanity, the artist sank into deep despair. In hopelessness, he concluded that he could never measure up to such holy divinity.

Peace came later, when the artist came across these words written by a terribly flawed apostle named Paul: *Christ died for the ungodly.*

The words brought the artist face-to-face with Christ, who provides hope for those who can never match God's perfections. Jesus rescued the sinful, not the holy. He died for the unrighteous, not the righteous. His grace is not for those who don't need it, but for the needy—like Tiemier and you and me.

Such gracious provision, not anyone's personal perfections, is the source of our peace with God and with ourselves. God's mercy dispels the darkness of despair and ushers in the dawn of peace through the sacrifice of God's Son for sinners like us.

PRAYER: *Heavenly Father, dispel the darkness of my despair and usher in the dawn of peace through my personal embrace of the sacrifice of Jesus Christ for sinners—like me.*

338

Let anyone who thinks that he stands take heed lest he fall. No temptation has overtaken you that is not common to man. God is faithful, and he will not let you be tempted beyond your ability, but with the temptation he will also provide the way of escape, that you may be able to endure it. Therefore, my beloved, flee from idolatry. (1 Corinthians 10:12–14)

In these verses, we learn to resist temptation by following Paul's instruction to *stand ... endure ...* and *flee*. The first two instructions are about resisting the force of temptation, while the last is about removing ourselves from its influence.

At times spiritual leaders may give counsel that seems inconsistent with a strong faith. A leader may advise a struggler, "Now you listen to me. Do not take that road home from work. If you take that road, you will be tempted by a place or person beyond your strength to resist. So take another road home."

Such instruction recognizes that it may take as much strength to flee some temptations as it does to endure others. Don't let anyone mislead you; often the best way to stand for God is to flee from seductive evil. Such flight confesses our humanity and trusts God's provision.

Overcoming temptation by faith is not like sitting on a sofa with a box of chocolates and insisting God make them disappear. God doesn't magically teleport us from temptation, or it from us.

When God graciously provides His way out of temptation, take it. Have enough faith in Him to flee down the path He provides for your spiritual safety.

PRAYER: Lord, as I face temptations this week, help me to trust and take Your way of escape, so that I can flee from danger to stand for You!

Be sober-minded; be watchful. Your adversary
the devil prowls around like a roaring lion,
seeking someone to devour. (1 Peter 5:8)

Several years ago, my wife, Kathy, and a friend gathered up their kids and took a trip to the St. Louis Zoo. "Big Cat Country" had just opened, allowing lions and tigers to roam in large enclosures.

Our two preschool-aged boys ran ahead of the moms, who got distracted by a crying infant. The boys innocently squeezed through a child-sized gap in the fence undetected by employees. They clamored to a perch above the lion's den and proudly shouted, "Hey, Mom, we can see them."

Suddenly Kathy realized where the boys were! The boys had no idea how much danger they were in. But Kathy knew, and she also knew this was not the time to scold. Instead, she knelt down, spread out her arms, and called to her children, "Come get a hug." The boys came running to her embrace, saved by love from a danger greater than they could perceive.

In Scripture, God cautions us about our spiritual adversary not merely to scold, but to warn of danger greater than we can fully understand. At the same time, He draws us to safety by loving arms spread wide on a cross to receive wandering children into His eternal embrace. Come running to His hug!

> **PRAYER:** *Lord, I know that Satan is like a hungry lion, seeking to devour me. When he threatens my soul, help me run to the arms of Jesus that are spread wide to receive me.*

There is no fear in love, but perfect love casts out fear.
For fear has to do with punishment, and whoever
fears has not been perfected in love. (1 John 4:18)

If God threatened to punish us for every sin in our lives, then terror would be an appropriate response. But the Apostle John tells us that perfect love for God casts out fear. How can that be?

The answer lies in understanding the difference between God's punishment and His discipline.

Punishment is the infliction of penalty for a wrong. For the Christian, the fear of such punishment has passed. How can that be?

On the cross Jesus took the punishment for all our sins—past, present, and future. God's love may still discipline to turn us from sin's consequences, but the penalty for our sin was entirely paid by His Son. That's why we sing, "Jesus paid it all."

Punishment and discipline are not the same thing. Punishment exacts a price; discipline edifies God's people. For believers, all punishment is past, and all discipline is grace.

As a result, Christian obedience should never be an attempt to placate the "ogre in the sky" who's just waiting for us to step out of line so He can punish us. The fear of that kind of punishment should be gone for the children of God.

In fact, the Apostle John says that we haven't been "perfected in love" if such fear rules our hearts. The peace of God is the true blessing of hearts that are ruled by Scripture's assurance that Jesus's love has cast our fear of punishment far away!

PRAYER: Lord God, please help me to respond to You out of a heart trusting that there is no condemnation for those who are in Christ Jesus. Because He took the fear of punishment away, rule my heart with the peace of knowing Your enduring and edifying grace.

341

How sweet are your words to my taste, sweeter than honey to my mouth! Through your precepts I get understanding; therefore I hate every false way. Your word is a lamp to my feet and a light to my path. (Psalm 119:103–105)

A nature trail that my family enjoys meanders through woods, parallels a stream, and circles a lake as it leads us to trees and rocks identified with placards explaining each landmark's significance.

The explanations help us understand and enjoy the features of the forest around us. But as interesting as these descriptions are, no trail sign is more important than the one at the beginning—the one with the arrows and the words Begin Here.

Without a proper beginning we will struggle to find our way, see our path, or reach our destination. The same is true with God's Word. We get on the proper path of Scripture when we start reading with the understanding that God will be revealing His heart in all the features of His Word.

His instructions are sweet and He lights the path that is good for us because He intends to share with us the beauty and wonder of His care. Every path that begins with any other understanding is false and we will end up hating it.

Jesus is at the end of the path designed by God's Word. Knowing that destination *as we begin* will help us read Scripture's landmarks as revelations of God's heart—a heart that reveals our sin only to make us desire a Savior and delight in His path.

> PRAYER: Lord, may Your Word guide my steps today, leading me closer to my Savior, Jesus Christ. Help me to delight in the words that reveal Your care for me, my need of Jesus, and Your path to Him.

342

Who shall separate us from the love of Christ? Shall trouble or hardship or persecution or famine or nakedness or danger or sword? ... No, in all these things we are more than conquerors through him who loved us. (Romans 8:35, 37 NIV)

Guilt and fear can cause us to question our usefulness to God. But His love for us, and His power to hold us, are the basis for our ultimate confidence that He will not separate us or any that He loves from His care.

We sometimes hear Christians question whether it is right to bring children into such a troubled world. We need to remember that God's promises to us are no less powerful for the generations that follow us.

God created us and our children for the precise moment in time that each is needed to conquer the challenges to His divine will that we are designed to overcome. Every child of God has been raised up with the personalities, gifts, and circumstances that God knows are best to further His mission and glory.

He raised up David for Goliath, Daniel for the lions' den, and Hannah to provide Samuel to anoint kings in preparation for the Messiah. Generations later, God raised up Jesus for the cross, then Peter and Paul to build and expand the Church that would follow.

God is not now wondering how He will maintain His purposes until Christ's return. He is raising up moms and dads and children who are integral to His plan.

Nothing can separate His children from His heart or His plan. All are more than conquerors through Him who loved us.

> **PRAYER:** *Heavenly Father, help us remember the grace that preserves Your people and purposes through all generations, so that we raise the next generation of conquerors of hatred, bitterness, and evil.*

343

But seek first the kingdom of God and his righteousness,
and all these things will be added to you. (Matthew 6:33)

In my senior year of college, I thought that I had to make a decision whether to pursue broadcast journalism or to attend law school. The more I prayed, the more I recognized I was evaluating my choices solely by how much fame or fortune I could achieve. My Christian principles were hardly in view.

A wise friend suggested that I "briefly" attend seminary in order to study God's Word and get my priorities back in order. I'll confess, I went largely because he offered a scholarship that appealed to my pride. Yet I still had regrets that I was losing ground in my career.

But God is good. The Holy Spirit took me down a path I had never considered. Soon I was learning and sharing the treasures of God's Word—and seeing it change hearts.

By God's grace, on that ministry path I met my wife, led historic churches, raised a godly family, became a leader of the same seminary I once hesitated to attend, and got to see grandchildren start on the same path.

When we follow the paths that God marks for us, there may be challenges —but no regrets. By seeking His Kingdom's priorities first, all that is most dear to our hearts will ultimately be granted according to God's wisdom and love.

PRAYER: *Father, as I look to the future, help me to be guided by the priorities of Your Word and Spirit. Where I have forgotten or neglected them, remind me of the grace in Your heart that will make me want to seek You first.*

344

Each one of you also must love his wife as he loves himself,
and the wife must respect her husband. (Ephesians 5:33)

The women the Bible presents as the most desirable are those respected by their husbands. And the wives the Bible presents as most faithful are those who respect their husbands. Still, our corrupted world can tempt each woman's heart with a desire to *control* more than to *respect* her husband. That's not new.

When Adam and Eve sinned, God's said from that point forward, women would long for authority over their husbands. That makes sense, of course, because all of us naturally want to control our own destiny by doing what is best for us.

But God's redeeming influence changes our thoughts and priorities. The heart controlled by love for Christ beats to love as He loved, and to love those that He loves. To love as He loved is to give oneself in sacrifice for another; and the call to love those He loves cannot bypass those He places closest to us.

Christ's grace changes our priorities from doing what is best for us to giving what is best for another. Jesus redeems our hearts and restores appreciation for the family God designed to thrive by how a man loves a woman with Christ's heart, and how a woman respects a man for Christ's sake.

Human joy and spiritual oneness in a marriage will not come by efforts of self-serving control, but by selfless efforts of Christlike support—which is what is best for all.

PRAYER: *Lord, may I never desire to dominate my spouse but rather to demonstrate sacrificial love and respect so that we would be knit together by living in harmony and humility with the grace we have received from Christ.*

345

Everyone who believes that Jesus is the Christ has been born of God, and everyone who loves the Father loves whoever has been born of him. By this we know that we love the children of God, when we love God and obey his commandments. (1 John 5:1–2)

Motivation is as important as obedience to truly please God. Doing right things for wrong reasons is wrong! That's why God sometimes rejected the prayers and worship of his people in Scripture.

Prayer is not wrong, and worship is not wrong, unless we are using them to try to bribe God to do what we selfishly desire. God's heart cannot be bought by our good deeds. He is never indebted to us or managed by our merits.

God motivates us to do His will out of gratitude for His love and grace. True obedience is always a loving response to God's grace rather than an attempt to buy Him off. That's why love for God is necessary to obey His commands.

The heart that truly comprehends the greatness of God's grace loves Him. Such love finds its source in Christ's sacrificial provision for us, and then compels us to live for Him and walk in His ways. When we love God, we love those He loves and what He loves, making love for God the basis of all true obedience!

> **PRAYER:** Father, I'm grateful You enabled me to love You through Jesus's love. Now help me confirm that love by living in true obedience that comes from making my greatest motivation love for Your purposes rather than for mine!

346

Therefore, since we are surrounded by so great a cloud of witnesses, let us also lay aside every weight, and sin which clings so closely, and let us run with endurance the race that is set before us, looking to Jesus, the founder and perfecter of our faith. (Hebrews 12:1–2)

In every generation, God sustains His people through trials to provide encouragement to surrounding people and subsequent generations.

When the prophet Daniel was old, he remembered what God had done for his young friends—Shadrach, Meshach, and Abednego. When Daniel faced new trials, he remembered how God had helped Jeremiah in a previous generation. Then, when Daniel dreamed of trials yet to come, he also foresaw the Rescuer who would overcome.

So Daniel was helped through hard times by being surrounded on all sides by a cloud of witnesses to God's faithfulness. The writer of Hebrews offers similar encouragement. In a time of persecution, he reminds readers of the faithful witnesses in present and previous times to inspire continuing faithfulness.

Scripture reminds us of such grace that has come to instill trust in the good yet to come. We trust God to do as He has done. We do not base our trust on words alone, but on generations of God's care.

He's the protector of past, present, and future generations. If that cloud of witnesses seems remote or obscure, then you should remember the greatest present witness of God's goodness is the Holy Spirit bringing you to faith.

Even if all is taken from you on Earth, you still have Jesus. He is behind and before you, above and below you. You are surrounded by Jesus in the cloud of His ever-present grace!

PRAYER: Father, Your Word shows how You always provide what is best for Your children. When I face trials, surround my heart with this cloud of witnesses so so I can fulfill Your purposes.

*The book of the genealogy of Jesus Christ, the son of David,
the son of Abraham.... Judah [was] the father of Perez and
Zerah by Tamar ... and Salmon the father of Boaz by Rahab,
and Boaz the father of Obed by Ruth, and Obed the father of Jesse,
and Jesse the father of David the king. And David was the
father of Solomon by the wife of Uriah. (Matthew 1:1, 3, 5–6)*

Jesus's family line is not what we would expect. There's Tamar, who was abused and abandoned. There's Rahab, a prostitute and outcast; and Ruth, a foreigner to God's covenant with Israel. And let's not forget about Bathsheba, the wife of King David—who murdered her husband to have her.

Jesus's family tree is rotten.

Why does God use such an imperfect lineage for Christ? God is making plain that He isn't surprised by human frailty or put off by it. Imperfect people are the best candidates for receiving and displaying His grace.

This may not be a message that we desire to hear on the days that we are confident of our goodness, but it is the message that we are desperate to claim on the days that our imperfections—our rottenness—is plain to us.

God's light shines brightest in the darkness, and His grace will gleam through the dirt on us. He can work past the sin we thought was greater than He, and He delights to do so. God displays His grace so brilliantly to make His mercy plain and to encourage us to claim it readily!

> **PRAYER:** *Heavenly Father, thank You for the fact that You pardon and give purpose to messed-up people like me. Today, help me so to believe in Your grace that I rejoice to receive it and live to reflect it!*

The grace of our Lord overflowed for me with the faith and love that are in Christ Jesus. The saying is trustworthy and deserving of full acceptance, that Christ Jesus came into the world to save sinners, of whom I am the foremost. (1 Timothy 1:14–15)

The Apostle Paul seemed to get the Gospel backwards. In one of his earliest letters, he confessed that he was the "least of the apostles." Later he wrote to others that he was the "least of God's people." Finally, toward the end of his life and ministry he wrote that he was the "foremost" of sinners.

The more mature he became, the worse he saw his sin. Isn't that backwards? Shouldn't he have been getting better and better? Of course, we are right to expect Paul's behavior to improve as his walk with Christ matured, but that is not his point.

The more Paul understood the sacrifice of his Savior, the more he detested the sin that required it. Paul did not get worse; he simply saw his wrongs more realistically.

This perspective did not lead Paul to despair—quite the opposite. The more he recognized the magnitude of his sin, the more the cross of Jesus was magnified in his heart.

Yes, Paul's sin got worse in his estimation, but consequently the cross of Jesus got larger in his appreciation. So, far from despairing, he wrote, "The grace of our Lord overflowed for me."

We don't have to be afraid of confessing the magnitude of our sin to God. He already knows it, and our love and faith will only increase as His overflowing grace overwhelms our guilt and shame.

PRAYER: *God, be merciful to me, a great sinner in need of a greater Savior. Let me see the magnitude of my sin so that I am overwhelmed by the magnificence of the cross where grace overflows for me.*

349

*You, therefore, have no excuse, you who pass judgment
on someone else, for at whatever point you judge another,
you are condemning yourself, because you who pass
judgment do the same things. (Romans 2:1 NIV)*

In the play *The Best Christmas Pageant Ever*, we get to know the six Herdman kids. They are town terrors—they lie, smoke, cuss, and bully others at school. They *never* attend church. And, for all the other kids in town, this is a blessing.

Church is the one place the town kids can find some protection and peace—until the day the Herdman kids show up for Sunday school.

Invading the class, these inventively awful kids ask the teacher lots of questions like, "Why don't they call him Bill instead of Jesus?" and "Why don't they give Christmas a better name, like 'Revenge at Bethlehem?'"

How do kids like the Herdmans wind up in a Christmas story? The same way that we do. They receive patience and mercy they do not earn or fully understand.

Whenever wayward children of God receive grace they do not deserve, that's the real Christmas story—and what makes it real to us. When we witness blessings to wandering wisemen, lowly shepherds, delinquent Herdmans, or our wayward hearts, then the story carries the meaning God intended.

Ultimately, the beauty of the Christmas story touches us when we realize that we are in Christ's pageant story, too. We who didn't deserve to welcome Him were welcomed by Him, and can tell others of His love for kids as awful as we.

> PRAYER: Father, help me remember the grace that claimed me more than the merits I would claim. Make Jesus beautiful to and through me by the transformation in me that reflects how much I appreciate His patience and mercy toward me.

350

Behold, the virgin shall conceive and bear a son, and they shall call his name Immanuel (which means, God with us). (Matthew 1:23)

Jesus could have remained remote in Heaven's realm, but He didn't. As an infant in a manger, a child in Nazareth, and a Savior on a cross, He knelt down into the dirt of our Earth and our shame to demonstrate a holy love that is willing to come near to us.

Even the name those who prophesied His coming gave to him communicates such love: "Immanuel," which means *God with us*. Still, the announcement of our Savior's name was not the first affirmation of our God's presence.

When God walked with our first parents in the Garden of Eden, sealed Noah's family in the ark, spared Abraham's son with a provision of sacrifice, delivered Israel from Pharaoh and through the Red Sea, dwelt among His people in the wilderness, rescued them from enemies, spoke through prophets and apostles with His Word for us, and put His Spirit in us—in all these, our God was demonstrating the *Immanuel principle*: He is with us!

Why is the Immanuel principle displayed so often in Scripture? The answer is that we can face any trial, walk any path, and deal with all the pains of a fallen world so long as we know God is with us. He is!

By His Word and Spirit, God is with you every moment of every day, so you can face everything with Him. God is with you!

> **PRAYER:** Lord, thank You that You are with me. May the truths of Your Word be the witness of Your Spirit in my heart, assuring me that You will walk with me through anything. May I fear nothing because in everything my God is near!

For a child is born to us, a son is given to us. The government will rest on his shoulders. And he will be called: Wonderful Counselor, Mighty God, Everlasting Father, Prince of Peace. (Isaiah 9:6 NLT)

Isaiah wrote this passage during a sorrowful and somber time in Israel's history. God's people had turned their backs on Him, and the light of hope seemed all but extinguished.

That would be a sad story for sure—*if* that were the end. But it's not! Isaiah prophesied that God had a plan for turning His people back to Him! The prophet proclaims, "For unto us a child is born, to us a son is given." This prophesied Son would be the Savior of the World, offering God's counsel, might, love, and peace!

At times such a Son may seem distant from us, lost in the sentiment of a Christmas song, or banished from our hearts by serious sin. Whatever the cause of His seeming distance, recognize Isaiah wrote to a people whose sentiments were idolatrous and whose sin was great.

If you think you do not qualify for God's counsel, might, love, and peace, then think again. If people like these were to receive help from Jesus, then people like you and me can expect it too.

If we didn't need His help, then Jesus would not have come. Sin never needs to be the end of God's story. Let Him write Jesus's ending for you.

> **PRAYER:** *Heavenly Father, thank You that my sins need not be the end of Your story for me. Help me remember that my Savior came because I needed saving, and turn my heart to seek His counsel, might, love, and peace.*

352

The shepherds said to one another, "Let us go over to Bethlehem and see this thing that has happened, which the Lord has made known to us." And they went with haste and found Mary and Joseph, and the baby lying in a manger. (Luke 2:15–16)

Many of us grew up singing the Christmas carol, "Oh, little town of Bethlehem." But we may have become so familiar with the lyrics that we've neglected to marvel at the message they carry.

At the time of Jesus's birth, Bethlehem had become a town of little importance—fallen from its renown as David's city. In fact, most people avoided it on their way to Jerusalem.

Still, God's graceful design was to use the dingy town to bring His divine Son into the world. On that day, Bethlehem shone so brightly that we would sing of her, "The hopes and fears of all the years were met in thee tonight."

The King of Glory came to a forgotten town in an oppressed land to be laid in a cattle trough by a disgraced mother of a transient family and to be announced to the world by lowly shepherds. Where's the grace in all of that? You know.

God chose the weak and despised things of this world to display His glory, so that when we are forgotten, weak, disregarded, disgraced, displaced, poor, and lowly, we will remember that God does not despise coming to us. So do not fear to come to Him.

PRAYER: *Father, just as You used the flawed features of the insignificant town of Bethlehem to display the glory of Jesus's grace to people like me, so also convince me that you can use me—even me—to bring His good news to others.*

353

For to us a child is born, to us a son is given; and the government shall be upon his shoulder, and his name shall be called Wonderful Counselor, Mighty God, Everlasting Father, Prince of Peace. (Isaiah 9:6)

God gave His Son many titles: "Wonderful Counselor," "Mighty God," "Everlasting Father," and "Prince of Peace." Each reminds us that God provides blessings for us that we cannot provide for ourselves.

He gives *counsel* beyond our wisdom. He provides *might* beyond our strength. He offers *fatherly* care to orphaned hearts. He sends His *peace* to comfort anxious hearts, relieve burdened souls, and transform troubled lives.

Christ's titles display the essence of the Gospel to reveal the grace of God. His names signal His provision—not for those who think they have their lives all fixed and tidy, but for those who call on His name to provide their wisdom, strength, love, and peace.

When we call Him by the names His Word supplies, we are confessing He must provide what we cannot. Professing His titles invites His provision: to our cries will come His counsel; to our weakness will come His might; to all who call Him "Father," He says, "My child;" and, to our anxiety will come His peace.

Hallelujah! What a beautiful name for the Savior of a world of sinners like me!

PRAYER: *Lord, thank You that when I am confused You give me counsel; when I am weak You give me strength; when my childish resolutions do not last You remain my Everlasting Father; and when I am anxious You give me peace in Christ!*

*Be strong and courageous. Do not be afraid or terrified
because of them, for the Lord your God goes with you; he will
never leave you nor forsake you. (Deuteronomy 31:6 NIV)*

A generation ago, the captivity of some American hostages in Iran had stretched into the Christmas season. Bowing to political pressures, the terrorists allowed the hostages to celebrate Christmas together with TV cameras rolling. That's when hostage Kathryn Koob, an American embassy worker, softly sang "Away in a Manger."

The last verse, sung in the terrorists' presence, was the most poignant: "Be near me, Lord Jesus, I ask Thee to stay close by me forever and love me, I pray."

The words conveyed the hope and courage that is available to Christians in all generations and circumstances. It is the strength that comes from knowing that our God is always with us.

Jesus came to this earth to be with us despite our sin, and He sent the Holy Spirit to abide with us until our Savior comes again. He will never leave us or forsake us. We can face the greatest of trials or terrors with assurance that nothing separates us from His love.

Circumstance will change; His love will not. Trials will vary; His presence will not. Problems will pass; His purposes will endure. He is near. So take courage.

PRAYER: *Lord, You are with me through hardships. With You I can face anything. You will never leave or forsake me! So give me the strength and courage that come from trusting Your constant presence.*

355

For God, who said, "Let light shine out of darkness,"
has shone in our hearts to give the light
of the knowledge of the glory of God in the
face of Jesus Christ. (2 Corinthians 4:6)

A friend described looking into a Christmas sky where geese flying in V formation reminded him of Christmas trees celebrating Christ's birth. The more he looked, the more he realized the wonder of God's work.

The reason my friend could see the geese in the night sky was because the moon was reflecting off their breasts. And the reason that the moon shown so brightly was that it was reflecting the sun on the other side of the world.

When God shines into our hearts the glory of Christ, in whose face is revealed the glory of the One who gave the sun its light, then we are seeing the magnificence of heavenly grace beyond our world.

The glory is displayed in us, but it is not from us. Our lives reflect the glory of God who delights to shine His grace from His Son into our hearts.

We rejoice in the beauty we are able to receive and to reflect because of the glory that shines from the goodness and grace of Heaven.

PRAYER: Father, help me today to rejoice in the light of Christ that You have shined into my heart and to reflect Your love and grace revealed in Him to those around me.

You were once darkness, but now you are light in the Lord.
Live as children of light—for the fruit of the light consists
of all goodness, righteousness, and truth. (Ephesians 5:8–9 CSB)

Beautiful. Significant. Righteous. Worthy. That is what God sees when He looks at you! While you might question how God could be so fooled, know this—He isn't.

He knows you aren't perfect, but He sees you in His light. He knows your lackluster obedience, but He colors you with the radiance of His righteousness.

Our church's Christmas program draws the churched and the unchurched to hear the seasonal music and admire the Advent presentations. Still, as a pastor, knowing the fears and flaws of many of the participants, I tend to see things in a different light.

As the choirs line up, I may observe a struggling couple or wayward child preparing to sing to our community of the beauty of the Savior. A part of me thinks that it is a strange, even inappropriate, witness. How can we allow those so flawed to sing of the perfections of Jesus? How does this help anyone?

Then the program starts, and all is bathed in the colors of Christmas. The stage lights wash away the shadows and the ordinary colors, turning every object and every person into a brilliant display of beauty not their own. That's the witness my heart needs!

Despite the darkness and difficulties of our lives, Jesus shines His grace upon us to wash away our sin and color our souls with His righteousness. If only perfect people sang of Jesus at Christmas, it would truly be a silent night. But because Jesus makes righteous those touched by His light, we can all sing "Joy to the World."

PRAYER: *Lord, may the light of Your grace cover my sin and color my soul so that I live as a child of light for You.*

But you, O Bethlehem Ephrathah, who are too little to be among the clans of Judah, from you shall come forth for me one who is to be ruler in Israel, whose coming forth is from of old, from ancient days. (Micah 5:2)

When the Old Testament prophet Micah foretold the birth of our Messiah in Bethlehem, he emphasized that this little town was nothing much—too little to even count among the people of Judah. But its name suggests a hidden significance.

Did you know that in Hebrew the name "Bethlehem" means *House of Bread*? How clever (and wise) of the Lord to have Jesus, our "Bread of Life," come from the House of Bread.

Like bread, Jesus is basic nourishment for life. When the lives of His people were threatened in the wilderness, God provided bread from Heaven—manna. When our world became a wilderness of sin, God promised and sent the Bread of Life—Jesus—to nourish and rescue us.

Jesus said, "I am the bread of life; he that comes to me shall never hunger!" That was not an afterthought. His birth in Bethlehem assures us that God's intention was always to provide spiritual bread for the life and eternity of those who come to Him. So come!

PRAYER: Lord, thank You for providing my daily bread and for sending the Bread of Life to provide for my eternity. May the wisdom and heart You revealed when You birthed the Bread of Life in Bethlehem nourish my faith to trust You and to come to You now for the eternal sustenance I need.

358

Because of him you are in Christ Jesus, who became
to us wisdom from God, righteousness and sanctification
and redemption, so that, as it is written, "Let the one who
boasts, boast in the Lord." (1 Corinthians 1:30–31)

When the wisdom of God provided for our sin by spiritually uniting us to Christ by faith, everything that would separate us from God's love was obscured by Jesus's identity. The Son of God placed His mantle of love over us, identifying each believer before God as His own child.

One Christmas, we gave our grandchildren superhero capes. As each child donned his mantle, he became that hero in his own imagination.

Grace is so much better! When we trust that Jesus puts His mantle over us, God actually makes us His own child, covering us with the identity of Jesus.

Our guilt was covered by Jesus's righteousness, our impurity hidden behind His sanctified life, and we were redeemed from the debt of our sin by the riches of His grace. So much are our sins and weaknesses eclipsed by Christ's characteristics that we are called the children of God (1 John 3:1)!

It is in this "new" identity alone that anyone could possibly boast before God. Such boasting comes not from anything we have done. After all, what good would it do to boast to the God who knows all our weaknesses, doubts, fears, and shame?

So the Apostle Paul teaches us, "Let the one who boasts boast in the Lord." Because your sinful self is now covered by Jesus, His identity is yours! And what is even better than that? Because you have His child's identity, the Heavenly Father loves you as much as He loves Jesus. That's super grace!

PRAYER: *Heavenly Father, I praise You for giving me a new identity in Jesus Christ. Help me to believe that You love me as much as Your own child so I will trust and live for You.*

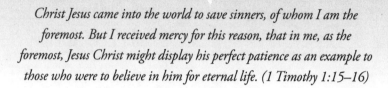

359

Christ Jesus came into the world to save sinners, of whom I am the foremost. But I received mercy for this reason, that in me, as the foremost, Jesus Christ might display his perfect patience as an example to those who were to believe in him for eternal life. (1 Timothy 1:15–16)

In the play *The Best Christmas Pageant Ever*, a twelve-year-old named Imogene is a bona fide delinquent. She does her best to convince the church pageant director to kidnap a *real* baby to play the part of Jesus. When the director explains that kidnapping babies isn't a good idea, Imogene simply doesn't get it.

Still, the show must go on. So Imogene does her best to play the part of Mary. The role doesn't fit her any better than tattered bathrobes fit the kids trying to act like shepherds.

But as Imogene cares for the doll the church uses for a Christ child, something amazing happens. Her face softens, her love for her "child" seems to bathe her and her audience in a holy light, and she seems to understand something of God's love for her.

The story is fiction; the transformation is not. When we gain even a childlike understanding of the love that sent the Christ child, our hearts soften, our love for the Son causes us to be bathed in His holy light, and God's love becomes real.

We love because He first loved us—sinners in need of a Savior. Even the worst of us can love Him, and when we do His perfect patience and profound mercy are on brilliant display for all us Imogenes.

PRAYER: *Heavenly Father, if You can save sinners like Paul and Imogene, then I know You can save anyone—including me! Thank You for Your perfect patience that claimed me; now help me be patient as Your mercy claims others.*

360

You ... were taught in him ... to put off your old self, which belongs to your former manner of life and is corrupt ... and to put on the new self, created after the likeness of God in true righteousness and holiness. (Ephesians 4:21–22, 24)

Oak tree leaves flapping in the cold winter wind are a sign of their obstinate nature. After other trees have shed their leaves for winter, an oak tree will keep the brown, shriveled leaves of its former life all winter.

Only when the warmth of spring activates latent life in the oak tree do new leaves grow, pushing off the old. New life replaces the old that has hung on.

We spiritually grow in a similar way. As the Holy Spirit stirs new life in us, we respond with new habits of speech and conduct in how we relate to others. The new life is already in us; the ability to grow is already present. But we do not mature if we hang onto features of a past life.

As we use the power of the Spirit to replace old ways of life, new life matures. We grow in grace, thriving in new ways of relating to others by pushing out old habits and patterns.

We never want to conclude that new life is impossible; the Spirit in believers is already sending spiritual power through us. Our responsibility and privilege is to act on the grace already present, cultivating new growth by expressing the new life that pushes out the remnants of what is already dead.

> **PRAYER:** Father, You have made me alive in Christ. Help me to live with new power You have given, pushing out dead remnants of the past with new patterns of speech and life.

361

*You have put off the old self with its practices and have
put on the new self, which is being renewed in knowledge
after the image of its creator. (Colossians 3:9–10)*

What does it mean to be a new creation in Christ? One dimension of this new reality is how the Holy Spirit works inside of us to teach, train, and rewire our minds for growth and maturity.

The supernatural rewiring of the Holy Spirit reminds me of the electric trains I played with as a child. When I wanted the train to go in reverse, I did not push it with my hands. I used a switch that changed the wiring, so the same train that had rounded its track in one direction would now move in a new direction.

In a similar way, the Holy Spirit changes our thoughts and desires. In one sense, we are still the same person with the same body and appearance. But in another sense, all of those aspects of our being are now moving in a new direction.

Once we were moving away from Jesus; now we are moving toward Him with thoughts and desires controlled by the knowledge of the One who loved us and gave Himself for us. Even when we sin, our betrayal of our Savior convicts our hearts. We long to put off sinful practices, and actually have the power to do so.

What has happened? God has supernaturally rewired our hearts to love and serve Him—something impossible prior to the indwelling of the Holy Spirit. Knowing and experiencing His rewiring gives us confidence to move in the direction He empowers.

> **PRAYER:** Father, thank You for the fact that my old life is past, and I have new life in Jesus Christ. May the new life the Holy Spirit is wiring into my thoughts and desires motivate me to love, serve, and obey You more each day.

Your eyes saw my unformed substance; in your book were written, every one of them, the days that were formed for me, when as yet there was none of them. (Psalm 139:16)

Have you ever faced a trial and thought, *This is because I have not done enough for God.* You're not alone. My missionary friend, Richard, confessed to having the same thoughts when his child was born with multiple medical concerns.

Richard wrote of how every medical setback led him and his wife to wonder whether their righteousness and repentance were enough. The questioning was leading them into a dangerous quandary of wondering whether to blame themselves or God for their child's struggles.

Then the Lord turned their hearts back to the truth of the Gospel: *We will never be right with God by depending on what we do, but by trusting in what Jesus has done for us.* When we trust in the sufficiency of Christ's work on our behalf, then we need not doubt Him or blame one another for the troubles of a fallen world.

We trust the Good Shepherd to carry us through dark valleys of this world because He has proven His care, giving us access to it by His cross. Now nothing enters lives hedged about by the grace of Christ except what is eternally best for us and our families.

We don't trust our goodness to insulate us against all earthly trials, we trust the goodness of Jesus to take us through them to Himself.

> **PRAYER:** Father, I know we live in a fallen world that You will someday make right. Through the grace unquestionably revealed at the cross, teach me to trust Your sovereign love through inevitable trials until Jesus comes or takes me home!

363

I will show my love to the one I called "Not my loved one."
I will say to those called "Not my people," "You are my people";
and they will say, "You are my God." (Hosea 2:23 NIV)

For well-known author Anne Lamott, life was full of sinful pursuits and relational ruins. In so many ways, she was seeking God in all the wrong places. She wrote about her journey toward faith and how she came to understand God's grace.

When her despair caused her to ask a pastor what it meant to be "saved," he gave this answer: "It's like discovering you're on the shelf of a pawnshop—dusty and forgotten and not feeling very worthy—when Jesus walks in and says, 'I'll take her place on the shelf, let her go out in the sun.'"

Ann Lamott is still on a journey of faith. Those who know her life acknowledge it has lots of twists and turns. But through that pastor, she started down a new path toward a new life in the sun.

God used her destitution and despair not only to show the futility of past paths, but also to reveal that He is willing to take those who think of themselves as *not God's people* and make them His.

That's the same message for us. Jesus took our place in the darkness and dirt of the cross and put us on a new path in His light. So even if we think of ourselves as *not God's loved one,* when we say, "You are my God," He says, "You are Mine."

> **PRAYER:** Lord, thank You for taking me off a dusty shelf and putting me in the sunshine of Your grace! I praise You that when I thought I was not Your loved one, Jesus took my place so that You now say to me, "You are Mine."

364

These people honor me with their lips but their hearts are
far from me. They worship me in vain; their teachings
are merely human rules (Matthew 15:8–9 NIV)

My unbelieving jogging friend joined me on our path with a new resolution: "I need to go to church more to learn to be good." I wrestled with knowing how to say to him that simply learning to be good isn't really the point of church.

Spiritual growth that honors God requires heart change, not mere behavior improvement. Our behavior is important, but not as important as developing a heart of love for our Lord. That is why bare moralism is never equivalent to the Gospel.

While there is nothing wrong with being moral, moralism substitutes prideful performance for humble devotion, and legalistic obedience for loving discipleship. Hands and hearts should work together in biblical obedience, but the heart must be the command center of our lives.

Because of this, the enemy will always begin his attacks on us or our loved ones by attempting to alienate affections. He goes straight for the command center, often by tempting hearts with love for sin, but also by convincing us that God will be satisfied with simple obedience rather than dependence on Jesus.

We combat Satan's ploys by filling hearts and minds with understanding of God's grace. Love for God results from knowing His mercy to us. True discipleship springs from a heart devoted to Him who gave Himself for those who confess their sin—not those who claim their goodness.

PRAYER: *Lord, draw me nearer, always nearer, to Your heart by the wonders of grace that make my devotion an offering of praise for Your grace, not proof of my deserving it.*

365

This grace was given us in Christ Jesus before the beginning of time, but it has now been revealed through the appearing of our Savior, Christ Jesus, who has destroyed death and has brought life and immortality to light through the Gospel. (2 Timothy 1:9–10 NIV)

Baseball player Mickey Mantle asked for this to be sung at his funeral:

> Yesterday when I was young,
> The taste of life was sweet as rain upon my tongue....
> The game of life I played with arrogance and pride,
> And every flame I lit too quickly, quickly died....
> I ran so fast that time and youth at last ran out....
> The time has come to pay for yesterday when I was young.[5]

Mickey turned to everything this world had to offer for happiness: fame, fortune, formal religion, physical prowess, physical pleasure, the bottle. Each in turn promised fulfillment, and all came up empty.

So at the end of life, Mickey turned from himself to another. He asked Jesus to forgive him and to save his soul. Perhaps that's clear from the final words Mickey Mantle asked to be sung at his own funeral.

> Amazing grace, how sweet the sound / that saved a wretch like me. / I once was lost but now am found, / was blind but now I see.
> Twas grace that taught my heart to fear, / and grace my fears relieved. / How precious did that grace appear / the hour I first believed.[6]

Such grace is available for all who confess their need of Jesus and trust Him to forgive them forever.

PRAYER: *Heavenly Father, I confess that I am a sinner in need of the grace of a Savior. I believe Jesus is my Savior.*

NOTES

1 Laura Story's song, "Blessings," was released through INO Records February 21, 2011 and the story of the faith and family challenges behind it are described in her book, *When God Doesn't Fix It* (Thomas Nelson, 2015).

2 Tony Snow, "Cancer's Unexpected Blessings", *Christianity Today*, July 20, 2007, http://www.christianitytoday.com/ct/2007/july25.30html?paging=off.

3 Jeremy Lin, "Happy New Year!" *The Official Website of Jeremy Lin*, January 1, 2015, https://www.jlin7.com/blogs/journal/16502868-happy-new-year

4 The hymn "It Is Well With My Soul" was written by Horatio Spafford in 1873.

5 Originally titled "Hier encore," written by Charles Aznavour and released in September 1964, later recorded as "Yesterday When I Was Young" by Roy Clark, who sang it according to Mickey Mantle's request at the ballplayer's funeral. See Catalog of copyright entries—Volume 10, Part 1, Issue 1— 1967, p. 232.

6 The hymn, "Amazing Grace," was first published by John Newton in 1779.